THE FAIRLADY COLLECTION

THE

FAIRLADY
C O L L E C T I O N

40 YEARS OF FINE WRITING

EDITED BY
MARIANNE THAMM

JONATHAN BALL PUBLISHERS
JOHANNESBURG & CAPE TOWN

Published in 2005 by
JONATHAN BALL PUBLISHERS (PTY) LTD
PO Box 33977
Jeppestown
2043

ISBN 1 86842 228 3

Design, typesetting and reproduction by
Triple M Design & Advertising, Johannesburg
Set in 8,5/12,5pt Stone Serif
Printed and bound by
CTP Book Printers, Duminy Street, Parow, Cape

Contents

Introduction

Forty years. A lifetime some might say but also a mere blip in time. For most South Africans though, the past forty years have been particularly momentous. From surviving the calculated brutality of apartheid to celebrating the installation of our first democratically elected government to facing the challenges of the global 21st Century, it's been an emotional ride.

It would be safe to assert that *Fairlady* can lay claim to having played a unique role in this country's history. Apart from amusing and enlightening readers, the magazine also tried to challenge its audience. I doubt whether a mass-market woman's magazine anywhere else in the world would have tackled the political and social issues *Fairlady* has consistently done since its launch in 1965.

Editors (from Jane Raphaely at the start to the uncompromising Dene Smuts who was fired for her insistence on publishing stories that exposed the burning political issues of the time, to current editor Ann Donald) have consistently challenged the status quo, sometimes with subtle finesse and sometimes defiantly. Between the décor, the fashion, the food and the celebrities, *Fairlady* published provocative pieces by some of this country's leading literary talents. Writers like Alan Paton, Richard Rive, Miriam Tlali, Sindiwe Magona, JM Coetzee, Rian Malan, Es'kia Mphahlele, André Brink, and Nadine Gordimer all contributed to the magazine. Some of this work is reproduced here.

Apart from these better-known writers, *Fairlady* has also published pieces by a crop of the country's finest journalists including Madeleine van Biljon, Denis Beckett, Chris Barron, Lin Sampson, Sue Grant-Marshall, Jamie Carr, Erica Platter, Mike Behr and others.

This collection includes some of the best of forty years of writing in *Fairlady*. We could have published three volumes of work but were confined to around 100 000 words. Editing this collection has been a gratifying but irritating task. I found it hard to leave out so many of the pieces that had originally held me in thrall when I initially explored the *Fairlady* archives.

Ultimately what makes this collection so significant and readable is the immediacy of the writing and the diverse styles employed by these accomplished writers. These are not dry historic accounts, neither are they formal academic writings. They are raw, moving and often humorous glimpses into a not-so-distant past. These features, opinion pieces, book cuts and profiles on significant South Africans are lively and vivid and bring to life the taste and textures of life in the country in the last forty years.

It is rare to find this kind of writing in contemporary mass media and this collection is not only a tribute to our past but a reflection on how we have chosen to tell it.

Enjoy.

Marianne Thamm   *July 2005*

Editorial Contributors

Chris Barron

Denis Beckett

Mike Behr

Chené Blignaut

Wilna Botha

Nechama Brodie

Jamie Carr

JM Coetzee

Ellen Fitzpatrick

Sue Grant-Marshall

Ingrid Hudson

Cathy Knox

Rian Malan

Margaret McAllister

Khanyi Mjindi

Es'kia Mphahlele

PJ O'Rourke

Judy Olivier

Flavia Pascoe

Debora Patta

Erica Platter

Iman Rappetti

Richard Rive

Lin Sampson

John Scott

Dene Smuts

Rory Steyn

Jim Thorne

Amy Thornton

Miriam Tlali

Madeleine van Biljon

Marianne van Kuik

A Valiant Heart

What's it like to be the wife of the most famous patient in the world? Eight days after her husband's historic heart operation Mrs Louis Washkansky talked to Flavia Pascoe about the weeks of strain, the publicity, the continuous questions. Here in her own words Ann Washkansky tells the story of the world's first heart transplant.

Flavia Pascoe

Fairlady 24 January 1968

Mrs Ann Washkansky was lying in bed reading *The Life and Loves of Ali Khan* when the telephone rang. It was 15 minutes after midnight – the very early hours of Sunday morning, 3 December, 1967.

Her legs went weak. It could only be the hospital. 'They've phoned to tell me Louis had died,' she thought.

But when she lifted the receiver, a doctor from Groote Schuur Hospital said: 'We're wheeling your husband into the theatre, Mrs Washkansky. We're going to operate.'

Ann knew what this meant. She had been told about the heart transplant that the surgery team was going to do on her husband. She had hardly believed it – a new heart seemed impossible. Ann couldn't wait alone. In response to her telephone call her brother, Solly Sklar, Louis Washkansky's brother, Tevia, and his wife Annie, and two friends, Mr and Mrs Solly Cammerman came to her attractive upstairs flat in Sea Point.

Through the night they sat and waited, drinking gallons of coffee and smoking endless cigarettes. Every hour Ann's sister-in-law, Grace, who had stayed at home with her children, telephoned. 'Any news?' And every hour Ann telephoned the hospital: 'Any news?'

It was a long night – they watched the sun rise, glinting on the Atlantic Ocean as it topped the mountains, and the birds get up. Ann didn't dare think even one minute into the future. She could only hope.

Ann and Louis Washkansky were married 21 years ago, in 1946. Louis and Ann's brother had been buddies during the war. They came home on leave from the North once, but Ann, a schoolgirl in a gym, had hardly registered her brother's handsome soldier friend. When the war ended Ann was 19. She married when she was 20. Louis was more than 12 years older than Ann, but as she reflected, he was 'always young at heart'.

Six years later they had a son, whom they named Michael. They were

Professor Barnard sprang from a position of eminence in medical circles to worldwide fame. And Louis Washkansky emerged from obscurity to being the best-known patient in the world.

happy. Louis had that rare quality of making those around him happy. He enjoyed everything they did together. He liked people and they liked him. When he had a heart attack seven years ago, it was a blow to Louis. But he fought back and soon resumed life quite normally, working as the travelling partner in the family wholesale grocery business.

Almost three years ago he had another heart attack – much more serious this time. A third of his heart was damaged beyond repair, and it got progressively worse. A photograph taken at Michael's Barmitzvah two years ago shows an aged and dying man. But still Louis fought on. He wouldn't have a driver – he continued travelling three days a week, driving through traffic, looking for parking.

In September 1967 it became too much for him. Even he realised that he couldn't go on living like that. He was admitted to Groote Schuur Hospital.

The room was getting lighter. Six people, haggard with tension and lack of sleep, started as the telephone rang. It was 6.20 am. Ann jumped up to answer it – half crying with fear, hope.

'Mrs Washkansky, this is Doctor Bosman. The operation is over.'

'Is he alive? Is he all right?'

'Yes.'

'Do you mean the new heart is beating?'

'Beautifully. Just beautifully.'

'Can I come up?'

'Not till 10 o'clock.'

Ann still didn't appreciate the implications. This was important to Louis, Michael and her. It was important to the small world of their relatives and friends. It was important to Miriam, their domestic worker.

But she didn't know that this historic operation – the first transplant of a human heart – would carry the name Washkansky all over the world.

When Mrs Washkansky arrived at Groote Schuur, she was met at the lift by Professor Christiaan Barnard, the leader of the team of surgeons who had carried out the operation. He looked as if he hadn't slept for a week. Men were flopped out all round her – the exhausted, but elated team who had worked for six solid hours to give her husband a new chance of living. They didn't know how long he would survive the operation – they had no previous experience to draw on.

Then Ann Washkansky learned of a strange coincidence. As she had left the hospital after visiting hours the previous afternoon with her sister-in-law and a friend, she had driven down Main Road, Observatory. In the road, a great crowd of people was gathered. A policeman waved her on – Ann hadn't intended stopping – and as she drove past she shouted, 'Oh no, a woman lying in the road ...!'

Her sister-in-law said, 'Don't look, Ann, there are two of them ...'

The next day she learned that the women were Mrs Myrtle Darvall and her twenty-five-year-old daughter, Denise. Mrs Darvall died instantly, but Denise lived until that night. When she died, her heart, young and strong, was the one to give Louis Washkansky a new lease on life.

On Sunday the news of the operation was being carried all over the world on news-agency lines. Professor Barnard sprang from a position of eminence in medical circles to worldwide fame. And Louis Washkansky emerged from obscurity to being the best-known patient in the world.

But something was disturbing Ann Washkansky. Would having someone else's heart change Louis' personality? How much meaning was there in phrases like 'young at heart ', 'of good heart', 'a change of heart' and

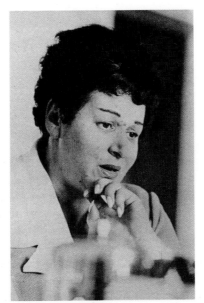

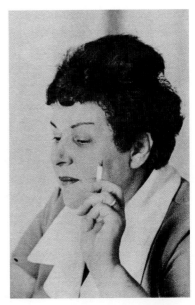

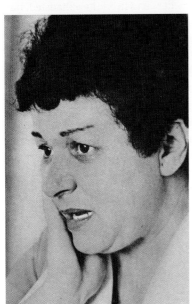

Ann Washkansky
waits for news of her
husband, Louis.

(Photos: John Thornton)

all the others? The professor assured her that they meant nothing. The heart was a pump, vital, but just a pump. Ann was exhausted. The cumulative worry of all those weeks while Louis was in hospital; the near-certainty that he couldn't go on living; a bout of pneumonia two weeks before; the tension every time the telephone rang had taken their toll. All she wanted to do was sleep. But sleep was the last thing Ann Washkansky was going to get.

It started on Monday morning. Louis had become a world figure and with him, his wife. The doorbell rang incessantly as visitors and telegrams arrived; the telephone never stopped ringing; and reporters, cameramen and television teams began to arrive.

Everyone wanted to know everything. The doubters argued with Ann that the operation was impossible.

being fired from all sides, without even becoming ruffled. She spoke quietly and naturally about the husband she loved and admired. A long-distance call from Perth, Australia, and an interview with their broadcasting company left her unmoved. Her only real concern was for Louis. She wanted him to live. Every day, several times a day, she telephoned the hospital. At first the bulletins were non-committal. 'Satisfactory', 'As well as can be expected' and 'Fairly comfortable' did not give her much cheer. But after the second day they became more encouraging. On Wednesday morning, she asked the inevitable question: 'Can I see him?' 'Yes,' she was told, 'come at five o'clock.'

She went into the ward wearing a sterile gown over her clothes and a mask. To her Louis looked better than he had done for three years. 'You're famous, Louis,'

She asked the surgeons why they chose Louis for this operation when there were many younger people, just as sick, who could have been the first. She was told, 'Because of his great will to live.'

She let them argue. Impossible it may seem – but in the Groote Schuur heart clinic it had become possible.

For two days Ann didn't even have time to bath. Michael became upset – his schoolwork began to suffer. Miriam had a breakdown. The doctor who attended her discovered that nervous tension had built up in the woman because her friends would not believe what she told them about her employer and his new heart.

Ann, a small plump woman, with the darkest, most expressive eyes, had never faced anything other than an amateur's camera before. But she faced the television cameras, her mouth dry under the hot light, questions

she said, taking his hand. 'Your name was even on the telecast on Sanlam Building.' (Sanlam Building, one of the highest on Cape Town's foreshore, has the 'largest electric newspaper in the world'.)

Louis looked pleased. But he still had no idea of how famous he had become, literally overnight.

'The food is awful,' he said. 'The fish looks as if it had died on the plate.' Ann smiled. Her Louis wasn't likely to take kindly to invalid food. Take him to the best restaurant in the world and he ordered steak and eggs.

Eight days after the operation, Ann was sure Louis would live. But in her happiness there was one dark cloud: Denise Darvall – the girl who had died to save Louis' life. Ann visited Mr Edward Darvall and tried to comfort him for the loss of his wife and daughter.

'I must forget about it,' she said. 'I can't live with the thought of that girl.'

Ann has a friend in Sea Point, an elderly Jewish man who, when asked, 'How are you?' always answers, 'I don't know.' Ann realises that he is right. No one can know how they are – there is always the hidden factor. She knows that this is true of Louis, and in her brave way – she only weeps when she is alone – she is prepared. She also knows that the heart transplant operation was Louis' only chance. With his heart as it was, he couldn't have gone on living – even his valiant fight was flagging. He should have died two years ago, doctors say. It was only his indomitable spirit that kept him going. Ann believes in God. And she believes that there was a plan that brought her sick husband and the brilliant professor together at this point in medical history. She asked the surgeons why they chose Louis for this operation when there were many younger people, just as sick, who could have been the first. She was told, 'Because of his great will to live.'

'He's got to live,' she said. But eight days after the operation, she still tensed when the telephone rang ...

'They've phoned to tell me Louis has died,' she thought that history-making night of 2 December.

Louis Washkansky lived for 18 days after the operation and died from complications after contracting pneumonia. Today heart transplants are commonplace.

Ann Washkansky died in Cape Town in 2003.

Our Woman in Oxford

In the mid 1970s, beating all odds, anthropologist Dr Harriet Sibisi became one of the first South African women to pass and shine through the hallowed halls of Cambridge and Oxford universities.

Jim Thorne

Fairlady 5 March 1975

Dr Harriet Sibisi – 'I was like a starving cow within an enclosure watching another cow freely grazing in a vast expanse of green pastures.'

(*Photo:* Bryan Wharton)

Carved along a high wall overlooking the central quadrangle of St Anne's College, Oxford, is wise advice: 'Get knowledge, get riches, but with all thy getting, get understanding.'

If this is what the founders of St Anne's hoped for the girls and women who were to pass through its halls, their hope could not have been better fulfilled than in Dr Harriet Sibisi, this year's Loma Evans-Pritchard Fellow at the college.

At first, the small, compact Zulu woman amid the trees on the lawn of the quad seems incongruous, but then you perceive the confidence and authority, which proclaim the rightness of Harriet Sibisi's presence.

Many dubious practitioners of dubious arts call themselves 'doctor' with no more authority than some plumbers call themselves 'hydraulic engineers'; Harriet Sibisi does so with the full authority of the three years (1969 to 1972) she spent at that other famous British university – Cambridge. This was thanks to a chance encounter in Durban with Professor Meyer Fortes, who was visiting South Africa at the time.

Nor was her doctorate achieved through easy options – it was earned in Social Anthropology at Cambridge, one of the more challenging and difficult studies.

Harriet is not only good at her subject, she is brilliant.

Said Dr Edmund Leach of the Department of Social Anthropology at Cambridge: 'I first met Harriet at Professor Fortes's senior seminar for graduate students and I remember the occasion well. The paper was being read by a gentleman who was just about to complete his DPhil at Oxford on the basis of research he had conducted in Tanzania and who now holds a teaching post at a British university.

'In the discussion that followed, Harriet – a shadowy little figure tucked away in a corner of the room – began to ask questions, very politely, almost tenderly. The reader began to get flustered and the audience gradually re-

'Working at the university again I was continually reminded of my predicament as a black person as I watched my previous classmate, a white student, proceed with her senior degree.'

alised what was happening. Harriet showed up her opponent as a complete amateur and did it without a touch of malice. It was a superbly professional academic performance.'

It was as a result of that performance that Harriet had her intended one-year stay at Cambridge extended to three. But she is not only academically brilliant; she is an all-round nice person, as Dr Ray Abrahams, also of Cambridge's Department of Social Anthropology, can testify.

'She left a deep impression on many people here,' he says, 'and she is remembered by them with a combination of love, admiration and respect not often encountered. Her devotion to her work and her family and her immense perseverance and optimism in the face of what to others would have been insurmountable difficulties has been quite remarkable.'

One can understand why Harriet would be sought out in this way. Impatient though she may sometimes be with the pretentious and overbearing, she is gentleness itself with those less clever and less equipped to make use of their opportunities than she is.

The tragedy of our time is that privileged people grossly underestimate the intelligence of the underprivileged, she says gravely, and the struggles of her own past put a sombre shadow across her words.

Harriet left school after passing Std 7 and then trained as a primary school teacher, which she was when she married Jethroe Sibisi, now a lecturer at Zululand's Ngoye University.

She already had two children when she passed her matric by correspondence. All the time she read, devouring every book she could could beg or borrow. Soon she found she could not tear herself away from her books and she moved around her small home then at Marianhill, housekeeping with one hand and turning pages with the other. By the time she registered for her BA at Natal University, Harriet was a mother four times over. At the university her career in anthropology began almost accidentally. She had chosen it along with Zulu and History as a subject, but it was only when it became clear that she had a particular bent for anthropology that her lecturers encouraged her to pursue it in greater depth. It was a revelation to discover how other people did things, she said of her early reactions to her subject. It was the beginning of understanding another world. When Harriet graduated in 1957 having in the meantime been ill with a rare blood disease, she went back to teaching, this time at a high school.

By now her husband was Supervisor of Schools in Ladysmith and to keep their Marianhill home – a schoolhouse – one of them had to remain on the staff. So until 1963 Harriet taught, studied for her BA Honours and started work on her Masters degree. Then the law changed, enforcing separate education for blacks and whites at South African universities. There was no suitable course for Harriet at a black university and the University of Natal applied for an exemption for her to continue studying there. The application was refused. It left a bitter feeling, said Harriet. She went back to teaching, but Natal University had not forgotten her and she was soon offered a job as a research assistant at the Institute for Social Research. It was not an altogether happy time.

'Working at the university again I was continually reminded of my predicament as a black person as I watched my previous classmate, a white student, proceed with her senior degree. I was like a starving cow within an enclosure watching another cow freely grazing in a vast expanse of green pastures.'

But things changed when Harriet met Professor Fortes, head of the Department of Social Anthropology at Cambridge.

'I heard of my predicament and he wanted to size me up, so he spent three days talking anthropology to me, grilling me to see what I knew, and I realised I didn't know nearly enough,' she said.

Professor Fortes, however, thought otherwise. After he returned to Cambridge he wrote offering Harriet the chance to do a one-year postgraduate course in Social Anthropology. For many reasons, not least that her seventh child was barely a year old, Harriet could see no way of taking up Professor Fortes' offer.

'I can't go,' she said wretchedly.

But her mother and her family were made of sterner stuff. 'You must go,' they said. 'The chance will not come again.'

Thus it was that Harriet arrived at Cambridge late in 1969 for the start of the academic year – 'still very much the mission-trained teacher' according to Professor Leach. 'Her English was hesitant, she clearly found the conventions of social life at Cambridge baffling and she was shy.'

But Harriet's determination and brilliance – including her encounter with the DPhil student from Oxford – overcame all the initial obstacles. Professor Fortes soon saw that nothing less than a full three-year research degree would be just or fair for her. With the help of the Oppenheimer Foundation, it was arranged – including a trip back to South Africa for additional fieldwork

on the thesis that brought her doctorate in 1972.

Her thesis was highly praised and is, again according to Dr Leach, 'a work of considerable theoretical interest'.

Then it was back home to Durban, her house in Claremont and a resumption of work at the Institute for Social Research. But the academic fraternity of Britain had not yet finished with the brilliant Dr Sibisi. She had not been back in South Africa six months when Selly Oak College, Birmingham, offered her a one-year William Paton Fellowship.

This trip, Harriet brought her four youngest children with her – 'They spent their time glued to the television set,' she says – and one senses that they made all the difference to her. The fact that she had them there almost certainly played a key role in persuading her to accept her next well-deserved break – the Ioma Evans Pritchard Fellowship which was founded to allow graduates the time in which to write for publication. Harriet is now as at home and as at ease in the atmosphere of a great university as it is possible to imagine. Although she refuses to be drawn on the subject of which of her three English universities she most prefers, a careful ear will soon discover that Cambridge is her favourite.

It was there that Harriet learnt what she calls 'The Discipline of Doubt', which allows her to question even the most firmly-held assumptions when she is confronted by new theories.

'It links up with one of the curious

facts I observed at Cambridge,' she said. 'That examination questions each year tended to be remarkably similar to those of previous years. Professor Fortes said it would make little difference because even if the questions may remain the same, the answers are always changing. Because we live in a world of dynamic ideas and changes there is a pressing need to cultivate an open but critical mind.'

The rising generation, she believes, must always be given an ear, no matter how young it is, and in this she points to Newton, whose greatest contribution to science was written when he was 22, and Einstein, who published epoch-making theories when he was a scant 19.

'This may sound a note of despair for older people,' she said, 'but there is scope for us as well ... if we want to preserve the ability to acquire knowledge we must preserve those things which seem to come naturally only to younger people – a sense of wonder and newness.'

In Harriet's view the best teachers – among those she met at Cambridge – are the ones who are not afraid to help students to get ahead of them in the academic hierarchy. 'They realise that the light of truth is not the blazing sun but the sum of a million little lights each helping to illuminate the infinite night of human ignorance.'

Professor Harriet Sibisi lives in Pretoria. She is currently writing a book and also works as a researcher for the Freedom Park initiative.

The Other Jubilee

The symbol of South African white women, whether you like it or not, is our dreadnought but delightful political diva, Helen Suzman. She celebrates 25 sessions of undaunted and enjoyable opposition this year. She's sexy, sixty, supremely outspoken and altogether admirable.

John Scott

Fairlady 23 November 1977

'History tells us of the beautiful Helen of Troy and the heroic deeds undertaken because of her,' wrote Schalk Pienaar in August 1959, just after the split at the UP congress in Bloemfontein. 'So it is not so incredible that the beautiful Helen of South Africa should also be the cause of men being led to do strange things.'

'It's not true, you know,' said Helen Suzman in September 1977, matter of factly discounting the effect, and indeed the fact, of her alleged and legendary beauty. 'The others felt just as strongly as I did. I know Graaff always thought I was the one who did it all. At that congress in 1959 I was in my car already with Kathleen Mitchell, just getting ready to drive back, and I said to Kathy: "That's it for me. Let's go back and tell our people in Houghton."'

She was the Houghton municipal councillor. 'Then, as I reversed the car, I looked in the rear-view mirror and saw Zac de Beer and Colin Eglin in earnest conversation. I said to Kathy: "Hang on a minute, I think something's going on with the others, too." And I hopped out of the car and said: "What are you two talking about?" and they said: "We're out" and I said, "Ooh, whoa!" parked the car and went back inside. So they were going to do it anyway.' We are sitting in the study of her Hyde Park (not Houghton) home, but the house and its garden are certainly imposing enough to confirm the worst suspicions of her detractors who accuse her of being able to buy her own apartheid.

'If I could find some mad Free State farmer to buy this place, I'd be very happy,' she remarks at one point. She bought the land in 1945 when her husband, Moses, was still in the army. It was out in the country then and, with the exception of a bluegum tree, just a bare piece of veld. Now it is a woodland of poplars, cherry trees and yellowwoods. At some point during these turbulent years Helen planted them all. I've known Helen for ten years, ever since I moved into the parliamentary Press gallery, but this interview is special. It is in celebration of her political silver jubilee, her first 25 years

'Don't forget, I took a very tough line from the beginning. There was no feminine charm exerted by me, in any way. I think at the beginning the Nats were quite intrigued – or perhaps the men, if you like. Quite intrigued. I was young and, you know, I was much better looking when I was 35. Obviously, I don't mean to say I'm much better looking now ...'

in parliament – a distinction she shares with only three other sitting MPs: the Prime Minister BJ Vorster himself, the Minister of Bantu Administration, Mr MC Botha, and the MP for Carletonville, Mr Cas Greyling, a rebel Nationalist.

'We're the last of the Mohicans. What a quartet!' she chortles. But the 25 years also encompass a unique accomplishment in South African political history.

For more than half of them, from 1961 to 1974, Helen Suzman was the sole parliamentary representative of her party. It was a sustained one-woman stand par excellence. She not only fought 170 males single-handed, but at times had them reeling against the ropes. She has also just turned 60.

How do you think being a woman helped you in politics?

'I don't think it helped at all. Don't forget, I took a very tough line from the beginning. There was no feminine charm exerted by me, in any way. I think at the beginning the Nats were quite intrigued – or perhaps the men, if you like. Quite intrigued. I was young and, you know, I was much better looking when I was 35. Obviously, I don't mean to say I'm much better looking now ...'

I would say you're better looking than all those males.

'Ja, ja, there's no competition. Anyway, I suppose the idea in this patriarchal society of a woman standing up and talking solid economics, which I used to do, quite intrigued them. But then, of course, the enormity of what I was proposing overcame that. There was no give on their part towards me. And I didn't want any.

'There was many a time during those years alone when I told myself: "This is madness, I can't go on." But when the chips were down and elections came round again, it was always "one more time". But in 1974, if we hadn't got any more, I told Colin I would resign. It wouldn't have been possible to carry on. It seemed to me there was no point in keeping a party going which could

only return one member after 15 years.'

A photograph in the large, cluttered study expresses, more than any words, the relief she felt when her 13 years of parliamentary loneliness ended. She has just thrown herself into the arms of René de Villiers on hearing, late on election night in April, 1974, that he had won Parktown for the Progressives. Yet it was those 13 years that not only established her reputation as the fiercest fighter for the underdog in South Africa, but made her an international figure – as well-known as Gary Player and Chris Barnard, which isn't bad for an opposition politician. Foreign universities showered honorary doctorates on her. In the house itself, the response was often something less than adulation. Mr PW Botha, her least favourite minister, last year said she was a 'hen cackling as though the air is full of falcons'.

She admits she can be shrill. Her interjections can be as pointed and witty as any heard, but if she is angry they tend to degenerate into a *sotto voce* commentary, unintelligible from the Press gallery but infuriating to the member trying to make his speech.

In April this year Prime Minister Vorster could take no more.

'I will give the member ten minutes of my time if she would just stay quiet,' he offered.

At times the attacks on her have been bitter and rancorous, with allegations of disloyalty to her country, particularly when she has criticised security legislation and detention without trial. But she gives as good as she gets.

'I wish the minister would emerge from his medieval miasma,' she said to one of them. When the backbenchers interrupt her she is apt to snap: 'Oh be quiet, you silly little man.' Then there was the occasion when Dr Willie Kotze, the MP for Parys, referring to her questions about conditions in prisons, and about detainees' deaths, said:

She admits she can be shrill. Her interjections can be as pointed and witty as any heard, but if she is angry they tend to degenerate into a *sotto voce* commentary, unintelligible from the Press gallery but infuriating to the member trying to make his speech.

'One can but ask what the member's purpose is with these questions.'

'To get information,' she retorted.

'To get information,' repeated Dr Kotze, as though he couldn't believe it. As for her speeches, this is how one commentator viewed them: 'Without the interjections, Mrs Suzman's speeches are like meringue without the glacé. They draw her out, sharpen her wit and add astringency to her asides.'

She herself says: 'I always like feeling I covered a speech well. I often feel dissatisfied with myself because afterwards you think of things you should have said, and quite often you think of things you shouldn't have said, that you did say.

'But I do prepare my stuff very carefully. I like the satisfaction of getting a good speech across, even if it's greeted with cries of rage from the other side. I don't often look back through the Hansard, but there are times when you have to check something and I'm pleased with some of the stuff I did in the '60s, particularly on civil rights. I really did hammer them.'

What other satisfactions?

'Well, a lot of things get done behind the scenes. You can help a lot of people just by picking up the phone and asking to speak to the department. They are quite co-operative.'

Do you get results?

'I do get results. I had an interview with a guy once when I picked up the phone – this was Bantu Administration – and I said: "This is Helen Suzman, MP for Houghton." And the voice at the other end said: "Ooo, God."'

She giggled at the memory. 'There was such a wealth of ... disgust in his voice. And I yelped, and then he gave a nervous giggle and said: "Ag, I didn't mean that, Mrs Suzman. What can I do for you?" So I get things done. It

gives you a feeling that you've got a useful role.

'Being a senior MP now is particularly advantageous, because you are on more familiar terms with cabinet ministers.'

When you eventually retire from politics, what will you do?

'I could never do nothing. The thought of reverting to type and just being a housewife and shopping in Rosebank and playing bridge every afternoon and perhaps golf once a week if I can still totter round the course would drive me mad. The sort of thing that could take its place is perhaps some lecture tours ...'

A lectureship?

'No, not a lectureship. No one would employ an old dame of 60. But what I certainly could do, because I've done a lot of it already, is give lectures in America, on South Africa, which is all I know anything about. One could do, say, two or three months of that a year. And then I've also been asked by several people to do a book. I'm not keen to do an autobiography. I would like to do memoirs.'

What's the difference?

'Big difference. Autobiography is tracing your life. Memoirs are selected things you want to record. The trouble is, I've never kept a diary. I've made no notes. I just hope that going through the Hansard and newspaper cuttings and so on will revive memories of things.

'But it would be a lonely existence, you know, doing that. In a way I'd miss the company ...'

And the limelight?

'I suppose in a way I would. I think all of us are failed actors. All of us politicians must have a very strong extrovert streak. Because you are putting yourself on display every single day of your life while parliament is sitting, and a good deal of other days when it's not sitting.

'I must say I get embarrassed at sitting around while

Helen Suzman – 'PW Botha, her
least favourite minister, said she
was "a hen cackling as though the
air is full of falcons".'

(Photo: Brian Astbury)

people go on and on about me. That I really don't enjoy.'

Do you mean when they are attacking you?

'Oh no, that I quite enjoy. And I've really been one of the fortunate ones, you know, who has been very honoured while alive, if you know what I mean.'

Well, stick around, won't you. Don't regard this as a signal to depart.

'When I think that they made me the honorary life president of the Young what do we call ourselves now? … Progressive Federal Party. I've got to think twice to remember our name. Anyway, I think that's a sure signal they think it's time I retired.'

She put her head back and rocked with laughter.

Is Cathy Taylor older or younger than you?

'Older. She'll never admit it (a naughty conspiratorial giggle) by a couple of years.'

The former MP for Wynberg was a complete contrast in style to her fellow female MP. They sat fairly close to each other, Mrs Suzman all tailored elegance, Mrs Taylor often in above-the-knee skirts and red sandals.

Did you have much rapport with her?

'No, I think she was jealous of me. I don't know whether you noticed, but she always used to make a point of getting up and walking out whenever I stood up to speak. And in a very obvious way. She used to gather up her books, slam them around and walk out. I used to do exactly the opposite. If I was about to go out when she stood up, I sat down again and listened.

'She had ability and worked hard, and I think she was a damn sight better than most of her male colleagues, from the point of view of conscientiousness.'

But clearly there was little sisterly love lost between them.

Would you ever consider doing what she did – emigrate?

'No, I haven't got any thoughts of emigrating.

Helen Suzman rises at 7 am, has breakfast in bed, reads the paper and then, if necessary, does some shopping – mostly by phone.

'My domestic work is done with the most remarkable speed. I streamline the whole damn thing. I've got a very good domestic who's been with me for 37 years. She comes to Cape Town with me for the session.

'So I don't do any cooking, I don't do my own smalls – I leave those things entirely to her. It's really just bed and breakfast. Lunch I always have at the House (of parliament), and I'm very often out for dinner.'

Until seven years ago she rented flats in Cape Town for the session. Then she bought a flat in Newlands, which she locks up for seven months of the year when she returns to Johannesburg. 'I love my little flat. It's as bright as a button. I did the whole thing in a morning with the help of a decorator. My sitting room's in orange and white, my bedroom in pink and white …'

Her mornings in parliament are always very busy, with the usual parliamentarian's correspondence, bills to study, speeches to write, interviews – every visiting journalist, guest of the SA Foundation and even of the Department of Information lands up in her office.

'I'm like the Kruger Park. I'm on the itinerary.'

And caucus meetings: 'These are great time-consumers. I never had a problem until 1974 because I was a one-woman caucus. I have discovered that men talk like mad. They love to mull over things. I have had to curb my impatience.'

About the younger male members of her burgeoning party: 'I've been trying not to be too bossy, which goes against the grain, because I am by nature a bossy person. I'm also inclined to be short-tempered and very irritable. I don't say: "Maybe you've got a point." I say: "Don't be so damned silly." It's not very tactful.'

Who can take offence when you say it like that?

'Everybody. You'd be surprised. But I like having the chaps around. They're mostly very nice people, which has made such a difference. I mean, I don't like them all equally. There are some that I don't like very much at all.'

She never works in the evening: 'I'm not a night worker. I like to have at least seven or eight hours' sleep a night to function properly the next day. And another half-hour at lunch-time if possible.'

She flies home to Johannesburg every second weekend, sometimes more often, and travels light.

'I just take my handbag. Sometimes a little overnight bag, but never a suitcase. It saves hours of waiting for luggage to appear on conveyor belts.'

The whole large Hyde Park household is organised around these fortnightly visits: 'I'm lucky in having good staff. The house is run extravagantly, but that's the price you have to pay them when you're not around, and I don't care. When I'm home I stock up the house for the next two weeks, seeing that everybody will be fed. My dogs are priority number one, now that my daughters have gone.'

She has four dogs, a poodle and three shih-tzus – a combination of a Tibetan terrier and a Pekinese, trained to guard temples. Her two daughters were aged 13 and 10 when she went to parliament for the first time: 'I have no doubt that from their point of view it wasn't easy. But they coped, and both graduated in their respective fields. They seem quite normal.' Frances, with a PhD in art history and married to a professor of public law, lives in London. Pat, still single, is a medical doctor in Boston.'

Her husband, Moses, is also a doctor and is apparently content to merge into the background of his renowned wife's political career. When the children were younger and their mother was in parliament, he used to take them to many musical concerts. 'Mosie is very absorbed in his work. He works every night with papers and preparing material for congresses.'

How do you spend your nights?

'In Cape Town there are a couple of dinners a week you go to. And I do have some close friends in Cape Town who are very nice about my phoning them and saying: "Can I come and watch telly this evening?" but I shall buy a portable for next session, so I don't have to go out on those stormy nights if there's something I want to watch. And I play some bridge over the weekends when I'm there.'

What are your interests outside politics besides gardening, golf, bridge?

'Reading. I read a helluva lot. I read every night. I've got very catholic tastes: travel books, biographies, novels. I don't read stuff on my work at night. I leave that to the morning.'

She's a careful eater with a weight that rarely rises 500 grams above or below 54 kilograms; wine doesn't agree with her and she sticks to Scotch at dinner parties; and she gave up smoking about 20 years ago.

'I used to smoke quite heavily from the age of 16. Then I chucked it. I stopped overnight. But I dreamt I was smoking years afterwards, and woke up in a panic.

Because I know – one drag and I'm gone.'

Where do you get the energy from?

'I'm a lucky enough to have good health.'

Physical exercise?

'No, but I've done a lot of exercise in my life as a little girl, and even as a young woman, until I got involved in parliament. I was mad about sport, you see. I was in the swimming team, the tennis team, the hockey team, and I rode a lot.'

She's sorry she gave up tennis for golf, which is more time-consuming and less concentrated exercise: 'Of course, you do walk in golf ...'

But it's a slow walk.

'Not with me it isn't. It's a brisk walk. In fact when I played at Wanderers there was a little cloud of dust on the fairway – there she goes.'

You have got enormous energy.

'I'm against self-indulgence. I'm not a procrastinator. And I have found if you do things immediately, you dispose of them and don't worry about them. The longer you leave them, the more difficult they are. My correspondence is never really left longer than a week. I'm meticulous in answering mail the week I get it. There are times when I'm away, obviously, when there's an accumulation. Then it's sheer hell to catch up.'

She calls herself a minister-watcher: 'If I ever send anything to a minister he can be sure of a follow-up letter if I don't get any reply from him.

'I have got energy, but I get very tired during the day and then, if I can get my 10 or 15 minutes passing out, I'm all right.'

Mrs Suzman is always immaculately dressed, without a strand of hair out of place.

How do you manage it?

'I don't enjoy shopping. I'm not a shopper. At the beginning of the season I go in and spend a morning getting a wardrobe. I shop at very few shops. I've got two or three favourites where the people know me, they know what I like, they don't bother me with fussy stuff they know I won't look at. They'll bring out the sort of clothes they know I like.

'In Cape Town I've got one or two such places as well, round the corner from where I live, and equip myself for the session in a morning.'

'Pomposity, for instance, infuriates me but I also find it amusing. I can't take it seriously: People who sit around pontificating about their patriotism, for instance. All these damn, pious remarks get on my nerves.'

You're not a slavish follower of the fashions.

'I'm essentially a tailored girl. I'm very fond of skirts and blouses and comfort. I can't stand things in which I can't move my broad shoulders. I don't like being restricted.

'When you sit all day you've got to worry about two or three things. One is comfort. Another is that your clothes must not look as though they've been through a washing machine when you stand up, although I don't like artificial fabrics at all. This is a problem. I like linen and cotton and silk. But today most materials have some artificial quality about them, and I suppose it's good because it stops them from creasing.'

Her hair: 'I'm very faithful to my hairdresser. I stick to the same chap; it's probably not such a good idea. I could get some new ideas. If I find someone who gives me satisfactory service I stay with him. I've got a thing about old friends and old shops. I have my hair done once a week, in the early morning. I haven't got easy hair. It's got to be managed. It's very curly and it's got to be handled firmly or it looks like a mad bush. I've been known to write speeches under the drier, too.'

In 1968, a British journalist, Anne Edwards, wrote of Helen Suzman: 'She has the gentlest manner of any woman MP I have ever met and she is by far the prettiest. There is none of the shrill aggressiveness, the tendency to squeak and thump that overcomes so many British women politicians.'

Helen commented: 'Well, then they must be pretty bad in Britain because I think I get pretty shrill at times. And I am quite aggressive.'

I would say that one of your characteristics is your lack of political reverence.

'I've got a rather wicked sense of humour in many ways. That's what has really carried me through this. I often look up (at the Press gallery) and you're laughing at the same nonsense thing that strikes me as being terribly funny.

'Pomposity, for instance, infuriates me but I also find it amusing. I can't take it seriously: People who sit around pontificating about their patriotism, for instance. All these damn, pious remarks get on my nerves.'

I read that the one person you were in awe of was Dr Verwoerd.

'Well, I was really quite frightened of that guy. There was something so … well, to my mind, so sinister about him. Because he was so convinced he had this divine mission. And those people frighten me because you can't touch them. You can't get to them.

'I could talk to Vorster when he was Minister of Justice. He would never smile, he was never friendly. But I could at least get to first base with him.

'I never really ever had a conversation with Dr Verwoerd. He never greeted me. I never greeted him. I think he hated me.'

Did he ever refer to you in his speeches?

'Oh yes, he did, always in a way that showed he hated me. "I've written the honourable member off," he once said. And I retorted: "The whole world's written you off." That was shortly after Sharpeville.'

In 1963 Cas Greyling said: 'This member's time in the House is getting short.' (And Helen had replied: 'Are you going to house arrest me?')

'Every year somebody said that. Blaar Coetzee came to me right at the end – I had a nice relationship with Blaar. We used to fight like hell, but he was always quite jovial and friendly if he met me in the lobby or on an aircraft, which you certainly couldn't say about Vorster.

'Vorster had a couple of years where he didn't greet me at all. He just snubbed me dead, and was very vicious in the House, to such an extent that Louis Louw, in *Die Burger*, actually wrote an article asking: Why this tremendous hostility? That was round about 1970/71. I don't know what engendered it, because I was no worse that year than I had been before, no more provocative. They just couldn't stand me any longer; they had had a belly full, I suppose.'

When did the United Party stop defending you? There was a stage in the beginning where, if they felt you were getting too much of a rough time, they would object, particularly Gray Hughes (chief UP whip).

'The only man who ever did. And once Douglas Mitchell did.

'And very often when I was hammered by that man PW Botha, for instance, and I took point after point of order with the chairman, and he wouldn't make the man withdraw, one of the UP should have stood up – if only for the House – and insisted that he withdraw.

'I was actually rather bitter. There were times when I was rather sorry that Harry Lawrence hadn't stayed in the House with the UP, though we were all tremendously pleased that he joined us, and he could never not have done so. But I used to think to myself if Harry Lawrence were still in the House on the front bench of the UP, he would never have let these things go by unchallenged. He used to stand up and help Margaret Ballinger time and again when she was having a rough time from Verwoerd.'

What is the mainspring of your philosophy? You're not an orthodox Jew.

'No, I'm not orthodox, but I'm Jewish. There's no question of that ...'

But in terms of religious faith?

'I'm not religious. I don't go to the synagogue and I don't go in for the whole concept of religion. It doesn't mean anything in my life. Justice means a lot in my life. I can't bear people being handled unjustly. That's all really. I try and be just in my own life. I hate bullies and the way blacks are kicked around; and the way they are at the absolute mercy of officialdom.

'I'm not a complicated person. I haven't got a philosophy, really. I just react to injustice.'

Helen Suzman retired from politics in 1989. The memoirs she refers to in this piece appeared in 1993 titled In No Uncertain Terms.

Fats Dike – 'The day will come when
it is the culture of Europe that will feel
foreign in this country.'
(*Photo:* Brian Astbury)

Meet Fats

Meet Fatima Dike, who says we should be contributing to one South African culture instead of each cosseting his own. She is one playwright who is doing just that.

Dene Smuts

Fairlady 19 July 1978

A big black woman in a white bush jacket stood up at a poetry reading in Constantia one night and brought the house down. 'Please Madam,' she boomed, reciting the song from the musical *Phiri,* and even with those first words people had the feeling that someone had arrived.

Fatima Dike has that sort of presence. She also has her own world, and a touch of the storyteller that whirls you away to her own world. And a visceral grasp of essentials. These talents brought her audiences up and down the land just three years later, and made her a prize-winning playwright.

The poetry reading was held in aid of The Space, the dilapidated, dynamic, independent and perennially poverty-stricken city centre theatre that has produced some of South Africa's most stimulating plays and talented players. Fatima was introduced by friends and became involved because it was thought she might be a potential actress.

She waited in the wings, working on backstage jobs and on her own poetry. She had progressed to the post of assistant stage manager ('the worst we ever had', grins Space director Brian Astbury) when dramatist Rob Amato found a book of her poems in the locker room one day and told her to sit down and write a play. She produced one, *The Sacrifice of Kreli,* that put her on the map and also on the permanent payroll of The Space, as resident playwright, in which capacity she now sits down at the theatre's old IBM to grind out some groundwork, then gets up again, moons about getting more and more 'pregnant with an idea' for the months and months it takes to come to term, and finally sits down again to deliver, writing 'straight from the gut', as her boss Brian says.

Fats, as she is fondly known, is gutsy; she has an unabashed vibrancy about her. She keeps sophistication where it belongs, in the mind and not in the manner. When she is excited, her language is gloriously impolite and she plays the fool with everyone in sight. When she is serious, she will drop her voice an octave, grab you by the knee and quite simply bewitch

> 'It is a vicious circle in which one group will do tomorrow what the other does today.'

you. When she makes a point, she punctuates it with a Xhosa click and pauses to watch it sink in. Even her slang is utterly sincere. She will call a recently deceased friend a 'dead cat' without blinking. The intelligence is there all the time, controlling, but she remains totally uncontrived. Rob Amato thinks it is this quality that 'enables her to relate to any human being'.

In the Cape, where black people are isolated from white people more than anywhere else in the country because the island of black life obscured under township smoke is so small amid the sprawl of white and coloured suburbs, it takes some doing. But Fats has brought Langa to Long Street and managed to make it part of The Space. She has also made it a part of our cultural repertoire – with a purpose.

When an audience settles down to watch her play, *The First South African*, it is confronted by the carefully reproduced interior of a township house. The lino is there, the scrap of carpet painstakingly placed at an angle to the settee that serves as a bed at night, the tub of water that first fills the kettle and then serves as dishwashing water.

Whites in the audience sit up and take notice. They wouldn't bat an eyelid at a British or a French or Russian setting, but this feels … well, foreign. By the time the play's last line has been spoken, the audience has taken its first steps towards becoming South African. The play, like the playwright, speaks directly to everyone, making an audience of every class and colour respond with what Amato calls 'a special kind of unanimity'.

The day will come, says Fatima Dike, when it is the culture of Europe that will feel foreign in this country. At the age of 12, Fats had read Dickens and *Black Beauty* and all the classics that establish English attitudes and affections in a child's mind. And because her mother had sent her to a Sotho instead of a Xhosa school so that she could learn Afrikaans, *die-osse-stap-aan-deur-die-stowwe* had become as much a part of her as the gallop of the Light Brigade, as much a part of her as the beat of her heart. At about the same time, she was so much a stranger to the people whose inner lives she shared that she thought whites were always given lots of room on trains because they were so soft and pink and would begin to bleed in a crush.

She had, she agrees, a bad case of cultural schizophrenia from which we all suffer in one way or another. What else can you call the gap between our cultural 'personalities' and the way we live?

Living the Western way in the city all day and returning to traditional rules at night causes schizophrenia. So does sending your sons to imitation Etons and thinking home is a host of golden daffodils when you have buried three generations under African earth. So does commemorating an ancient interracial battle like Blood River to keep an outdated identity going when your children grow up with the farm klonkies and your cities buzz with as many languages as the tower of Babel.

Fats nods, firmly. 'Listen: when I was at school, we had an inspector, an Afrikaans cat (man), who wept when we recited *Amakeia*. '*In die skadu van die berge, bosbeskut aan alle kante, staan alleen die hartbeeshuisie, op die grens van Kafferland …*' she begins, softy. 'When we got to the second verse, when we got to the story of the black nanny who gave her life trying to save a white baby from the warriors, that was when he wept. He never said a word, but he cried because he knew the reality of this country was in that poem.'

You can't keep politics out of the picture. Politics have always dictated our identities here, and will probably go on putting us in compartments.

'It is a vicious circle in which one group will do tomorrow what the other does today,' Fats says, facing one of life's more conspicuous facts.

But you can look beyond political passion and see what is really there. Fats does that because 'my trip, as an artist, is people and not politics'. And her formula is radical and simple.

'This country was meant to be a melting pot. However if we are going to order our existence together, we should be contributing to one culture, not making ourselves miserable by each cosseting a culture of his own. It is the next step in this country, and the cure for that schiz. The day will come when our children will not read the English classics. Noddy has nothing to say to South Africa.'

The first step in becoming a South African is to see those political identities for what they really are.

'Take a case,' says Fats, shoving her big glasses onto the bridge of her nose with a forefinger, 'where a man is born of a white father and a black mother and he is physically white, but is brought up by his mother as a black, with all the traditions like circumcision, so that he has a black heart. Then the law comes along and classifies him coloured. My question is this: what is that man? He is not black – he is the shadow of a black man. He is not white – he is the shadow of a white man. And he is definitely not coloured.'

The case is symbolic and it is the story of *The First South African*. 'Zwelinzima, called also Ruben or Rooi,' she goes on, 'believes himself black but is sent by the Group Areas Act to a place where he has to start a whole new life with people he doesn't know. Those three 'identities' start pulling him apart, he goes mad. Anywhere else in the world there would have been no question – he would have been accepted for what he is, a man, a South African.'

Once you have found out that we are all people and all South African, it follows that you have to set about consciously becoming one by making yourself familiar with all the South African lives that felt foreign before. Seeing a play like *The First South African* does that for you. It brings township life and its rhythms and rules and traditions to life before your eyes.

So does talking to Fats. She lives in an attractively decorated household of women in Langa where her widowed mother presides, in a very real sense, over a family of grown children and grandchildren.

Fatima has to watch her ways with Mrs Annie Dike and so do her son Seth, 9, and daughter Thembi, 7, who belong to their grandma because Fats is not married. According to custom they will become hers only if she marries and her husband agrees to have them, a situation she doesn't see arising.

'I like to be free, man. If I want to go to Johannesburg to write a play, I want to be able to go.'

Fats will undoubtedly go far. But her taproot will always lie in the township that bred her. In township life there is a quality called *ubuntu*, sharing.

'If my mother gets sick or someone is stabbed, we can't pick up a phone and call the ambulance. We have to go to the police with the patient, they call, and only then will the ambulance come. So you go to a neighbour who has a car and he will get up in the middle of the night, gladly. It is like a deep well. You are not alone. If anything happens, the others are there. In seven years, white neighbours will not get to know each other – they have their phone, their TV, their car. They don't need each other.

'And you know what else black cats have? They have what I call jive,' she goes on, erupting into an enthusiastic description of the stylish clothes on view at a black soccer match or the outfits the kids at mission school in the Transvaal used to wear to infuriate the head: pointed shoes fitted with false soles to make the toes turn up, sunflower-yellow socks with two black stripes worn with an equally sunny waistcoat and with considerable swagger, Barathea blazers, Pyramid hankies sticking out of Monatic pockets ...

'You must understand,' she says, slowing down and sobering, 'that blacks have nothing but their dignity. Dressing up is almost the only available way to express it. Clothes become very important to us, and the label all-important. In hats,

It is not happiness, it is the spirit of survival you hear in that laughter.'

It is not just a gay black girl you see in Fats Dike either. The spirit of survival is the black quality she celebrated in her first play, *The Sacrifice of Kreli,* which won the *Star*'s Play of the Year award. She woke up one morning in 1975 and realised that 18 million people in this country had no history. Rob Amato brought her two clippings from 1890 editions of The *Daily Dispatch,* interviews with King Kreli, and she had her history. Or some of it. Getting information on the king proved difficult. Imperialism wipes out more

The poetry reading in Constantia in 1972, seen from her side, was a kind of culture shock. She remembers watching the whites arriving and glancing at the 'Black is Beautiful' badge sewn onto her bush jacket arm with something like alarm.

the first choice is Dobbs, in jackets, Hector Powe. Shoes should be Florscheim even if you have to fork out R60 to get them, shirts are Arrow, and so on.'

In *The First South African* there is a sassy character sporting flamboyant outfits who steals clothes in the city and sells them in the townships.

'Who do you think that character is to us?' Fats wants to know.

'That character is Robin Hood!'

A lot of things look different seen from the opposite side of the system. Laughter is one of them. 'Whites always think blacks laugh so much because they are happy.

than warriors. But the available material was enough to excite her.

'Here was a man who went to war with the British for 40 years. He started with 12 000 warriors and ended up with 500, in exile in The Hole above the Bashee. The war cost the British £200 000, which in 1877 was a fortune, and at one stage there were only three men in the Castle at the Cape. The Cape Government couldn't pay for the war. Queen Victoria had to supply most of the funds.

'So who won? Who do you think really won the war?'

Kreli was Fatima's contribution to

Black Consciousness. It should logically have been written in Xhosa, but because it is also a contribution to the common culture, it was done in double text: Xhosa rhyme on the left page and a literal English translation in Xhosa rhythm on the right. 'Show us then, you our father/Be the light in our darkness...' It is hypnotic, and it is a melting of the kind that perhaps only Herman Charles Bosman has produced before, with his Afrikaans written in English. Since her girlhood days when her knowledge of whites was less than skin deep, Fats has had to do her discovering of the foreign side of South Africa too. After her school days, first in Langa and then at a high school in the Transvaal, she worked in a black bookshop and butchery owned by a wealthy brother-in-law and then in a steakhouse in Newlands ('Yes, in the kitchen, where else?') where she got swing-door glimpses of whites. It was her friendship with poet Sue Clarke that gave her the opportunity to meet the other half of mankind and that led to her involvement with The Space. The poetry reading in Constantia in 1972, seen from her side, was a kind of culture shock. She remembers watching the whites arriving and glancing at the 'Black is Beautiful' badge sewn onto her bush jacket arm with something like

alarm. Such suits she had never seen before, such silks and furs. And real diamonds, sitting there twinkling away on real fingers and throats. Her mind was already boggling from walking in and seeing the other readers, people she had known in newsprint only.

'Percy Sieff, in the flesh! And Janet Suzman and Athol Fugard and Yvonne Bryceland ... imagine meeting them!'

Now this – the fur and finery. And then, the reaction when she read *Please Madam*: 'Please Madam, before you laugh at the night watchman's English, try talking to him in Zulu; Please Madam ...' 'Sock it to them,' Constantia cried, and stomped its well-heeled feet. She had thought that was madam out there in the audience?

Now, six years later, she understands us very well, all our contradictions and convolution.

'I went to see a white friend today and a woman at the flats asked me: "Who are you looking for, Nanny?"' she laughs.

'She is not a racist, that woman, it is just that she is conditioned,' and she points her forefingers at her temples. She understands, so she can laugh at herself too, when that small sign of panic in the face of privilege, the great divider, recurs.

'Do you know so-and-so's house? Awoo – in her house there are such riches. A small table with porcelain, so delicate, a soft lamp, so,' and she evokes that atmosphere with the curve of a hand, then begins to grin, 'I felt *kaffer*!' When they asked me what I'd have to drink I had to do some quick thinking (oh hell, white cats drink certain things at certain times) and I said: "Ah, whisky please," as though I did this every day.'

Peals of laughter. Her next play is the next step towards the common culture: a consideration of separate societies living together in changing times. *The Glass House* will be the story of two girls, one white, one black, one the daughter of the house, the other of the housemaid, who inherit a house together. Outside, the world is changing. The black girl likes the way the feeling and features of a township are coming to this dilapidated, once affluent white area. The white girl feels threatened. Inside, they turn to each other with mixed emotions. The stage is set.

Fatima Dike still lives and works in Cape Town. She continues to be involved in the theatre. In 2005 the country she once imagined is in the process of being born.

Down Second Avenue

Es'kia Mphahlele

Fairlady 23 April 1980

You never knew Pretoria was like this ... A location comes to life in this extract from *Down Second Avenue*, the early biography of one of our foremost black writers.

When I was about 12, I noticed something that had already begun to take shape in that part of north-eastern Transvaal that fell under the rule of Chief Mphahlele. The young able-bodied men were leaving the villages to seek work in answer to the call of the city. Vaguely I understood that Pretoria was the Mecca.

At Christmas-time they came back in dashing clothes. They brought gramophones which they said they had played all the way in the train. They said the things we saw in Goldstein's general store were for chickens and not eagles compared with those that glittered in Pretoria shop windows. For a long time they made us believe that there were very small people singing inside the gramophones. They probably believed it themselves. At Christmas-time Jeemee Roe-Jars (Jimmy Rodgers), then in fashion, yodelled plaintively from various parts of the village.

I never dreamt that I should go back to the city where I was born, which I couldn't picture in my mind anyhow. We thrilled at the idea of riding a train, my brother, sister and I, when mother came in the middle of the year to tell us she had come to fetch us. The train arrived. I was too dazed to be happy. Too frightened to ask questions. We found ourselves at Pretoria station the next day. In the midst of a winter's morning we were whisked away by a taxicab to Marabastad, a black location.

This is how a country bumpkin dived into slum life. The springboard was Second Avenue, where my maternal grandmother lived with Aunt Dora and three uncles, all younger than my mother.

The water trickled down into tin containers. It seemed an age waiting for a four-gallon tin to fill up. More and more people came to wait, the queue got longer and longer, stretching down in snaky fashion. A few of us small boys were also in the queue.

It trickled into a bucket, or a dish, and the queue grew longer, not able to hear itself anymore. You could hear a click of the tongue from many souls

> Marabastad, like most locations, was an organised rubble of tin cans. The streets were straight, but the houses stood cheek by jowl, rusty as ever on the outside, as if they thought they might as well crumble in straight rows if that was to be their fate.

waiting there; a click of helpless disgust and impatience. A pilgrimage at a communal water tap. It was like this in Second Avenue; you knew it must be like that at every other communal tap in Marabastad.

Sometimes the people quarrelled, then they laughed, then they eavesdropped and they gossiped. Some sat on their tins. One or two suckled their babies while they waited. The tins filled at their own good time.

'Tck, tck, so much water in the seas, but none in Marabastad,' said someone. Another tightened her large jaws and clapped her hands and clasped them behind as if to say: 'Wait and despair.' And you knew she had a capacity for waiting.

About midday the water queue got shorter, and at about one the place was clear. It was most annoying to us boys because we missed going to the market to work for a few shillings for bread and atcha – mango boiled in 'hot red curry mixture' – during school recess. It also meant that we'd have to collect our pennies and tickeys from boys

who owed us – a thing that brought poor results.

Marabastad, like most locations, was an organised rubble of tin cans. The streets were straight, but the houses stood cheek by jowl, rusty as ever on the outside, as if they thought they might as well crumble in straight rows if that was to be their fate. Each house, as far I remember, had a fence of sorts. The wire always hung limp, the standards were always swaying in drunken fashion. A few somewhat pretentious houses could be found here and there. These were, like the rest, of corrugated iron. But they had verandas paved with concrete too. The grim old man down our street who worked for the Portuguese Legation had such a house. There was one in Tenth Avenue, and two in Thirteenth Avenue. The other verandas, where any, were paved with mud, and about four poles supported the roof unevenly.

There was only one house which had a flower garden. This faced Barber Street, and it belonged to a

man who boasted a coloured wife, Gertie, and a large brood of uppity children who were good at insulting their father because of his dark complexion. In fact, this family was reputed to be the only one that had a coal stove. It was possible, because at Christmas-time long queues of Marabastad residents stood waiting with dishes of dough in front of the Indian-owned ABC Bakery, to have bread or cakes baked at a shilling for a standard dish.

In the mornings and afternoons Marabastad was always covered by a blanket of smoke coming from the coal braziers which were put in the yard to burn out before we carried them into the houses in winter, or in the backyard in warm months.

The backyards were always inclined to be dirty, much as the people swept them continually with home-made grass brooms. Most of the houses had a room or two to a family or single persons. So it was not uncommon to find about three braziers blazing away in the same yard.

Ra-Stand, as we called the inevitable white superintendent of the location – *Ra* is Sotho for father – was always particular about keeping the streets free of dirty water and dead cats and dogs. But the backyards seemed to be beyond him. The only time we ever saw this personage was when we went to pay our fourteen shillings rent or when he drove up the only tarred road, Barber Street, which was the reason why he was thought of only as the owner of Marabastad stands. Otherwise, the location seemed to be the property of the police. Farther into the location, dirty water and flies and dead cats and dogs and children's stools owned the streets.

We were getting used to Second Avenue life, my brother, sister and I. Avenues and streets were new to us. Now why would people go and build houses all in a straight line? Why would people go to a bucket in a small building to relieve themselves? Why would we want to be cut off from one another by putting up fences? It wasn't so at Maupaneng where we had come from. Houses didn't stand in any order and we visited one another and we could sit around the communal fire and tell one another stories until the cocks crowed. Not in Second Avenue. And yet, although people didn't seem to be interested in one another, they spoke with a subtle unity of voice. They still behaved as a community.

My grandmother was head of a large family. She was a Mopedi, whose father had also been a Mphahlele, but no blood relation of my father's.

My mother, Aunt Dora, and three uncles were born in the district of eastern Transvaal. Aunt Dora, her three children and the three uncles lived with us. And we had two rooms. Both were bedrooms and the room which had a table and four chairs was bedroom and sitting room. We cooked on the back veranda. Granny leased three rooms. My mother, eldest in the family, worked in one of the suburbs as a domestic servant and lived in. She came to see us one Sunday in a fortnight.

Here the young men who migrate to the cities to work still fight as they did on moonlight nights in the country. And so every Sunday afternoon they marched with big broad slabs of human flesh they called feet to some place outside the city. They moved in rival teams. In Pretoria these *malaita* were provided with a piece of ground and they marched under police guard. In this way, the 'Natives let off steam', as the Pretoria City Council said.

Our house faced Barber Street. It was a family recreation to sit on the veranda on Sunday afternoons. The *malaita* beat on the tar with their large feet past our house; the police dispersed in front of our house before going each to his beat; visiting domestic workers from the suburbs passed our house before they swept into the locations, and passed in front of our house again on their way out. It was a common Sunday afternoon spectacle for a policeman to pass in front of our house propelling a man by the scruff of the neck to the police station. Women particularly fascinated us in their various styles of dress. Some hobbled past in awkward high heels, evidently feeling the pinch; others were really smart and enviable.

Our fence needed constant pulling up because it was always falling. Grandmother said how she wanted to plant flowers. We tried valiantly, but none of us had the guts to fetch water for the plants. We gave it up. The best we ever got to doing was to set up a grapevine creeper which made pleasant shade for the family to do washing. The rusty iron gate was a particular nuisance. The ants kept eating up the standards underneath, and we kept digging in the poles until we, the gate and everything else about it resigned ourselves to an acute angle and we piled stones around the standards to maintain the status quo.

We swept the yard, however, a ten-foot border on all sides of the corrugated walls. The women made a lovely path from the gate to the front door, branching off the back of the house. This was skirted on either side by small mud walls, and the floor was paved with mud smoothened with a slippery stone, then smeared with dung. Small pebbles had been worked in in repeated triangular patterns. A small wall separated this path from our ash dump, where we constantly scratched for coke to use again in our braziers. The ash we then poured into the garbage can.

Towards the front end of our yard, facing Barber Street and Second Avenue, we often planted maize. From this patch we harvested exactly seven cobs most years. We, the smaller members of the family,

> I can never remember Marabastad in the rainy summer months. It always comes back to me with its winter. And then I cannot remember ever feeling warm except when I was at the fire or in the sun.

netted half a cob each. Our backyard was fenced with a four-foot mud wall. The floor of the yard was made with mud because that was where we cooked – we and the tenants in the two back rooms. These rooms, together with our passage that ran from the back to the front doors, opened onto a small veranda. This we used as a kitchen in the winter.

The ash around the fireplace was a perennial problem. The corrugated iron walls were always sooty, except towards the edge of the porch, where Chipile, the Indian soft-goods hawker, often pencilled his invoice.

I did most of the domestic work because my sister and brother were still too small. My uncles were considered too big. I woke up at 4.30 in the morning to make fire in a brazier fashioned out of an old lavatory bucket. I washed and made breakfast coffee for the family, which we often had with mealie-meal porridge from the previous night's left-overs. Back from school I had to clean the house as Aunt Dora and Grandmother did the white people's washing all day. Fire had to be made, meat had to be bought from the Indian butchery in the Asiatic Reserve. We were so many in the family that I had to cook porridge twice in the same pot. We hardly ever bought more than a pound of mutton in weight.

Weekdays supper was very simple: just porridge and meat. When there was no money we fried tomatoes. We never ate vegetables except on Sundays. We never had butter except when we had a visitor from Johannesburg.

At breakfast bread was cut up. The grown-ups were given theirs first in saucers. Then I rationed the remainder in slices and bits of slices. Our youngest uncle, not much older than I, picked his first, which was the greatest quantity. Then I followed, then my brother and then my sister. We ate supper out of the same plate, we children, and meat was dished out in varying sizes and the ritual was repeated. We never sat at table. Only a visitor was treated to such modern innovations.

On Monday mornings, at about four o'clock, I started off for the suburbs to fetch washing for Aunt Dora. Thursday and Friday afternoons I had to take back the washing. If I was lucky enough I borrowed a bicycle from a tenant of ours we called simply 'Oompie' – uncle – when he was not using it on his rounds in the location collecting numbers from gamblers for the Chinaman's fah fee. If I couldn't get the bicycle for the morning or afternoon I carried the bundles on my head and walked – about 11 kilometres

a single journey. When I walked I couldn't use the pair of tennis shoes I'd been bought for Sunday wear. Winter mornings were most trying when the air penetrated the big cracks round the edges of my feet.

I can never remember Marabastad in the rainy summer months. It always comes back to me with its winter. And then I cannot remember ever feeling warm except when I was at the fire or in the sun.

I was cycling one Monday morning from Waterkloof suburb with a large bundle of washing on the handlebars. It was such a cold midwinter morning that I was shivering all over. I had on a very light frayed and torn blazer.

I came to a circle. Instead of turning to my right I didn't. I couldn't. The handlebars of the bicycle couldn't turn owing to the pressure of the bundle. From the opposite direction a handful of white boys came cycling towards me. They took their bend, but it was just when my bicycle was heading for the sidewalk of the bend. They were riding abreast. For some reason or other I didn't apply my brakes. Perhaps my mind was preoccupied with the very easy yet not so very easy task of turning the handlebars. I ran into the first boy in the row, who fell on the next, and their row was disorganised. The vehicle I was riding went to hit against the curb, and I was riding down on the ground almost in a split second.

'Barstard!' shouted the boy who had fallen first.

His friends came to me and about three of them each gave me a hard kick on my backside and thighs. And they cursed and cursed and then rode away, leaving me with the cold, the pain, the numbness, and the punctured and bent front wheel.

I picked up the bundle and dragged myself to the sidewalk and leant against the tree. At first I was too bewildered to think. I started off again and limped ten kilometres home. My aunt and grandmother groused and groused before they had Oompie's vehicle fixed.

'Say it again,' said China from the lower end of Second Avenue. I related the story of my collision again.

'You country sheep!' said Moloi, the boy next door, laughing.

'What d'you think this is – Pietersburg forests?' was Ratua's sarcasm.

It was a joke to all but Ratua. He was a grave-looking boy. Little Links looked indifferent. Even when he said: 'That's the first lesson, you've got to go about town with your eyes open.'

I had stopped worrying over being called *skapie* – sheep. I was told that's the label they stuck onto anybody fresh from the country.

Darkness had set in. Already the streetlights were on, and Marabastad location was steeped in misty light. A few moths were circling playfully round the electric bulbs. It was a Saturday night. Usually Saturday nights are far from dull in slum locations. Everybody is on the alert, particularly the womenfolk.

So it was this Saturday night. An ominous scream pierced into the darkness of the night. I was kicking my legs about for any slight glimpse of a torchlight. I think now how harassing that torchlight was. It was always like this: Saturday night and police whistles; Saturday night and screams; Saturday night and cursing and swearing from the white man's lips. Yet one never seemed to get so used to it that the experience became commonplace and dull from beginning to end. And I was 13.

My aunt was straining the last few pints of beer to pour into a gallon oil tin; and I was keeping watch outside in the yard.

It had to be like this always. 'Go and watch outside, my son'; 'Dig the hole deep, my son'; 'Stamp hard on it, my son'; and so on. The same old cycle. Leave school, my daughter, and work. You cannot sit at home and have other people work for you; stand up and do the white man's washing and sell beer. That's right – that is how a woman does it; look at us, we do not sit and look up to our husbands or fathers to work alone; we have sent our children to school with money from beer selling …

Yes, it had to be thus; always. You are on white man's land; you must do his washing; you must buy his bread with his money; you must live in houses built by him; he must police your area …

The other tins were in their holes already. The last one must be coming through the window soon. She must hurry, or … I heard heavy footsteps. Two big men had jumped into the yard, and a big torchlight flashed all over swallowing up every little object around. Before they turned the corner I had received the tin. In a split second I flung the tin into the next yard. It landed with a splashing thud. I was cursing my fate for the sound but thanking my gods that it had landed in a tank of dirty water, when a white and an African constable came round the corner and focused that terrible blinding light on my face, so that I could only see the big shoulders of the white man on the sides. I became stupid with terror and trembled.

'What are you doing here, my jong?' the big white man asked in Afrikaans. He had switched off his terrible light.

'Nothing.'

'How can you stand here alone and do nothing, Kaffir?'

Silence. Even at this moment I could picture my mother running about to dispose of the remains and the utensils.

'What was that I heard when I came in?'

'I was throwing a stone at a dog,' I said. I must keep them here until my mother would have finished. But I little thought what it was going to cost me.

'Hold the bastard's arms, Jonas, and pin them behind his ass.' The black constable had hardly reached my hand when the big white hand crashed full on my cheek so that I seemed to hear my name called, and staggered and hit against a pole that was supporting a vine. The black man pulled me away with a jerk that sent a pain shooting through my side.

'Are you going to tell the truth, jou donder?' I didn't care now. Let anything happen, I thought. I got a backhand on the mouth, and in an instant I tasted something salty. While I held my mouth the big white man caught me behind the neck and pressed my face against his other massive hand, so that I began to suffocate.

'Now, this is for your bloody lies, you son of a stinking Kaffir!' With the last word he thrust me away from him. I went down on hard ground.

A big terrible light ... Shining steel pokers with sharp points for destroying beer containers ... Heavy footsteps ... Clanging of steel ... the sound coming faintly ... I felt sick. The earth was turning and I seemed to hang precariously on the edge. Everything became dark and black before me ...

Marabastad continued to brew beer. Police continued to raid as relentlessly and to destroy. There were Saturday and Sunday mornings when the streets literally flowed with beer. The Chinese and Indian shopkeepers were not prevented from selling corn malt either. Each yard had several holes in which tins of beer were hidden.

Women brewed some of the most terrifying compounds.

'It's heathen!' Grandmother said indignantly. 'My beer's the pure and healthy food a man's stomach needs.'

And we never had the fighting type of customer. 'But even with that, send my children to college.' By which she meant either high school or teacher-training school. She did send three of her sons to high school and a teacher-training institution.

Saturday night. Darkness. Sounds of snoring from my uncle at the corner. Like the muted lowing of a cow. Tomorrow the other uncle sleeping with him on the floor will complain that he has been roused from his sleep by snoring. My younger brother doesn't stir beside me. Nor the youngest uncle the other side of him under the same blanket as we. They say I'm a bad sleeper and when sleep descends on me there is going to be a tugging and tossing and rolling among three of us. I know the cold air coming through the hole in the flooring boards will whip us out of sleep as it plays upon bare flesh, else one's leg will rest on my neck and then I shall dream that some fiend is slitting my throat and I shall jump up with a scream.

My sister also on the floor is kicking the leg of table she's sleeping under. Grandmother and three of Aunt Dora's children are lying quiet on the old double bed. The only door and the only window are shut. Hot. With two frayed blankets on us it's good to feel hot. I can't sleep, I can't get up to walk about in the yard because my bones are aching because I was cleaning the house and turning everything up and choking in the dust I was making. Sweating. Blowing off the salt water from my lips. Kneading my nose to ease the tick-

ling sensation inside it. No use. The boxes and some of Grandmother's worthless collections on the boards resting on the rafters will never be free from the dust ever.

And then the boxes on the floor containing old handbags and hats and trinkets given by some long-forgotten missus, had to come down from their high stack. But Grandmother said to leave them as I found them. Tins of beer dug into the floor behind the stack and the strong smell of fermenting malt and grey spots on the floor around the holes. No policeman will find it easily. Policeman? Saturday night. The men in uniform may even now be sniffing about in the yard.

Far to the west end of Marabastad a police whistle, the barking of dogs – no, it must be in Fourth Avenue maybe because I hear heavy booted footsteps; it's sure to be a person running away from the law, the police cells, the court and jail. Saturday night and it's ten to ten, I can hear the big curfew bell at the police station peal 'ten to ten, ten to ten, ten to ten' for the black man to be out of the streets to be at home out of the policeman's reach. Year after year every night the sound of the bell floats in the air at ten minutes to ten and the black man must run home and the black man must sleep or have a night special permit. The whistle is very near now and the hunted man must be in Second Avenue but the bell goes on pealing lustily and so, black man, you must run wherever you run, run. Whistle sound dies away, the bell stops but still I cannot sleep because my back is aching and

'The white man is strong,' funny this comes to me as I seem to hear my mother say it: 'the white man's strong I don't know you mustn't stand in his way or he'll hurt you, maybe when you're big I don't know you will open your mouth and say what is in your heart but remember now the white man has a strong arm.'

I am trying to stop my tears of pain so I jump over the others and feel my way to the door opening out on to the ten-foot passage where there is a bucket of water.

I take a gulp and go back. Take care not to run your head into the leaning stack of boxes or night will come to an unholy end soon. Music of U-NO-MES band at the Columbia still travels along the night which is what the handbills meant by *Daybreak Dance*. Still no sleep, only things to remember like Saul and Rieta down our Avenue. This morning they woke up to find Rieta had rolled onto her new baby and killed it and they are in the cells this moment. Saul and Rieta. One seldom spoke of Saul without saying Rieta. Drank too much beer, the two, and quarrelled and sometimes Rieta bit one of Saul's fingers and they cried together, all which made Grandmother say those two are Sodom and Gomorrah and now they went to fetch God's infant from where it had been lying in peace and then killed it. Saul and Rieta, two thin people, thin as Satan's messengers, Grandmother said, as thin as water-reeds walking forever as if blown by the wind.

The Saturday night buzz has now been ruffled. Siki is walking down the street playing his guitar, the one he carries about on him, the guitar he plays while he coughs on and on, for he has been coughing ever since I knew him, a long time. Siki's music comes and goes and I can see him passing on the side of our house, see him as if I were outside, rolling down to the house where he lives with his brother who feeds him and clothes him. Is he with – no, he can't be playing like that if he's with Katrina, Katrina his girlfriend who looked after him often. The music fades and fades and is gone with the night.

'The white man is strong,' funny this comes to me as I seem to hear my mother say it: 'the white man's strong I don't know you mustn't stand in his way or he'll hurt you, maybe when you're big I don't know you will open your mouth and say what is in your heart but remember now the white man has a strong arm.' Saturday night and I'm thinking of school and my classmates. I feel so weak, inferior, ignorant, self-conscious. Saturday night and I'm still thinking and feeling. Tomorrow and the *malaita* marching through in bright uniforms led by a beautiful and loud brass band who play so that you can hear and a banner floating, beating in the air. But now it's Saturday and I want to sleep.

Wonder if that poor man has been caught. Police, police. Mother I fear police Grandmother I don't want police Aunt Dora Uncle I fear the police I hate them. Mother says my child when you're grown up when you're big ... What's the matter with your herbs? Aunt Dora asks Mathebula the Shangana witch doctor of the family, now sleeping on the back veranda as always. We feed him and give him sleeping room and he gives us strong herbs when we are ill and throws his bones and asks them to tell him why we are so poor and why the police give us no peace and why my uncles and my aunt sometimes quarrel.

Mathebula is asleep maybe but I think through his herbs he can see me wide-awake. He put a stick into the fire when he went to bed as he always does to keep away other people's baboons but he cannot tell us how to keep the police away. I wonder what the matter is with Mathebula's herbs ...

Reprinted with permission of Picador Africa, from Down Second Avenue *by Es'kia Mphahlele.*

A Life in Service

Ingrid Hudson

Fairlady 7 October 1981

Leah Tutu was the daughter of a domestic worker. Today she is the 'mother' of millions of domestics. Loved and revered, she holds a position unique in South Africa.

The tall, regal figure, the deep forceful voice, and the bold kaftans and turbans attract attention everywhere she goes. This attention turns to reverence when people realise who the wearer is.

'Leah Tutu' – the whisper spreads like wildfire. People crowd round to hug and kiss her, or stand talking to her, holding her hand affectionately.

Leah Tutu is the wife of a controversial leader but she is also something more; a female figurehead, the voice of millions of black women.

Her life with Bishop Desmond Tutu has had a great deal to do with the flowering of her own qualities of leadership and the unique position she holds in South Africa today. She gained her first insight into the machinations of the race relations which lie at the core of the country's problems when she went with her husband to England in 1962.

Leah had grown up in Munsieville near Klerksdorp – a typically dusty township. She went to a Catholic high school and teacher's training college and married the son of the former headmaster shortly after qualifying.

He too was a teacher but left the profession after the Bantu Education Act was passed. He turned to theology and when he was awarded a scholarship to study at King's College, London, he and Leah and their two young children left home to live in London. It was a crucial period for Leah.

'I learnt I was not inferior. Of course, if you'd asked me if I felt inferior to whites or anybody before I left for England, I would have said: Not on your life. But I was taken aback when people, accidentally bumping into me in the street, apologised, or when a shop assistant said "Can I help you?" Ordinary courteous behaviour, but I was amazed by it because I wasn't used to it at home. The whites I had come into contact with were rude and I had accepted their treatment because I must have felt deep down that I was not as good as them.

'Whites don't know what generation after generation of growing up as second best does to a person. You get to accept that status without even

Leah Tutu – 'The whites I had come
into contact with were rude and I had
accepted their treatment.'
(*Photo:* Ingrid Hudson)

> She gained her first insight into the machinations of the race relations which lie at the core of the country's problems when she went with her husband to England in 1962.

knowing it. This feeling of inferiority will have to be exorcised in order for things to change.'

While learning to understand her feelings of inferiority, Leah also recognised her own prejudices.

'I hadn't met many whites up until then but those I had met were hardly pleasant. But I suppose you shouldn't base your assessments of a whole race on its shop assistants and post office workers, especially in South Africa. Living in London I met a wide range of people. I got to know whites as individuals and became aware of my own prejudices for the first time. Now I know there's no such thing as a dirty race – only dirty people.'

Like thousands of young, student families before them, the Tutus had very little money, no one to babysit. They went out only for the odd cup of coffee after the children had been put to bed.

They returned after four years in London to life in Africa in the Eastern Cape.

'It was good to be back home – in some ways,' says Leah.

'One day we took the children for a swim at East London. We settled ourselves on a "black" beach next to an amusement park with swings, slides and a little train. My youngest daughter, Mpho, who was three at the time, wanted to ride on the train but I had to say: "No, it's not for us." She wailed: "But it is for us. Look, there are children on the train." We left the beach and have never been back.

'It never occurs to black children who've grown up in South Africa to enter a park; they just don't think it could be for them. But Mpho was different because she had grown up in England. This is what I mean when I say people grow up with an ingrained feeling of inferiority.'

Bishop Tutu's meteoric career took the family from Alice to another four-year spell in London and then on a switch-back ride from Johannesburg to Lesotho, Johannesburg, Lesotho and back to Johannesburg.

'It's enough,' says Leah. 'We've never yet stayed in one place for five years. I'm not moving again.'

Now they live in a pleasant house in Beverly Hills, Soweto, down the road from Nelson and Winnie Mandela's daughter Zinzi and around the corner from Kaiser Motaung of Kaiser Chiefs soccer fame.

They first moved into their house after Desmond was made the first black Dean of Johannesburg in 1978. They were offered the deanery in posh Upper Houghton but agreed it would be wrong for them to accept a privilege denied to other blacks.

I first visited Leah's home to interview her on a Saturday afternoon and was met at the door by Mpho, now a lovely, laughing 17-year-old. She entertained me while we waited for her mother and engagingly told me: 'Dad's not really strict, doesn't much mind us saying shit, but don't say "God", then he really gets mad. Crazy, isn't it?'

When Leah arrived she told me they'd just heard Mpho's O-level results – six As and two Bs – and that she invited a few friends around to celebrate. She asked me to stay and drink a glass of champagne and apologised about the interview.

I stayed. Guests arrived and the Bishop, woken from an afternoon nap, joined in, slightly bleary-eyed and barefoot. He sat on the floor and made some hilarious remarks to the ladies before toasting his daughter and retiring to his work. It was a justifiably proud moment for loving parents and I was privileged to share it.

All four Tutu children have been educated at private schools, in England and Swaziland, during the periods when the family was living in South Africa. This is a contentious point in the black community, with some resenting the privilege only the successful can buy.

Children leave school poorly educated and with feelings of inferiority which often manifest as aggressiveness. This Leah did not want for her children.

I asked Leah why their children had been sent to private schools and she looked me straight in the eye and said from the depths of her being: 'Any parent would do anything in their power to avoid Bantu Education.'

Children leave school poorly educated and with feelings of inferiority which often manifest as aggressiveness. This Leah did not want for her children.

They are all doing extremely well. Trevor, the eldest, has a scholarship to King's College, London, where he will do a Master's degree in computer science. Ntombi is in the United States studying political science and languages. Thandi is at university in Botswana studying physics and chemistry. And the youngest, Mpho, wants to do an arts course in the USA.

The day Mpho's O-level results were celebrated was not the last time a planned interview was postponed. The next date was abandoned when the Tutus were delayed at a service in Regina Mundi, the large Catholic Church in Soweto, to commemorate the deaths of ANC members killed by the SADF near Maputo in February.

I waited for them for an hour but after being manhandled by a drunk Sowetan decided I'd had enough and went home. Our arrangements were also sabotaged by a couple of funerals which Leah, who is much in demand, attended. Eventually we got together and over endless glasses of diet cooldrink, talked about Leah, her family, home and role in South Africa.

Because of the publicity Leah has received as the wife of Desmond Tutu and the director of DWEP, the Domestic Workers' and Empowerment Project, you may be forgiven for imagining her as someone fanatically involved in takeover politics. But seeing Leah at home or in her carefully tended garden, she begins to resemble an ordinary northern-suburbs housewife rather than a revolutionary. And this is exactly the role she played when the family returned to London for a second stay.

'In England you can enjoy yourself. I used to go to floral arrangement, car maintenance and yoga classes. They were stolen moments of leisure between hours of drudgery, driving children to and fro between Brownies, music lessons and rugby games.'

But that was England. Back in South Africa there were wrongs to be righted and Leah was catapulted into the role of spokeswoman for domestic workers. With her husband frequently away and the children scattered at their universities in London, the USA and Botswana, she had the time and energy to act as director of DWEP. She also had the background. Her father had a small farm near Brits but the family was not well off and when he died her mother became a domestic worker to support her growing brood.

DWEP is a two-pronged project. It aims to persuade employers to provide domestic workers with better conditions and wages, and alerts domestic workers to their potential, making them aware of their dignity.

At the DWEP head office domestics call in for advice and legal assistance. Many tell harrowing tales of wages of R25 per month, of very little time off and appalling accommodation. It is these concrete examples of exploitation which fire Leah's commitment to change the situation which is heading us for disaster to one of understanding and co-operation.

'We try to explain to employers that they can't expect a high standard of work if they don't pay high wages. And if the working conditions of their employees are poor, the work will also be poor. Of course not all domestics are reliable but mostly you can see the difference in the attitude of a woman who has a good employer – she is proud of herself and her work.

'A good employer is someone who respects her domestic worker as a human being, pays her a decent wage and allows her enough time off – eight hours a day, five days a week is what we work, so why should they be different? – plus a paid holiday once a year. Domestic workers should also have a room with enough space for their clothes and for a guest. Space is desperately lacking. You find suitcases under the bed, on top of the cupboard. If a burglar should break into the room the domestic worker couldn't even jump under the bed! Toilet facilities should be provided, preferably a bathroom but at the very least a toilet and hot and cold running water.

'Whites sometimes wonder why blacks don't discuss their employers. It's because domestic workers feel insecure and inferior. It's difficult to feel good about yourself when others don't respect you – especially when you've come to assume that you are inferior. Take privacy. A black woman's privacy is not respected. Employers think they can put three women in a room together and expect them to dress and undress regardless of who else is in the room. It makes you feel you don't matter; you begin to think of yourself as nothing.'

Leah herself employs a maid. I asked her what she felt about joining the ranks of the employers.

But Leah assured me that the association's first objective would not be to strike.

'You just know that domestic workers, like any others, ought to unite to negotiate for recognition by the government of their status as a work force so that legislation will be passed to ensure decent wages and better conditions.'

Sadly, Leah feels that DWEP's 100 Centres of Concern country-wide are not making much progress. At the centres, domestics gather once or twice a week to learn sewing, cooking, literacy. But the internalised prejudices of both the blacks and the whites create problems. 'We had hoped that by bringing black and white women together we could help them to see one another with different eyes, just as women, not as "madams", and "girls".

'But unfortunately we haven't had much success in breaking the habit. Whites come to the centres to teach skills but at the same time manage to intimidate the black women. One senses that they feel better than the domestic workers and so treat them like children. It's terribly arrogant for one adult to treat another like a

'It's not exploitation to employ a domestic worker. There are thousands of women out there who are not trained to do anything else and who desperately need to be employed. Exploitation only arises when the salary is low and the conditions degrading.'

'It's not exploitation to employ a domestic worker. There are thousands of women out there who are not trained to do anything else and who desperately need to be employed. Exploitation only arises when the salary is low and the conditions degrading.

'Recently we formed the South African Domestic Workers Association which will give employees a chance to take part in their own liberation. 'Obviously employers are going to be scared stiff of any sort of coming together of black workers. It's a threat, and a threat to the white housewife is the biggest threat of all because she has a domestic worker right there in her house, in her bedroom.'

child. After all, the fact that you have been lucky enough to learn a few skills doesn't make you a superior human being.'

Living in Soweto is risky enough without the added fear that the government might lock up your husband. Bishop Tutu is one of the most outspoken black leaders in the country, squarely in the black books of the powers that be.

I asked Leah how she coped with what I assumed was the continual threat of her husband's imprisonment.

'Yes, I am frightened now and again. If I was permanently terrified I'd go crazy. It wouldn't be so bad if Desmond and I had to go to gaol together – oh, it's not just *being* in gaol that's so terrible, it's what may happen while you're there. Nobody's going to forget Biko. Desmond and I have talked about what may happen. Whether it's imprisonment or death, if it's for our beliefs, it will be worth it.'

Leah knows a little of what she is talking about because she has already spent a night in gaol. She describes it as not altogether five-star treatment. It happened last year when she joined the 'March of the Clerics' to protest against the arrest of an Anglican minister who she believes contravened an unjust law.

'Justice and the law,' she says, 'are not always the same thing. And it's stupid to say that walking down the street in peaceful protest is illegal. I'd march again tomorrow if need be.'

Fighting talk from someone who had to remind herself not to cry as the gaol door clanged shut behind her.

Hardly a day passes without a comment from the Bishop in the press. Depending on one's political outlook, he can sound like anything from a rabble-rousing terrorist to a charismatic visionary. Few of his statements appear to relate to his role as a bishop.

Leah disagrees: 'All those comments or statements concern religion because religion has to do with your whole self. Housing, toilets, food, work, they're part of you so they're part of religion. They could report Desmond praying but that would hardly be news.'

Asked whether she thought the Anglican Church could fulfil the spiritual needs of black people, Leah regretfully admitted that she didn't really think so. Some Anglican churches with black congregations have Africanised their services and these churches are full whereas the traditional churches are half empty, she says.

She feels Africanisation of the services has brought the spirit back so that church-goers are touched by warmth and fullness, refreshed and strengthened.

'But it also depends on the sermons. Sermons must relate to the everyday lives of black people and not be holy, holy pie in the sky.'

Leah has always avoided playing the role of a minister's wife, never taking Sunday school classes, or leading the Mother's Union.

'No, that wasn't for me. I just said: No. But I'm not a feminist. Desmond's the boss in our house – I allow him to be. Actually we share a great deal, and he has helped me to grow. There have been occasions – I won't quote you any – when I've been so daft that if I'd been him, I would have wondered what I was doing with this woman. But not him. He has allowed me to grow and at my own pace too.

'This is one of the problems with the Centres of Concern. Although the whites who are involved are well-meaning, they are so keen on making the centres run smoothly that they take over. Yes, it's important to have high standards but isn't it more important for people to grow in confidence and responsibility? And they can only do this at their own pace, making mistakes on the way and learning from them, just as Desmond has allowed me to be daft from time to time so that I could learn from the experience.

'Children with the guts of youth won't be intimidated by whites any more but millions of women with ingrained feelings of inferiority need sensitive help in realising their potential.'

Desmond and Leah Tutu celebrated their 50th wedding anniversary on 9 July 2005.

What Electricity has Meant to Me

Miriam Tlali

Fairlady 8 September 1982

Many South Africans enjoy countless benefits and conveniences at the flick of a switch. But many do not. Here Sowetan resident and author, Miriam Tlali, who has lived with and without electricity, speaks out.

Whenever I think of Nkhono (grandmother) I picture her kneeling near the open fire, with the heavy *lesokoana* (wooden spoon) in her hands, deftly stirring the contents of a piping-hot iron pot which she has balanced against her knee to keep it from swerving.

The thick, agitated, simmering mielie-pap spatterings keep popping out and flying around her face and neck. She has to wince and turn her head now and again to dodge the molten drops. What an agonising experience it is, this cooking of meals, I would think.

Keeping the smile on my face, although deep inside I would be hating every minute of it. I loved my grandmother, you see, and my heart bled to see her suffer though she would never admit it. I dared not show my disgust. How could I?

A few minutes later, being satisfied with the results of her undoubtedly painful performance, she would rub off the stiff pap against the brim of the pot, replace the lid, and remove the sweat from her forehead and temples.

She would look at us watching her from the other side of the pot and declare sternly: '*Ho re mosali ke ho re pitsa* (to say woman is to say pot), or '*Ho re mosali ke ho re lefiela*' (to say woman is to say broom). And we – my sisters and I – would be expected to welcome the announcement philosophically and smile! The brainwashing, indoctrination and conditioning processes had now begun in earnest. I was only about four then, and my sister a few years older and we were females; there was no way of avoiding what was in store for us.

That was in Sophiatown and it is now nearly four decades since my Nkhono passed away. I have often thought of her and wondered just what she would think of me sitting here holding the pen in my hand instead of wielding the broom in the yard first thing in the morning. No doubt she would consider me an undesirable, lazy, rampant female!

Nkhono would sometimes take us with her when visiting her relatives in

> I was determined that the pot and the broom were never going to bog me down and keep me in chains like they did with my grandmother and my mother.

the Orange Free State. All over, in the buses, trains and in the homes, the 'gospel' of the virtues of the slaving female would be preached and repeated by everyone, just to make sure it sank in and was absorbed by us and other doomed little girls as easily as possible.

Coming back to Sophiatown to us meant coming from the darkness into unending daylight where every night we jumped and skipped merrily under the street lamps as the adults sat on the stoeps chatting and watching us. Sunset did not mean the end of the day. Everyone looked forward to nightlife in Sophiatown and Western Native Township. The local cinemas of Balansky and Odin would open their doors widely every evening of the week to welcome the thousands of people who would crowd in to watch the latest Hollywood films and although we youngsters were not allowed to go, we did not envy them. We staged our own shows and plays on the bright pavements and the smooth tarred roads. When away on the farms we used to miss the street lights which, seen through our childhood eyes, seemed to welcome us back in an array of flowing glory continuing an uninterrupted stream from Park Station right up to my Nkhono's doorstep.

It was no wonder therefore that whenever one of us was sent on an errand down to my uncle's home, we all jumped eagerly to go. My uncle had his house wired. The brightness right from Bertha Street, all along Main Road swept graciously into my uncle's home. Inside the house, my aunt would be ironing bundles and bundles of washing. She would go about it with great ease, compared with Nkhono who always used the heavy *lieistere* (from the Afrikaans *yster*) to do her ironing. We would stand around the table and watch her enviously as her arm glided effortlessly over the starched white linen.

Why Nkhono stubbornly held onto her iron tripod and *lesokoana*, and still preferred to kindle the open fire,

I shall never know. Preparing our meals was always sweat and toil for Nkhono, and she went on suffering with all the advantages of modern technology around her.

After I was married and as soon as I got my own house in nearby Western Native Township, my husband and I saved hard, and had it wired in as short a time as possible. I was now a mother and had resumed my studies as a student of the University of the Witwatersrand.

I would find it almost impossible to fulfil my commitments. I was determined that the pot and the broom were never going to bog me down and keep me in chains like they did with my grandmother and my mother.

But alas, not very long after that, I knew that the days of my comparative comfort were numbered. The 'fatal' law had been passed in parliament. Sophiatown and Western Native Township were declared 'black spots' and we were soon to be removed some 25 km out of Johannesburg. We, the unfortunate inhabitants of the two townships, were infuriated by the move. We referred to the 'bundu' townships of Soweto as the 'Zoo'. Their great distance away from the centre of town, the lack of adequate and appropriate infrastructure were regarded as primitive and fit only for occupation by lesser beings.

We knew of course that these inadequacies were not accidental, that they were in keeping with government policy, which at the time regarded Soweto to be even less temporary than Sophiatown and Western had been.

We were informed that the houses in the township of Moroko where most of us were removed to would have electricity. We also learnt that buying a site there would give us some form of security. Accordingly, some of us took the plunge and bought. But we were soon disillusioned when we were told that those who had bought sites would have to pay for the installation of cables and the wiring of their houses.

Within months, we were moved to our Soweto

matchboxes. I was stuck. Obviously it would be a long time before we would be able to afford the soaring costs of electrification. For me it was hell. I was right back at square one. It was like being cut off from the rest of the world. What would I do with the baby waking me up in the middle of the night demanding, howling for her usual bottle of warm sterile water?

In addition, I had my aged in-laws to look after. What is more, I was already feeling the urge to write; sit down and write, for goodness' sake. The restlessness within me was growing and stifling me; I knew that I would burst and go to pieces if I did not put down all that was in my mind. One thing was certain … I would just *have* to make the time available to me and try hard to create the 'ideal' situation for writing. I would have to improvise *come what may*. I made a resolution. I had learnt the advantages of having electricity and pressing the button on the wall, and there was no going back.

As soon as my baby was a little older, I would go and look for a job and immediately start saving to electrify the premises. In the meantime it meant sweltering in a hot kitchen throughout the long summer months, not

I wasted no time looking for work. I obtained a clerical position at a firm of bookkeepers. But not long after I had been hired, the boss sold the business. I thought it was the end of everything. The saying goes that 'the darkest cloud has a silver lining'. The boss undertook the task of hunting for another job for me. I considered myself very fortunate indeed as jobs were not easy to come by in those days.

I was soon employed at a big department store selling furniture and household appliances. There were all kind of makes of used and new electrical appliances everywhere one looked. And many used ones had never been collected by their owners. These the boss sold at a reduced rate. I was delighted. It was like suddenly stumbling into paradise. I was allowed to have whatever used items I wanted on account. As soon as the house was electrified, I grabbed what I needed eagerly. In no time I had amassed a whole collection. … a toaster, a kettle, a polisher. Later, a customer walked in and offered me a used refrigerator because the boss would not accept it as a trade-in. It would do for me. If any of the goods I had acquired broke down and needed repairing, Donald

> If I were to grade the different so-called racial groups (whites, Indians, coloureds, and Africans) according to their worth or esteem in this country, the African woman would undoubtedly be rock bottom. By deliberate arrangement, custom and accepted norms she is lowest on the totem pole.

to mention the drudgery of chopping wood and carrying coal from the coalbin outside into the house and then transporting the ashes out into the rubbish bin. It would mean scraping and removing the soot from the whole stove and chimney from time to time. Just thinking of the hours it would take to cook meals, do the washing and ironing for the whole household, scrubbing and polishing the floors alone made me lose hope of ever having time to do the things I really wanted to do.

My dream persisted and I kept building castles in the air. When my baby was old enough to leave home

– the coloured mechanic downstairs – promised that he would always be in a position to help me. From then on, all I would have to do would be to plug in the machines and switch on and I would have all the aid I had ever dreamed of. I could now devote some of my time to relaxation, daydreaming and my creative pursuits, thank God.

If I were to grade the different so-called racial groups (whites, Indians, coloureds, and Africans) according to their worth or esteem in this country, the African woman would undoubtedly be rock bottom. By deliberate arrangement, custom and accepted norms she is lowest on the totem pole. And what is worse, even though she toils along for some 20 hours a day, following in everyone's trail, picking up this and straightening out that – doing the donkey work for everyone in the home – she is never regarded as being employed. She is the least worthy immediately below the African male (except perhaps to those who love her). But certainly, legally she is the least worthy and most oppressed. The law even goes to the extent of condemning her to a status of a perpetual minor, always under the guardianship of some male, sometimes even her own minor son! All these factors make her unable to realise her full potential as a human being.

Richardson in his book *The Creative Balance* writes: 'Self-fulfilment implies the development and exercise of individual capacities'; also, 'A person with high self-esteem is someone who has a high estimate of his own value and finds that others agree.'

It is not difficult to see why in the customary marriages, the virtue of giving domestic services to others is so emphasised in African woman. The status of being 'Mrs' automatically qualifies her for 'respectability', which is full compensation for those services she is expected to render to her in-laws especially. Some may want to argue that some men also help with the housework, but how many? A negligible few. In any case, I have never heard such titles as *makoti* or *ngoetsi* used in the case of a man. It is not necessary to explain what is implicit in those words. Every African man or woman knows.

We hear such phrases as 'raising the quality of life of the urban blacks' and 'raising living standards' reiterated by the industrialists, economists and the powers that be. Whatever their self-centred motives may be in this apparent change of heart, where there is economic growth, change is inevitable. Economic and social transformations are inherent in development, and time is an important commodity (an expensive one) if growth and progress have to take place.

The African housewife is in most cases forced to seek employment. She is forced to play the dual role of housekeeper and breadwinner. Ever-growing numbers of black women are turning the wheels in our textile factories, in all types of manufacturing firms. They can be found hammering on the keyboards of typewriters and accounting machines in many offices. Not to mention the technicians in operating rooms; the thousands of nursing sisters, hospital clerks and attendants; and many many more in the teaching profession. We even have African women replacing men as drivers in many firms and private homes. Obviously these women need more time to cope with the demands of their dual capacity. And electricity saves time. I wish I could say it saves money too. Experience shows that it is not always the case, especially in Soweto where the occupants of the matchboxes sometimes find their electricity bills exceed those of tycoons in Parktown!

The African woman has proved her endurance and ability to withstand monotonous, uncomfortable, repetitive household tasks. She deserves all the aid and relief scientific methods and modern technology have to offer. To the African woman the use of electrical aids is more than just a necessity; *it is a dire need*. In fact, a law should be passed to make the supply of cheap, readily available electrical power compulsory. Electricity should be sold to us at a cost we can afford. We are the unsung heroines of this country and without us it just would not tick.

Miriam's first novel, Muriel at the Metropolitan, *was the first to be published by a black woman in the country. She currently lives in Johannesburg and hopes to soon publish her*

Dr Allan Boesak

'Flip not Thine Wig'
is the injunction
on a plaque which
stands on the desk
of this devout and
remarkable man
who feels it his duty
to speak out on
the injustices in our
society.

Madeleine van Biljon

Fairlady 20 April 1983

'No, I'm not a crusader! I hate the word! For me it symbolises someone who wears blinkers, someone without a sense of humour who
spends his days and nights obsessed with one thing. That's not me!
But there are certain basics which allow no compromise.'

Dr Allan Boesak and I are sitting in the living room in his comfortable
family home. His wife, Dorothy, who is making coffee, has already pulled out
the plug on the telephone, which has, by early afternoon, rung 17 times.

The sound of voices in the background indicates that their children are
home from school.

On the surface, a typical suburban home, a typical suburban atmosphere.
But Allan Boesak is neither typical nor suburban.

He is president of the World Alliance of Reform Churches, which declared
apartheid a heresy. He is assessor of the NG Sendingkerk, chaplain to the
students at the University of the Western Cape, the Bellville Training College
and the Peninsula Technikon. He is minister of the Bellville congregation.

One of the most widely-quoted men in the country, Boesak dines with
diplomats, has the ear of students, is seen as a spokesman for the powerless
and the oppressed. He has been given many labels: political firebrand, a minister of the church who mixes politics with religion, a man who addresses
himself to the gallery for overseas consumption, one who cares more for his
image than for his Christian beliefs.

Allan Boesak brushes aside such tags. He is serene, a man committed to
his beliefs, and the need for stating them.

'In the Christian faith there can be no compromise on the subject of
justice, or human dignity, for everyone on earth.'

Allan Boesak believes that in South Africa, church and politics are indivisible and he has called South Africa a 'pigmentocracy'.

'But I would hate to think that I'm so eaten up by these beliefs that I
can speak about nothing else. Friends, for example, are intensely important
to me. I feel lost without friends to love and to share things with. I enjoy

One of the most widely-quoted men in the country, Boesak dines with diplomats, has the ear of students, is seen as a spokesman for the powerless and the oppressed.

cooking for them, opening a bottle of good wine, making a meal a festive occasion. No ideologue can appreciate good wine!'

Dorothy comes in with the coffee and she and her husband discuss a typical day, something that doesn't exist.

'At the moment I'm not working,' she says. 'I'm unpaid secretary to Allan, answering the telephone calls, attending to letters. But this year I'm going to lectures at UWC, hoping to get a BA in Xhosa and Biblical Studies.'

The couple has four children, Lieneke, 12, Belen, 9, Pulani, 6, and Allan, 4. Although Dorothy has household help, she does a great deal of the work herself and is wholly responsible for the garden.

Religion is the driving force in the Boesaks' lives. They have family devotions every night, however brief, and the children go to church and Sunday School and are members of the 'Kinderbond'.

'My faith dominates my life,' says Dorothy. 'It helps me when things are going badly for Allan and it's a great comfort to know that the struggle is for justice, not personal gain. We work according to what God wants from us and what should prevail in a Christian country.'

While Allan's day may well have included breakfast with a visiting fireman, a speech at a university, lunch with a diplomat, and an interview, he is primarily a pastor.

'I attend church meetings, speak to members of the congregation who have personal problems and, of course, on Sundays I deliver a minimum of two sermons.'

He is fully aware that this programme leaves too little time for Dorothy and the children and is consequently very jealous of the time they do spend as a family. 'Ideally I would like to have an hour each afternoon with the family as no minister has time over the weekends. On Saturdays I prepare sermons, on Sunday I preach.'

For Allan Boesak it's a far cry from the barefoot boy from Kakamas to one of the most important positions in the Christian world. He was born 38 years ago to deeply religious parents. After his father died, his mother moved to Somerset West with her seven children. Working as an alteration hand, this extraordinary woman who played, and still plays a great role in her children's lives, had two things to give them: faith and an education.

The first posed no problems. The second demanded that each child give up a year's schooling to work, making enough money to give the older ones a chance to complete their education.

All, like two of his brothers, wanted to become a minister, and like them, did. His sister married a minister.

'When I was fourteen,' he recalls, 'I served as sexton in the local Sendingkerk. My task was to sweep and garnish the church for services. I'd lock the doors, climb up on the pulpit and deliver great sermons!'

There was no room for politics in his background.

Nor for dancing.

'Dancing! The word was not allowed to be mentioned,' he laughs adding rather wistfully: 'I'm sure I have an innate rhythm but it's too late now.'

At high school during the '60s, Boesak was taught to think critically, to read newspapers and to discuss affairs of the day. By the time he went to the University of the Western Cape to study for the ministry, the unquestioning acceptance of the political set-up in South Africa had become tinged with scepticism.

Bitterness followed scepticism, hatred followed bitterness.

The house in which his mother had lived for years was designated as being in a white area. UWC did not grant degrees to aspirant 'coloured' ministers.

[I remind Boesak that in an earlier interview, some years ago, he had taken almost violent exception to a wholly innocent remark on my part that he spoke a beautiful Afrikaans. He said then: 'What did you expect?

He denies that he ever would, or ever could, become a political leader.
'Whatever I do or say is bound by the parameters of the ecumenical movement.'

The patois of a street kid?']

That hatred, that chip on the shoulder, is no longer there. The pejorative term 'boer' is also no longer used to express contempt. The man who played a major role in overthrowing what Boesak calls 'my theory that all boers were bad' was Beyers Naudé (outspoken Afrikaner anti-apartheid campaigner).

The road to tolerance has not been easy. His first church, in Paarl, fell under the Group Areas Act.

'And today,' says Boesak, 'there is not a stone to record the fact that it ever existed or served a congregation.'

Dorothy: 'It was heart-rending.'

Time and again Allan Boesak mentions the solace of faith.

'Anyone with a programme as full as mine, can easily skimp on his religious life. I can say with all honesty that if I didn't have time every day to be quiet, to meditate or to read my Bible I would not have the strength to cope with the tensions.'

There is unusual empathy between him and his mother.

'She'll telephone to tell me that she's reading Psalm 70 or 72 on my behalf.'

He gestures, as he nearly always does when he speaks.

'People complain I've become politicised. It's very far from the truth, but I believe from the bottom of my heart that because of my faith in Jesus Christ it is impossible for me to be quiet in the face of injustice. It must never be forgotten that in our community there are very few people who have had the opportunities to study. I was given a position I never asked for and it lays a burden and a responsibility on me to speak for those who cannot.'

He denies that he ever would, or ever could, become a political leader.

'Whatever I do or say is bound by the parameters of the ecumenical movement.'

Boesak is quiet for a moment, his face still. Then he says: 'I have a dream. Because I started my international ecumenical career so early, perhaps I can stop at an early age and become a minister in a small village. That's what I want.'

More vigorously: 'It's hardly pleasant to be a target in newspapers, hardly pleasant to live under a cloud, to receive threats, but because I am in a certain situation, within a certain community, I must take responsibility. If I want to evade that responsibility, I must emigrate.

'I refuse to do that.'

Allan Jnr trails in, wanting his father's attention. Allan Snr says that he gets far too little exercise despite his son's insistence that they jog together.

'Playing with him on the lawn is more exercise than running with him. I try to play squash now and again and I watch my weight. I think it must be dreadful,' says the president of the World Alliance of Reform Churches, 'to walk around with a fat, round belly.'

He gives a mock sigh. 'My mother always tells me I'm vain – I do like wearing clothes that match. I find a person wearing a green suit with a brown shirt and a jazzy tie physically hurtful to look at. Not that I can afford expensive clothes. But if you're fat as well, then even good clothes don't help!'

He wishes there was more time for reading and writing.

'Two years ago I made a study of *Revelations* and gave a series of sermons. The students asked for copies but I don't write out my sermons. I make notes and then speak. It sounds very smart but it isn't because I've been trying to get them on paper ever since. Now I'm waiting for a miracle.'

He is also working on a series of small meditations for daily uses. 'Of the 52 needed, I've written 10,' he says,

> What would Boesak wish for his children? There is no hesitation when he replies: 'A South Africa without tension, without apartheid, where there is no question mark over their human dignity.'

somewhat mournfully.

The pressure of work resulting from his international status has increased immeasurably. By February he could no longer accept speaking engagements until the second half of this year. He has already been invited to visit Germany next year.

What would Boesak wish for his children?

There is no hesitation when he replies: 'A South Africa without tension, without apartheid, where there is no question mark over their human dignity.'

For the first time during the interview there is a faint trace of bitterness. 'If you knew how deeply it hurts me to know there are beaches my children may not use ...

'The essence of the South African tragedy is that no normal human relationships are possible here. Of course, we have huge problems but in Europe and America there are no lines drawn between people of different colours.'

Allan Boesak took his doctorate in Holland where his older children were born.

'They could have had Dutch passports. I refused. My children must know where they come from.'

Despite his wish for his children, Boesak does not believe that there is any chance of rearing children in this country who are not colour conscious.

'Parents in South Africa lose that battle before they start. The very words "white" and "black" are emotive, have a social and economic meaning, tell you what you may and may not do.'

He laughs with wry amusement when he says that even small Allan, reared according to their precepts, will ask of white visitors: 'Are they on our side, Daddy?'

What Allan Boesak would like to see is a country in which such a question would be unthinkable.

In 1980 Allan Boesak divorced his wife Dorothy and caused a minor scandal when he married Elna Botha, a white, Afrikaans-speaking former SABC journalist.

In 1999 he was sentenced to six years in jail for defrauding the NGO, the Foundation for Peace and Justice, of R400 000 destined for the poor. Boesak maintains his innocence. He served two years of the prison sentence before being paroled. In 2005 he received a Presidential Pardon and his criminal record was expunged. He is still married to Elna. The couple has two children. Allan Boesak's earlier dream of being a pastor to a small congregation has since come true.

Working Wonders in the Wilderness

In the desolate corner
of the north-eastern
Transvaal where she
was both banished and
banned, a remarkable
woman doctor,
Mamphela Ramphele, is
changing people's lives.

Judy Olivier

Fairlady 7 September 1983

The Naphuno district in the north-eastern Transvaal has a nickname. The locals call it the Valley of Death.

During winter, the dry dust from the arid earth is driven by an ice-cold wind. In the summertime the countryside is deceptively seductive. Trees and shrubs flaunt a lush, tropical greenness. But it's hot. Horribly hot and humid.

Few people have heard of Lenyenye. If you try to telephone there, the Post Office denies its very existence. Even residents of Tzaneen, 21 kilometres to the north, shake their heads unobligingly when asked directions.

About 8 000 people live in and around the township. Many are families who used to work on white farms where the right to graze their cattle and cultivate crops was considered part payment for their labour. But the State has put an end to that system, and throughout the country thousands of people have been resettled, usually in 'homelands'. The going rate for labour in this part of Lebowa is about R1 a day.

Many men leave their homes to find work in the cities within the confines of influx-control regulations and the migrant labour system. The result is a community typical of hundreds of others in resettlement areas, where poverty dominates and the problems of malnutrition and disease are endemic.

Before 1977, Dr Mamphela Ramphele was one of the vast majority of South Africans who has never heard of Lenyenye. She was running the Zanempilo clinic in King William's Town, which combined conventional community medicine with self-help projects. She was deeply involved with the Black Consciousness movement and its leader, Steve Biko. In April 1977, she was banished and banned to Lenyenye for five years.

It is a Thursday morning in April. The Security Police have come to her office at the King William's Town clinic. They've got an order with them, banning her to a place she's never seen, even on a map. She notices the wrong pass number at the top of the document, but when she points this

Mamphela Ramphele and her
five-year-old son, Hlumelo.

(*Photo:* David Goldblatt)

The women are eager to learn. For many of them it means that for the first time they are able to write to their husbands in the city. And it means they are able to read the prices when shopping at the local stores.

out, nobody wants to know. They won't allow her to pack, but offer to do it for her. She declines. She leaves within an hour without clothes, without money, without any of her friends knowing she has been taken.

She spends the night in a police cell in the Orange Free State. The Security Police sleep in a nearby hotel. A local policeman is horrified to find the respectable lady doctor in his cells, and produces a supply of brand-new blankets.

She arrives in Tzaneen at one o'clock on Saturday morning. She's travelled over 1 500 kilometres. She is taken to the nurses' home of the local hospital. She is told that she'll be working at the hospital, and she protests. She cannot even understand the local dialect of Sotho. She makes her way to the Sacred Heart Mission where she is met with suspicion by the Irish priests. Her story sounds bizarre. They think she's an informer, a police spy. But they take her in.

She phones King William's Town and tells her worried friends where she is. She contacts lawyer Raymond Tucker in Johannesburg. He drives up to see her, takes one look at the banning orders with their faulty pass number, and points out that they are invalid.

Within days she's free to return to King William's Town.

She is soon back with her friends. They celebrate with a party. The local police don't even know she's there. She goes back to work at the clinic, and is visited by the Security Police who apologise for the treatment she has received. She relaxes a little.

Within a fortnight new banning orders came through, and she's back in Tzaneen.

Ithuseng is a South Sotho word meaning 'help yourselves'. It's the name of Dr Ramphele's clinic, and underlines its philosophy. The emphasis is on preventive medicine, literacy training programmes and self-help

projects. The main thrust is to encourage the people to think of themselves as a community, to bring a little hope into lives which seemed hopeless.

The Ithuseng clinic grew out of one room. Stranded in the back of beyond, Dr Ramphele saw the typical problems of a resettlement area: poverty, malnutrition, alcoholism, venereal diseases brought home by migrant workers, typhoid … She did something about it.

'I began teaching the people how to work together. I started a brickyard because I saw many of the women were leaving their homes and children early in the morning to go to work for a pittance at the local brick factory. Of course I didn't know anything about the construction industry, but I didn't let that stop me.

'We started the brickyard close to the township so that the women could keep an eye on their children while working. And now they're producing bricks both for the new nursery school and for sale.

'I organised a communal garden in which the women grow vegetables. I've introduced a literacy training programme using the Learn and Teach method. The teacher is Moses Moshoma, who used to be a house painter but was crippled in a car accident.'

The women are eager to learn. For many of them it means that for the first time they are able to write to their husbands in the city. And it means they are able to read the prices when shopping at the local stores.

She's begun the equivalent of a Women's Union which meets regularly and is run on the most democratic lines. There are office bearers and the meetings (at which they learn to knit, sew and crochet) start off with hymns and follow a proper agenda. According to Professor Francis Wilson, Director of the Southern African Labour and Research Unit at the University of Cape Town, the results of Mamphela Ramphele's work are a model for rural health development anywhere in the world.

His mother doesn't tell him who his father is until he turns four. His reaction moves her tremendously. He immediately becomes very concerned for her, afraid that something might happen to her too.

'But she has achieved even more. She is not merely patching people up. She's helping to create a community with self-respect.

'She is nurturing a new feeling of pride in this desolate backwoods. What makes her particularly impressive is that she combines her professionalism as a doctor – and she is a very fine doctor – with her ability to draw on and use the resources of unskilled people.'

She will never forget 1977, the year she sinks into a bottomless pit. After surviving it, she feels she can handle anything that happens to her.

She is in hospital in Tzaneen when the news comes that Steve Biko has been arrested again in a roadblock on his way back to the eastern Cape from Cape Town. She is carrying his child. She has already had one miscarriage. She lives in constant fear of losing the baby. She is still in hospital in September when she hears of Steve Biko's death in detention. She remains in hospital another four months. Her son is born in January. His mother names him Hlumelo. It is a Xhosa word meaning 'sprig that comes from a dead branch'.

He becomes the pivot of her existence. She plans her life around him. He is beautiful and very bright. He loves to read and he's used to being the centre of attraction when visitors arrive. He is the spitting image of his father.

His mother doesn't tell him who his father is until he turns four. His reaction moves her tremendously. He immediately becomes very concerned for her, afraid that something might happen to her too.

When he hears that she will be going to Cape Town on a much bargained-for holiday, he becomes flustered.

'Mommy, have you got a permit?' he asks anxiously. 'My daddy went to Cape Town without a permit and never came back.'

Enforced isolation weakens the wills of the banned. Despite the visits by people from overseas who include her in their programmes along with Beyers Naudé and other influential restricted people, the lack of intellectual stimulation obviously bothered the lively doctor.

She was accustomed to a warm, vibrant atmosphere.

'I was born in Bochum, near Pietersburg, into a large

and lovely family. I have five brothers and a sister, and our house was always filled with children. My parents were teachers, and they made our home a haven for the poor children in the neighbourhood.'

She met the same warmth at the Zanempilo clinic in King William's Town where she practised after obtaining her degree from the University of Natal. She'd met Steve Biko at the university where he'd been a medical student (he dropped out to concentrate on community work), and he'd kindled her interest in politics. At the clinic in the Ciskei she practised on a large scale what she later engineered in the backwaters of the north-eastern Transvaal.

The Ithuseng clinic draws people from all over the surrounding countryside. They come on foot, by bus or in taxis. They come to see Dr Ramphele and, if there's a locum standing in, they turn around and come back the next day. The clinic also serves as a community centre and as a haven in which children can do their home-work. There is a makeshift library, ill equipped for its customers as the bulk of the stock appears to be com-prised of tattered editions of the *South African Medical Journal* and incongruous back copies of the intellectual British weekly *The Listener*.

In a situation in which most people would find it difficult to survive, let alone thrive, Mamphela Ramphele reveals few signs of bitterness. Instead, she exudes an earthy sen-suality and an outrageously raucous laugh. It comes out in great guffaws. Often. Photographer David Goldblatt regret-ted that it was impossible to capture on film.

In 1982, she married Sipho Magele, a lecturer at Turfloop University, who is studying for his doctorate in pharmacology. They have known each other since the mid-'70s. He was a friend of Steve Biko, and he supported her through the most traumatic times. On 16 March this year she gave birth to their son in the

Pietersburg Hospital. It was another difficult pregnancy and, despite the prescribed rest, Malusi was born two months prematurely, weighing only 1,7 kg. He spent his first month in an incubator, his mother feeding him every three hours.

She was soon back at work at her clinic, putting in as many hours as possible, perturbed about her patients, particularly the children who have suffered dreadfully in the drought. Sister Mankuba Ramalepe, who is in charge of the self-help projects, puts it quite simply: 'The people love her.'

The sister was born in the area, but she understands that the doctor doesn't like it. At the beginning of this year Sister Ramalepe said: 'She's only here because she has to be. When they allow her to, she'll go away, back to Port Elizabeth.'

On 1 July this year her banning restrictions were lifted, but Mamphela Ramphele, who six months ear-lier had eloquently expressed her intense dislike for the bundu to which she had been banished by 'the Boers', remains in Lenyenye.

'It's strange. I thought the moment I was freed I would be up and away. But I can't do it. Do you know that one out of every two children brought to see me is suffering from pellagra? I can't leave now. I've got a commitment to the people here. Maybe next year. Maybe ...'

Mamphela Ramphele was appointed the first black vice-chan-cellor of the University of Cape Town in 1996. In 2000 she joined the World Bank in Washington as managing director responsible for human development, becoming the first South African to hold this position in the institution. In June 2004 she was appointed as co-chair of the new Global Commission on International Migration and a senior advisor to World Bank President, James D Wolfensohn.

Changing Gear

One of South Africa's most brilliant young journalists, Helen Zille, gave up her job to go back to varsity, to read, learn, grow and expand her horizons. She hasn't regretted her decision for a moment.

Erica Platter

Fairlady 16 May 1984

You may remember the name Helen Zille. A few years ago it appeared constantly in the press and not only because Helen was the *Rand Daily Mail's* political correspondent, reporting on the affairs of state. She also made news herself.

There was the famous LAPA Munnik affair: Helen reported that the minister had declared the elderly could live on R20 for food a month, and sued Dr Munnik for defamation when he denied her report (he eventually paid her R4 000 in an out-of-court settlement).

She also tangled with ex-Justice Minister Jimmy Kruger – Helen's was the first story to reveal that activist and founder of the Black Consciousness Movement, Steve Biko, had been murdered in police custody and had not died because of a hunger strike. The minister's fury was swift, vociferous and much-publicised. During the lengthy Steve Biko inquest, it was Helen's verbatim shorthand reporting of the proceedings that kept millions informed.

A story she wrote in the early days of the Info Scandal had Minister Owen Horwood denouncing her by name in parliament.

Still in her 20s, she became one of this country's most devastating political journalists, her byline a sure guarantee of a story you couldn't afford to miss if you wanted to be thoroughly informed.

Then, at the age of 31, the trim business suits and high heels were exchanged for sandals and cotton prints, and Helen went back to varsity. She changed gear completely.

It was a decision that astounded her colleagues, who felt she was being groomed for higher things in the newspaper world. And she's always seemed so formidably serious about her career.

But Helen hasn't regretted the change in course for a moment.

'I suppose those people who see their lives in terms of job status would say I'd dropped out, but in the sense of growing, expanding my horizons, deepening my insight, it's been pivotal. It might have seemed a momen-

She also tangled with ex-Justice Minister Jimmy Kruger – Helen's was the first story to reveal that activist and founder of the Black Consciousness Movement, Steve Biko, had been murdered in police custody and had not died because of a hunger strike.

tous decision but it was very easy really. So many factors came together and crystallised.'

Her editor and mentor, Allister Sparks, had been fired. It was Allister who'd first seen Helen's potential.

'I had all sorts of ideals but I was a bit like an unguided missile, with no conception of how to pull news together. He took time, helped me say things coherently,' she remembers.

It was also Allister who started her on the political beat and who pushed her into the demanding political correspondent's job when it suddenly fell vacant.

She remembers 'the incredible strain' of her first week in parliament.

'When the bells rang for a division I thought there was a fire and rushed out. I didn't know a *thing*.'

What made it worse was that Helen had no time to blood herself on a few safe bills, a few run-of-the-mill debates. The Info Scandal had broken, the buzz was that the buck didn't stop with Eschel Rhoodie, and Helen's first assignment was to plunge headlong into this most complicated and explosive affair.

'That first night I sat in a cold sweat at my typewriter, reporting a new set of revelations.'

The next day Minister Owen Horwood hit back by attacking her in parliament.

'He tore into me. In my first week, I wasn't used to that type of thing and I was really upset,' she recalls.

Allister found her feeling really low and made no allowances.

'"If you can't stand the heat you'd better get out of the kitchen." Those words have lived with me.'

Helen hung in but always with the complete backing of Allister Sparks. When he left she thought long and deeply: 'He'd put his whole life into something and almost overnight it was cut from under his feet. That put so many things into perspective for me – my job, my relationships and the rest of my life.'

For three years her job had made it almost impossible to have any private life at all. A political correspondent is a nomad, spending half the year in Cape Town for parliament, the other half back home on the paper in Johannesburg, and in between, covering the hectic schedule of party congresses, political meetings, elections and by-elections and press conferences from Lusaka to George.

Home was often no more than a suitcase, and when she could get back to the little doll's house of a cottage she'd bought in Woodstock it was always late at night, after meeting her deadlines.

When she first invited Johann Maree, now her husband, over to supper, he took ages to find her place though he lived only a few kilometres away. She'd directed him via Chippy's take-away, Luigi's, Moosa's Samoosa Bar, and Jimmy's café.

'They were the only places that were still open when I drove home from work, starving!'

Johann played an integral part in Helen's change of gear, though she says, 'he would have been quite appalled if he'd known I was taking the decision to leave my job for him'.

Helen had been seriously involved with an Associated Press foreign correspondent, a dashing New Yorker with his own small plane and a gold mine in Zimbabwe ('more like a couple of holes in the ground', Helen says). He was the perfect partner during her most intensely career-orientated years. When they were together Helen would be out of her suits and into her jeans and off into a different life.

'We had this wonderful living-for-the-moment thing. Being apart didn't worry him; he let me be 100 percent. We'd agreed my career would take precedence for a number of years and he didn't ever put any pressure on me.'

Helen Zille – 'Helen doesn't chat. She discusses, debates, probes, questions, always stretching her mind and yours.'

(*Photo:* Mike Donnelly)

> '**I have a deep respect for certain people (Sheena Duncan of the Black Sash is one) but the battle is to find out what's right for you.**'

Which was what she needed to offset her job.

'It was high powered, full of pressures. I needed a totally relaxing relationship.'

But at the back of her mind was the knowledge that he ultimately wanted to return to the United States 'while I was involved in the issues here'.

Then she met Johann, a lecturer in industrial sociology at UCT. Helen can seem super-serious, formidably intellectual, and you expect her to describe a meeting of minds. But she's also devastatingly honest.

'I just loved his red hair.'

They plunged straight into a political discussion and 'differed on most issues. I realised how much broader a perspective he had and how many gaps there were in my knowledge.'

She'd been thinking about this for some time.

'Parliament is very important but there's something incredibly distorting about being in a situation where the PFP is regarded as being on the left. It's so unrealistic in the broader South African context. I knew I needed to go beyond that, beyond covering the politics of the system. I realised my BA degree should have been in political science and economics, not languages. I needed to catch up with the new approaches, the new history that was being written.'

Helen doesn't chat. She discusses, debates, probes, questions, always stretching her mind and yours. Johann gave back better than he got from her and she liked that. It was almost a week before he phoned and came over to see her.

She remembers his first words: 'I've come to discuss those economic issues you were interested in,' Helen laughs at herself. 'That was the *last* thing I was thinking about. I was totally speechless.'

All the factors coincided, and her choices became clear. She wanted to go back to university, she wanted to be near Johann, she wanted to put together the private life her job had cut into, to have time to read and think. 'There are times for growth and for consolidation in every life.' Now she was ready for both.

From childhood, Helen says, she's always been 'searching for some way that rang true for me. To find myself and live that uncompromisingly.'

She feels strongly that too many people try to base their lives on role models.

'I have a deep respect for certain people (Sheena Duncan of the Black Sash is one) but the battle is to find out what's right for you.'

She remembers her later school years as a particularly fierce battleground. The Zilles lived in Rivonia on a plot her father, Wolfgang, had originally bought for £100. The original old *pandokkie* grew as her father grew more prosperous and added on. It still has an iron roof, and fruit trees – sweet apricots, nectarines, almonds, plums and lemons.

Her grandmother, whom she remembers as 'very large and totally protective', tended the garden – 'nothing dainty like pansies – just big beds of cannas!'

She was a trained horticulturist, encouraged to take up a career by her mother, one of those doughty 19th-century campaigners for women's rights.

'She would throw her daughters' needlework into the fire, telling them not to sit round waiting for husbands, but to go out and learn to become independent individuals.'

The little local school Helen and sister Carla attended was within walking distance. Dual medium, it taught Helen 'one of the most important things in my life: to speak Afrikaans properly'.

The sisters and younger brother Paul often went barefoot. They played marbles and soccer.

'I don't remember learning anything – except about

fun and friends. The whole community's kids went there, there was no class consciousness.'

In Standard 4 however, she started at a much posher and pricier private school. It was a major wrench in her life.

'It was very English and our home was very German. You were expected to be reserved, not expressive, at school. At home we let it all hang out. I remember seeing the other girls carefully cutting their bread into quarters. We'd never done that. I went back to my mother and accused her of not teaching us manners. She said: "Forget it. The only important aspect of manners is consideration for others."

'At home we were brought up to believe there were no certainties, no ultimate truths. My parents were very, very liberal – children of Freud and Spock – and they tried to bring us up according to those new liberated values. They allowed us all to choose our options in life from a very young age – and learn how to handle freedom and responsibility.'

'Every night after supper was discussion time – my father would get out the old globe and we'd discuss geography, politics, religion – they took us through all the different religions (all branches of the same company, my father said). We were always encouraged to take our own positions on issues.

'It was marvellous: I have Protestant, Catholic and Jewish ancestors so I'd take Jewish holidays, go to Sunday school and mass; every Christmas we had a tree but with the Star of David on top. At school I loved chapel because I loved to sing, but I never understood the phrases and the symbolism.'

In her characteristically thorough way, later in life, Helen explored a variety of religions, including those of the East. She and Johann have recently become Quakers: 'very quiet, very socially and politically concerned, low-key, simple'.

But back in her school years religion merely aggravated the 'clash of values' she experienced.

She became 'a strong rebel, a difficult teenager. I took the freedom my parents had given me and really pushed it. When they tried to apply stricter controls, I would find some way of getting around them.'

She took up with a rough crowd. It was the flower power, op-art, mini-skirt age, with socials in the Rivonia Hall. Helen and a friend saw it as their mission to get the Beatles on top of the LM radio hit parade. They wrote scores of letter and when the group made it, regarded it as a personal triumph.

She remembers overhearing her parents discussing whether she'd ever find her feet. She was leading a sort of dual life. Though a teenage rebel at home and at school, and despite her misgivings about the system, she was head day girl, one of the top two of her class, in the debating society, and the school representative on the Johannesburg Junior City Council.

She even got her gym colours – more for her originality than skill. 'I couldn't even do a handstand.'

At 17 she was sent overseas alone – which turned out to be more of a test than a holiday. By the time she got to UCT she was tired.

'I just wanted to do the easiest courses, to have fun.'

She came back home after 18 months, seriously ill. She became thinner and thinner; there was even an exploratory operation to try to pinpoint the trouble.

Her mother, she says, knew instinctively what was happening. But anorexia nervosa was not common then.

It took seven years for Helen to be cured and she regards it as 'probably the toughest battle I have ever fought – a formative experience. There's a comprehensive book to be written on this subject and if I wasn't so involved in other issues I would sit down and write it.'

When she began slimming she was at that stage of her life when she wanted to get things sorted out: making strict rules, eating very little, seemed to simplify everything.

'Too many contradictions in my life came together at the same time. It was my way of getting control of the situation and defining my limits.

'When I came back from Cape Town, my parents laid down the law for the first time. I was not going back. I fought their decision but they were rock-firm. They gave me the most incredible support.'

She completed her degree at Wits while going through medical treatment, and is now 'one of the fortunate people who've recovered completely. It's really over. I enjoy food and don't think about it. And I don't put on weight. It was the greatest liberation I've experienced personally.'

She'd done a shorthand and typing course part-time, and took a vacation job on the *Rand Daily Mail*. Her first bylined story was a report on the Miss Southern Transvaal beauty contest – actually written by the news editor, she confesses, because she hadn't a clue how to approach it. After varsity she did some temping, and then a cadet journalism course led her on to the *RDM*.

'The paper had always been part of our lives, and I never thought of joining any other.'

Because of her interest in politics she accompanied political reporter Tony Holiday to meetings and learnt from him. When the UP split, the paper was short-staffed and despite her inexperience she was landed with what was then a very big story. She started writing about church and student politics and spent six months as the SAAN representative in Windhoek.

When the political correspondent's job fell into her lap she still felt she wasn't ready though she'd already covered the Soweto hearings and the Biko inquest. (Her extraordinarily good shorthand made her report in the *Mail* stand head and shoulders above others.)

Political reporting is a particularly demanding discipline. You need a radar-like instinct for homing in on the essence of what might be day-long debates: the ability to distil without losing accuracy; a speed reader's skill to dissect massive reports to meet early deadlines, and a wide grasp of the vast range of subjects that the pursuit of politics embraces.

Helen's far better equipped for varsity now than she was the first time around, she feels.

At 31 'I had enough practical experience to relish the theoretical stuff, I was more mature.'

She took a seminar course in Southern African economic history and went to 'any lecture that interested me. It was a magnificent time. I soaked it all up, worked on the student paper, taught in a school near Crossroads.'

She kept her writing hand in by freelancing for some American papers and *Frontline* magazine, of which she is an associate editor, and she explored a new avenue, community journalism. She was covering bus fare increases, water tariff hikes – 'tackling issues from the bottom up rather than interviewing cabinet ministers and assessing big political manoeuvres as I'd been doing before'.

UCT's Professor Francis Wilson asked her to co-ordinate the research for the Carnegie Inquiry into Poverty and Development and she jumped at the offer.

'I'd more or less come to terms with urban political issues but had neglected rural issues.'

It met her current criteria for a job: It was relevant and would expand her understanding. For more than a year she worked with 350 people preparing a 200-page paper for the massive poverty conference in Cape Town in April.

She is earning half of what she did as a newspaper reporter, but says

She'd done a shorthand and typing course part-time, and took a vacation job on the *Rand Daily Mail.* Her first bylined story was a report on the Miss Southern Transvaal beauty contest – actually written by the news editor, she confesses, because she hadn't a clue how to approach it.

her lifestyle hasn't changed much. She's not into possessions – 'they're a total handicap'.

The Zille-Maree house in Observatory (she's kept her maiden name – 'it's a normal part of me') is bright with posters. There are old wooden floors, a good Kelim, a cluster of bright artichoke flowers in a vase. But it's all simple and functional. Her hi-fi set was bought at a Black Sash market 10 years ago and the only real touch of extravagance (though it's more of a necessity) is an Apple that both she and Johann use in shifts – the only thing they ever argue about. They each have their own studies – Johann's is neat. Helen's is overflowing with books and papers. Soon one of the studies ('Johann's!' Helen says) will become a nursery. She and Johann are expecting a baby.

The baby will, she knows, change their lives dramatically. They're determined to share parenting as they share the cooking and every other aspect of housekeeping. 'My married friends all smile at my ideals.'

When they were married the ceremony featured readings focusing on the equality of a life partnership.

'Johann is totally insistent that I mustn't give up doing work that I find fulfilling. My main priority is still to be a good journalist. Eventually I'll go back to it full time.'

She'd like to do as good a parenting job as she feels her parents have done, but admits she 'may not have the guts to let my child be as free as I was'.

She's extraordinary close to her mother, Mila.

'She has incredible wisdom and insight. She's sensitive and aware, always questioning her values, never stagnating. The most growing person I know.'

She remembers once getting 0 out of 20 for her sums at school and coming home crying.

'My mother said: "It's easy to take success, much more important to be good at failing." Then she went out and bought a cake and we had a party when my dad came home.'

In 1938 Helen's mother and her parents managed to leave their home in Essen. In the infamous Kristalnacht of that year their splendid house was ransacked as the Nazis struck at Jews throughout Germany. Helen's grandfather hated the idea of being driven out of his country by a tyrant like Hitler, but he'd already sent his four other children away. During the raid his beloved Italian cello was smashed in front of his eyes and he was imprisoned. When he was released, having managed to avoid being sent to a concentration camp, he knew he couldn't stay any longer.

He and his wife and Mila, their youngest daughter (Helen's mother), fled to England where the once wealthy lawyer took a job as a night watchman. They lived in an attic. Helen's mother trained as a nurse and midwife and worked in London during the war. Her brothers had by this time found their way to South Africa and in 1949 the family was reunited here.

Helen's father had immigrated to South Africa in 1936, and despite his classical gymnasium schooling in Germany had to take any job he could find. He was a labourer at the Modderfontien dynamite factory and later a deliveryman for Atlas Bakeries. He served in the South African forces in North Africa and Italy, and when he returned from the war, he took an economics degree by correspondence and went into the scrap metal trade.

Helen remembers his office as 'a children's paradise'. During the holidays they'd play there amid old sewing machines, cars, stoves and bicycles, then eat greasy fish and chips from the corner café. There were hard financial struggles initially, though Helen has no memory of ever being deprived, and they've always lived modestly.

Helen's maternal grandparents lived with them and she remembers her grandfather trying to teach her Latin as a child. 'His room had a lovely smell of red wine and tobacco and during the lesson I'd always pinch some of his cigarettes, which my sister and I would later smoke behind the shed.' (Though her parents didn't stop any of the children from smoking, none of them does so now.)

'But Dad was always the rock of the family. Nothing could ruffle him – he's the opposite of the women in our family.'

Women and their roles is a subject Helen has come to fairly late in her life – while the first wave of feminism was sweeping the world she was involved in her own private battle with anorexia – and only now has she formulated her own feminist philosophy.

'The movement seems to have gone into two tracks and neither speak to my condition. There's the American brand – go-getting, career-orientated, ambitious, materialistic, self-seeking. That's reduced women to just another deprived lobby group scrabbling to get a share of scarce resources. The roles haven't been re-evaluated. Another cage has been created for women.

'Equally stifling are the born-again feminists who frown on lipstick, shaved legs and men. They've also reduced women to a minority group – an angry and revengeful one. They don't allow for any nuances, any seeking.

'It's time for feminists on both sides to evaluate their positions, sceptically. The whole basis of the movement should be justice for all.'

Helen's started a women's group among some friends 'to search the issues together'. It's all part of her constantly probing, in-depth approach to life. Giving up her job has meant much more, not less, involvement with all issues that touch her. And she seems to have changed: the prickly edges of the pressured career woman have smoothed out. She seems softer, more serene. Marriage and motherhood and time for learning and reflecting suit her.

'I love getting older. I really feel I'm becoming a more whole person ...'

Helen Zille is currently the Democratic Alliance's National Spokesperson, Education. The Rand Daily Mail *was closed down in 1985.*

Everywoman's Poet Laureate

Poet Antjie Krog Samuel has been hailed as a voice of her generation but this mother of four struggles with the dual identity of being a housewife and a writer.

Cathy Knox

Fairlady 13 June 1984

'I am of two spheres,' says Antjie Krog Samuel.

'The one I was born into – a conventional family-orientated life style. In this my husband is the indispensable compass guiding me in what to wear, what to cook, to teach, to say. I am blemished with guilt for being a selfish mother, an uncaring wife, a disloyal citizen, a conceited white, and a loveless Christian. To make up, I am neurotic about organisation and punctuality.

'The other sphere I was born with. The writing – it is the only thing I do with absolute confidence, devotion, freedom and ease. I cannot dispense with it. Many people grow out of one sphere into another. I must try to reconcile my two. I must convince myself and my children that this is the way it has to be.'

Another writer helped Antjie reach this point of equilibrium. She had been uneasy in the public role of poet since her high-school days in 1970 when her first book *Dogter van Jefta* thrust her rudely into the limelight. She was uncomfortably aware of the dichotomy between her domestic persona and the world's expectations of her literary persona. The reconciliation of homebody and working body was aided by a highly-evolved feminist author she came across quite by chance in 1975.

'Erica Jong changed my life,' Antjie says.

André Brink had read her volume *Mannin* and commented: 'Erica Jong would laugh at you.'

'Who the hell is Erica Jong?' Antjie asked, crossly assuming Brink was referring to a member of the Grahamstown set.

Then, by sheer coincidence, Antjie was flipping through an old magazine in a waiting room and saw a photo of Jong with some information about her books.

'She wouldn't laugh at me. She'd like me,' Antjie thought as she read the books.

'Erica Jong changed my life,' Antjie says.

'Erica Jong freed me from the Elisabeth Eybers image: the poet as a regal woman. Her ideas rid me of a lot of complexes. I felt free to be a housewife, to be frustrated, to be myself.'

Energy is irresistibly attractive to human beings. So is integrity, a person like Antjie makes you realise. She looks straight at you or an issue with those remarkable eyes – chips of pale blue fire in her brown face; it's a quest, not a threat.

She doesn't want to win, she wants to know, to understand, and to state as exactly as possible *everything*. From the sublime to the ridiculous. Life's mysteries; what makes Zola (Budd) tick; the universe; this wonderful peach dessert concocted by gourmet poet WEG Louw …

Powerful minds can be very intimidating. A high-school prodigy who slays the literary world with a red-hot bundle of political and erotic verse is awesome. When she doesn't burn out as predicted but fights through her travails of Everywoman – marriage, mother-hood, divorce – to become a major literary figure, you'd expect her to be terrifying. Antjie is all those things but also supremely likeable.

Unadorned, outspoken, unpretentious, welcoming, warm, fierce, and thoroughly human.

We women do have our strengths, Antjie reminds you. Everything feels better after you've visited her. You've grown. You feel as though you're a very interest-ing, very alive person when you leave her house clutch-ing your *padkos* – dried fruit or some other home-made country treat.

Antjie, the eldest of five, was born near Kroonstad in the old homestead of Middenspruit farm, where her par-ents still live. Her mother is Dot Serfontein, the writer. Her father is a farmer and a collector of books and an adoring grandpa.

'We had a very free childhood. I can't remember ei-ther of our parents interfering with our lives. They were just there. I wasn't really aware of my mother until I was about twelve. I was not conscious of being protected or having my life ordered for me.

'But obviously there was a certain atmosphere in the house – a special way of thinking about things. There was a succession of intelligent and unusual visitors dis-cussing all sort of fascinating things. I was always listen-ing in on adult conversations. There seemed to be no restrictions. We could think, say and read whatever we wanted. Never has my mother told me I shouldn't read this book or that.

'I learnt that being creative is not an esoteric activity you practise in a special place. It permeates everything. You don't have to be an artist to be creative. You can be original and imaginative in the way you think, talk, even dress.

'I value the freedom of my childhood, but I'm afraid I am a very different kind of mother. I am over-anxious, over-emotional. I have very tight control over my chil-dren.'

She has four – Andries, 9, Susan, 6, Flippie, 5, and Willem who had his first birthday on 9 April.

'Although I believe it's wrong, I know what they think, I know what they're doing – I know where every one of them is right now and whether his nose is running or not. They're not totally free and as a result they're losing out on fantasy.'

During her adolescence Antjie and her mother welded together a dynamic, often fiery relationship that has been a source of strength for both.

'A good mother-daughter relationship is a priceless gift. There is nothing that can match it. My mother and I have terrible fights and we differ a lot but it's a very stimulating friendship.

Antjie Krog – 'I am of two spheres.'

'I used to write compulsively, but I'm too old now. That intensity belongs to an adolescent life and I can't be like that again. A raw energy that I didn't understand drove me but I know I don't have it any more. During an intensely creative period you live in a state of heightened consciousness. You are so exhilarated, you see everything more clearly than at any other time in your life.'

'The main thing she taught me, the thing I want to pass on to the children, is the importance of formulating your thoughts and feelings. She taught me communication is not enough, you must formulate first. She would hammer away at me: *Why are you feeling that way? What is it that you feel? What is worrying you? What is upsetting you? Why?* She taught me to think hard, to analyse and to try at all times to formulate exactly what I felt. She taught me to put it into words and to listen to the way other people expressed their inner life.

'Communication is the secondary step. It's no use unless you can formulate what you feel. If I teach this to my children, even if I only teach them to formulate their complexes, I'll be more than happy.'

Andries is a bundle of knobbly knees, fire and air, and his intensely serious mental processes are almost tangible. Susan started school this year – a china doll in bobby socks, her blue-grey eyes wide behind their thick spectacles. Flippie is a knock-out charmer in his scuffed Batman tights and cape. ('I'm afraid he's going to be a minister or a professor just so he can wear a similar outfit,' says mama.)

Willem is everyone's love-object – a teddy-baby who endures the embraces of his smitten family with the detachment of the very young.

'I can do nothing without help in the house,' says Antjie, who makes absolutely no apologies for having a full-time domestic worker and a nanny for the baby. She keeps the mornings to herself for her literary life. She reads everything she can lay hands on, fighting isolation by working her way through book lists, absorbing all the new Afrikaans poetry and as much of the English as possible, making translations, reading, reading, reading. Training and exercising her mind like an athlete does her body.

Writing …

The work is addictive and consuming.

'Some things are complete in a day. *Susannah Smit* (based on the diary of a Voortrekker) took four years.

'I used to write compulsively, but I'm too old now. That intensity belongs to an adolescent life and I can't be like that again. A raw energy that I didn't understand drove me but I know I don't have it any more. During an intensely creative period you live in a state of heightened consciousness. You are so exhilarated, you see everything more clearly than at any other time in your life.

'I was terrified of losing it. My mother maintains that you can't be original after twenty-five. You're no longer totally free because you start getting responsibilities; you develop complexes and phobias.

'But during one visit to DJ Opperman, he taught me that time had passed. Experience has its compensations.'

A Stellenbosch professor, DJ Opperman is one of the finest poets this country has ever produced. In his time he was a great teacher who ran invaluable literary workshops for new writers.

'He said now I must use my brain and all the sources I could lay my hands on. I was shocked when I saw he had all sorts of encyclopaedias and dictionaries in his study. "You're an artist! How can you admit to using a rhyming dictionary?" I objected. "A writer can't be snooty," he told me, "I use everything. I even use *Scope*."

'He taught me to work everything over and over. The first night I battled with one line and dawn was breaking before I'd written it.'

Her guru's lessons are still very fresh in her mind as she beavers away among her books all morning.

Antjie's afternoons are spent taking the children to music, rugby, swimming. She shops and she gardens. ('I'm not into it – my husband forces me. But I think

I have quite a nice garden,' says Antjie of the emerald patch behind the low stone walls that demarcate their erf.)

'I live like this by choice. I want to be like this.'

In the words of one of her simplest and strongest poems:

I have a house
that I clean every day
I have a washing line
in the yard
between the vygies
that bloom in winter
I have a child
who eats porridge
and grows under my hands.
I have a husband
who goes to work in the morning
who comes back in the evening
at night, he falls asleep against me.

Like every mother she has days when she feels bloated with responsibility – 'a battleaxe at thirty'.

I pick snotlike things out of the sink sieve
so that oaty water and bacon rinds
can burp out into the drain
nappy liners are bailed-out into the toilet
the dirty nappies soaped with Sunlight
buttocks are washed and powdered

The one is crying of hunger
the other in fury
the oldest one with his nervous paring-knife voice
my husband closes the door against everybody
and turns the Mozart piano concerto a notch louder

and I go crazy

my voice shouts a mengermalermixermincer
my nose drips like a fridge
my eyes tremble like boiling eggs
my ears are post boxes pouting with orders
the children assault me with their loudness

selfish
impudent
destructive
their tears, complexes, doubts, threats, needs
beat my 'image as mother' into pulp on the floor
I smell of vomit and shit and sweat
of sperm and onion
I illustrate a kitchen
with hair whipped pale against the morose Novilon of
skin
the sticky milk coupons of spine bend disinterested
under the dishcloth colour dressing gown
the legs are veined with blue soap
slippers curl like scouring wool

I am fed up as a flour bag
chipped as a milk jug
my hands, older and drier than yesterday's toast
give half-hearted hidings against the noise

On this Saturday morning I
go outside
and sit on the step
neither soberly nor timidly
and wonder

how and with what do I survive this?

Later she says serenely: 'You're a mother for such a short period of your life. It's about 20 to 25 years.' (In poet's time that isn't much, take note all you frenetic rushers who skid along the surface of life.) 'The nice thing is that I'll be young – only about 45 – when the children have left me. I'm looking forward to it – organising my life differently, with no excuses for not doing things.'

Periodically Antjie lands in the creative doldrums, euphemistically known as 'writer's block' – a period of crippling inertia which combines the physical with the mental torment of insomnia. There are various ways out of it – all of them involving hard labour.

She was becalmed again this year because scruples came between her and the subject of her poetry – her house, her family and her life. 'What else can I write about? This is all I know.'

Praise and outrage greeted the powerful and unconventional subjects in her polished stanzas. Antjie was in the eye of the critical hurricane.

Now the children are growing up – reading, registering, remembering, and asking questions – is it fair to 'exploit' them in her writing?

Many readers have asked the same about the searingly erotic verses that plumb the depths of the relationship she shares with her husband John.

'I don't mind now,' John says lightly, 'but I might worry about what she says when I'm over the hill.'

Some of the love poetry is about wisdom and acceptance:

… long ago you started to love me
tender as evening smokiness surrounds all
now you care for me with demands and lamplight
with rows and roses you keep me normal
after every winter snug against you
I thaw.

'Ode to a Perfect Match' celebrates the spiritual homecoming of marriage:

'On this Monday morning
on which Mavis hasn't turned up
among laundry and toys
in my bra and panties on the carpet
John Lennon in the air
oh my lover for the first time in my life
my eyes can see
your children busy fighting
I let my hair frizz out
throw the front door open against the red double hibiscus
abandon the household
to write you an ode …
… divorces do not surprise you
you said
because one in a hundred finds a perfect match

that I love you is an understatement
that I can't live without you a cliché
amid our quarrels, our children, our stuttering household
the boredom of guests and statework
we stay a wonderful perfect match

tonight when I press my breasts against you
my wrists sliding over your thick shiny hair
when I rotate around your eyes
(after all these years still biting blue)
this Monday pastoral is telling me
that our love is all I know
all I need to know

Other poems are erotic, compulsive and startling but never shocking. They don't expose one particular couple's private life because they have an independent existence – one of the qualities that lend special significance to a work of art. A child once part of your flesh and blood grows into a secret separate entity. A poem moves like the soap bubble from the pipe until it is complete in itself, quivering with it's own resonance, sounding chords in the reader that the writer may never have heard. Sometimes surprising the writer herself with what she says.

Antjie's marriage poems are about humans in communion, not simply about what she and her husband do to one another.

This is her second marriage. She was married briefly to pianist Albie van Schalkwyk.

She was very young and still digesting the trauma of early fame.

'Wait until she is twenty-five, she can't cope with the attention now,' her mother was advised when schoolgirl Antjie had completed her first book of poems. She and her mother decided to go ahead and publish in spite of the warnings. *Dogter van Jefta* was an instant literary *cause célèbre*.

Praise and outrage greeted the powerful and unconventional subjects in her polished stanzas. Antjie was in the eye of the critical hurricane.

It was too much too soon. The marriage ended about the time Albie was awarded a scholarship to study in Britain.

'After such a failure you need to strengthen yourself again. You have to remind yourself of your abilities. You couldn't make a marriage work, what can you actually do? A lot of women go back to study when they reach a point like this in their lives. It gives you quite a kick to see. *Oh yes, this I can do. It wasn't luck. I can do it even better now.*'

So Antjie went back to Bloemfontein to study for an Honours degree in English. She'd majored in English, Afrikaans and philosophy for a first degree. And she picked up the threads with John Samuel, the tall architect who'd been her boyfriend in high school. They were married on 2 October 1976 in the Kroonstad Methodist Church. After four years in Pretoria John was offered a partnership in Kroonstad so they moved back and built their own house in Middenspruit. During this period Antjie completed an MA thesis on family themes in Opperman's work.

Kroonstad is halfway between Bloemfontein and Johannesburg. Huge mealie fields stretch out across the shallow curves of the earth. The sky is enormous – a 180-degree dome of blue with small flotillas of white cloud. You feel happily small. The Samuel house is not an oasis but part of the landscape. There are no trees to obstruct the view. The walls are all made of old stone, very thick for coolness in summer and warmth in winter. Both the structure and the furnishings are a pleasing combination of old solid tradition and a newer use of light and geometry. There are countless books and records, and fascinating paintings on the walls.

The town is not exactly a cultural Mecca – Dot and Antjie are always hassling the CNA to get more than André Brink for its literature shelf. But Antjie was not sorry to come back. 'We had a very happy childhood in Kroonstad. It's a nice town for children to grow up in. We have a lot of friends of all sorts.' John comes home for lunch every day and brings Susan and Andries back from school with him.

There's plenty of work for John in Kroonstad; the area boasts some of the wealthiest farmers in the country. Being rich and being seen to be rich is *de rigueur*. An unworldly mobile balance sheet with no outward and viable show would be as incomplete as a society wedding without a photographer. Consequently, lavish manor houses in the district are continually rebuilt or at least refurbished.

'In a sense I like living here because there's no chance of being lionised,' says Antjie. 'Here a poet is nothing.'

Today Antjie Krog is a leading South African literary figure. In 1998 she published the critically acclaimed, Country of my Skull, *based on the two years she spent covering the Truth and Reconciliation Commission as radio journalist for the SABC. The book was adapted into a film and featured French actress Juliette Binoche as Antjie.*

Antjie and John are still married, they both live and work in Cape Town and their children have all grown up. Antjie continues to write prose and poetry between editing, teaching and travelling.

Her response on reading about herself in Cathy's compelling interview: 'Jissis tog dis grillerig verby – afskuwelik! Kan jy dit nie met vyftig persent sny nie of heeltemal drop nie?' (God, it's beyond gruesome – it's awful. Can't you cut it by fifty percent or drop it entirely?)

The Black Prince

To some he's a shining light, to others he's an immovable object and an irresistible force rolled into one. A prince of the blood, prophet of reconciliation, hereditary political leader of the Zulu nation, a legend in his own time, Buthelezi is here to stay.

Cathy Knox

Fairlady 6 February 1985

'He is coming now! *Shenge* (the prince) is coming now!'

The chanting and ululating throbs with the drums of a fierce-faced Youth Brigade corps.

Faster than an agitated heartbeat, the compulsive rhythm runs though the tarmac, into the soles of your feet and up into your body like an electric charge.

'They are fetching the Chief Minister,' an excited aide explains.

The people, the chants and the drums are 'fetching' Buthelezi. His BMW pulls up at the bottom of the hill. He will walk the last couple of hundred metres to the meeting place. The excitement rises to an unbearable pitch. *Shenge* has come. His smile flashes acknowledgement of the homage, he brandishes his ceremonial stick high above his head and strides forward. The crowd surges towards him in a frenzy of excitement and that stick is all you can see of the leader. It's a short fibreglass *ntonga* in which Inkatha's yellow, green and black colours are embedded.

The singers and dancers run before the *Mtwana* (or Prince) Buthelezi. Great fringed Inkatha banners sway above their heads. The beat sweeps forward, upward into catharsis before the fun has even really begun! The spirit is alive and growing in Ulundi. It is a recent city, with more wide-open spaces than built-up areas. A few civil servants' bungalows cluster around the entrance to the legislative assembly buildings – a modern complex paid for by KwaZulu, not the South African government. A kilometre or so to the south there's the smallest Holiday Inn in the world, then another short but bumpy ride on a dirt road and you reach the dormitory area: single-storey bungalows encircling a large central oval.

There seem to be flowers everywhere – big swags of bougainvillea, bright clumps of geraniums. An emerald-green circus-size marquee has been erected in the oval. The minute the tent goes up, hearts start beating faster. It is the sign that there is going to be a big meeting. Far too big for the

> And so inspirational was his message, so powerful his oratory, I felt we'd surely all burst through the canvas roof above and fly straight to heaven.

small community hall. The months of preparation, saving, planning, wangling leave, are reaching their climax. The Inkatha conference is about to start. Busloads of singing delegates start rolling in from Friday midday. Taxis, combis, bicycles, bakkies, more and more buses. They come in all night. Travel-stained but hyped-up delegates spill out into the dusty parking area. Hundreds of loaves of bread are sliced, porridge bubbles in giant three-legged pots. Old friends are reunited. There is much hugging and hand-squeezing. By morning the open square is filled with thousands of Inkatha members – a seething mass of khaki and black, green and gold punctuated by the disc each wears on his or her beret. The round badge with the picture of Buthelezi. The Chief Minister. Inkatha President. *Shenge*.

Crowds lining his route take up the cry. *Shenge!* The Youth Brigade is very much in evidence. Proud and scrupulously groomed they show off the disciplines they have learnt in their youth camps. Junior drum majorettes go through their paces in formation. Other teenagers (there is no sex discrimination) march up and down with orderly purpose. Like a frieze of great red lilies behind them, the *nkehlis* (round-topped headdresses) of a group of women

in tribal dress sway and shift as the wearers move their heads. The marquee is bulging at the seams and the ululating and cheering only subsides when a priest ascends the platform. What could be finer than a good rousing sermon to set the day in motion? And so inspirational was his message, so powerful his oratory, I felt we'd surely all burst through the canvas roof above and fly straight to heaven. This was going to be a very tough act to follow.

A very tough man stood up next. A bull-necked colossus in a neat sports jacket. *Shenge*'s praise singer. Everybody rose as he fixed his eyes on the middle distance and his lips a few centimetres from the microphone. Then, fast as machine-gun fire but in the high expressionless tone of a charismatic, he chanted 25 non-stop minutes of passionate poetry about Buthelezi's history, virtues, and achievements. Names like Vorster, Koornhoof, and Botha came up a couple of times. It was an absolutely staggering display of verbal improvisation ... As he wound up, a rhythm came into his speech, and praises to the King of the Zulus climaxed in a great cry: *You of the elephant!* The crowd yelled with one voice. I felt frightfully white. But I was loving every minute of it. It could be addictive. Everyone was

given an English copy of Buthelezi's speech – 27 typed pages. Delegates would later take the document back to their branches to share the message with those who were left behind. The president's words will be chewed over a hundred times before the next conference. But when Buthelezi started speaking the printed copy paled and I said a silent thank you to Lefina Malinga who taught me to understand Zulu.

He spoke for only 140 minutes – he has been known to go on for up to six hours. But thanks to his superb sense of drama, clever timing, saucy humour, and earthy image-packed Zulu, there was never a dull moment. He's always been a mine of quotable quotes.

Example: 'If I see clouds in the sky and I say "It's going to rain", Mr Botha says "I'm making the rain."'

The mob hooted with glee when he made a ribald crack about Pretoria wanting to thumbscrew him. The guilty quaked when he reprimanded those groups that are not holding meetings regularly.

'I know who you are!' he bellowed with awful ire into the audience. Everyone collapsed into helpless giggles as he mimed the way a drunkard staggers about trying to remember where he lives. He reaffirmed important Inkatha standpoints.

At an official braai later, Chief Buthelezi fed sparingly on steak, teasing the waitress about the underdone meat.

Mangosuthu Buthelezi – 'He spoke for only 140 minutes – he has been known to go on for up to six hours.'

(*Photo:* Mlandeli Puzi/*Die Burger*)

'I say bluntly that we cannot wage a struggle for fine and noble objectives if we are ourselves dehumanised.'

He reminded us of the importance of fighting corruption and intemperance. And he went over the events of the past months, opening his heart and his mind to the people. He read out important letters he'd received and written. He gave the assembly logical ammunition to use when they debate in defence of Inkatha. When we poured out of the tent into the midday sun, everyone looked satisfied. They had been treated to a veritable banquet of a briefing. At an official braai later, Chief Buthelezi fed sparingly on steak, teasing the waitress about the underdone meat. ('This beast hasn't even been killed, let alone cooked'), joking with his hundred odd guests, making everyone feel special.

'I see you remembered a lot of your Zulu in the tent. I saw you laughing when I said some things,' he ragged me. 'Why did you leave your *putu* (stiff porridge)?'

How had he known that? I had been sitting five places down the table from him. It must be true what they say: He has eyes in the back of his head.

Chief Buthelezi's house is not a prime ministerial residence: it was built by his clan as their headquarters and chief's home base. A cattle kraal near the first set of highly efficient security gates lends a practical, homely air to the place. Beyond the gates, up on the right, shaded by big flowering trees and shrubs is the old homestead where Buthelezi's

mother, King Solomon ka Dinizulu's sister, Princess Magogo, lived until her death in November last year. It is probably thanks to her that Buthelezi grew up with a healthy respect for women and their potential. He works well with women and several hold senior posts in his administration. 'I find them very reliable,' he says.

His statement on feminism is simply: 'I was born of a woman, and I am married to a woman. What more can I say?'

A second set of security gates leads you in to 'Kwaphindangene No 2'. The name translates roughly as 'the place of coming back in again'. There is an enormous parking area. Buthelezi's BMW is usually parked under a screen where he can make a dash for the front door in bad weather. Simplified decorative motifs based on traditional designs decorate the walls. As we walk down the wide steps to the house, Buthelezi's two dogs – a Saint Bernard called Mandla and a Rhodesian Ridgeback called Freedom – rush out to greet him. He endures their affectionate welcome with a wry smile.

'I get angry when they jump up and put mud over my suit, but my wife says I can't reprimand them because they are acting out of love. She has a terrible soft spot for dogs.'

Several waifs and strays are in evidence about the place.

'She'd bring every dog she sees back to live with us if she had her way.'

Princess Irene makes me think of Edith Piaf with her huge melting eyes and the slim hands she presses over mine. She drops feather-light kisses on both my cheeks, French style. She is elegant in a wonderfully understated way in a metallic grey shantung Chanel-style suit and beret worn with a dark blouse, a couple of heavy silvery chains and black patent shoes. Flashy demonstrations of wealth and power are not the Buthelezi style.

In line with the Zulu tradition of deploying domestic activities under several different roofs, the house consists of three big square units. They are joined by wide corridors, but the feeling of three separate buildings is preserved. They are conventionally roofed, but something of the beauty of thatch has been captured in the carefully panelled wooden ceilings that slope up to a centre point. Inside there's an open, comfortable, contemporary feeling – the perfect setting for hand-woven rugs, and African arts and artifacts. A stuffed, full-grown leopard stands near the great front window of the sitting room, its glass eyes gazing out across the blue hills of Mohlabathini – layer upon layer of recumbent shapes powdered by the haze stretching back hundreds of kilometres ... centuries ... leading the eye into the heart of Africa.

The view spills into the room, bathing everything in the serene beauty of the timeless – a comforting, tangible, spiritual tranquilliser. But when you tear your eyes away from the eternal and back to the tea tray you can't help noticing that this is obviously a busy man's room. There are all the signs that people usually rush in and out. The simple but very capacious sofas offer seating for lively debates, not lounging cocktails. The leopard is clearly still standing where it was unpacked. It is the gift of a trade union that recently affiliated to Inkatha. Buthelezi strokes its head, smiling as he describes his surprise and pleasure at the magnificent gesture. There's a glass-fronted display unit running the length of the wall behind the leopard. In it are gifts and memorabilia that reflect the tradition of international political involvement of the chief of the Buthelezi tribe. There's the silver-headed cane presented to Chief Matole (Buthelezi's father) by the last Prince of Wales. There's an ancient armband dating back to the time of King Shaka. Countless tokens and presentations from the four corners of the globe – which speak of Buthelezi's diligence as a roving ambassador, and also of the close friendships he forges on his travels. Favoured items from his personal collection of African sculpture and artifacts are also displayed. 'I love art – but I know things are getting too cluttered here,' he says ruefully.

He has a genuine aesthetic appreciation of the sculpture of Africa. He points out the special features of a large carved mask from Tanzania with the reverent tones of the connoisseur.

The squad of domestics you would imagine appropriate in a princely residence is conspicuous by its absence. There's a certain austerity that dates back to the early days of Buthelezi's life.

> He says sometimes when he contemplates the human intransigence that unnecessarily impedes progress, he feels: 'I wish I had another life. I have not enjoyed a private life.'

'I was brought up in the king's residence. We were privileged in some respects, but we didn't live in luxury.'

As a pre-schooler, Buthelezi herded the royal cattle along with other youngsters from the 'palace'.

'When I learnt to ride I explored all the hills and valleys within range. My mother was always surprised at how many people I knew.' But when he first took office he had to motor every day all the way to Nongoma and back. There was no legislative assembly building then, no drivers, no proper catering facilities. 'My wife would sometimes cook for lunch for the entire legislative assembly – sometimes up to 60 people!'

One of the daughters of the house carries in the tea. Buthelezi takes a sachet of sweetener out of his pocket and empties it into his cup. Health-consciousness is part of his responsibility to his job. He watches his weight and cholesterol intake. He doesn't smoke and he's downright abstemious when it comes to alcohol. Exercise is always a problem for pressured executives.

'I try to fit in daily workouts on a rowing machine and exercise cycle. But time is the problem.'

In 1976 he discovered the benefit of an annual visit to a health hydro: 'That really charged my batteries up.'

He'd go with a small entourage of members of his immediate family, including his mother.

Alas, his schedule for the last couple of years hasn't permitted him to take a complete ten-day break. But he seems completely unscarred by the ravages of office. It's almost impossible to believe he's 56. He keeps his weight admirably in check. He's always immaculately groomed. He moves with the easy sprightliness of a healthy young man. And he smiles an awful lot. From a gutsy, eye-crinkling guffaw of pure delight to his famous quizzical twinkle – a subtle blend of amusement, outrage and amazement at human foibles. When you are introduced he slips almost instantly into informal friendliness. He listens with acute attention but he has a habit of closing his eyes while he talks. Is he resting them? I wondered. Or is he tuning in to some internal music that keeps constant time for his thoughts? Rest is a luxury largely denied him. For so-called relaxation he reads journals – the basics like *Time, Newsweek, Financial Mail,* and *Finance Week* and as many more as time allows.

'I have staff who are supposed to monitor the media and draw my attention to relevant items but I find it more satisfactory to do it myself.'

It is essential that he keep his finger on the national and international pulse.

'I like reading history and biographies. I enjoyed Nkomo's biography last year.'

He inherited a tremendous love of music from his mother

'My taste is pretty eclectic: Grieg, Mozart ... I love Handel – his work is very popular among blacks. I can't say I really enjoy music like the Beatles.'

Buthelezi was brought up in a Christian home and he has always been a staunch Anglican. His faith is a wellspring of strength: 'I wouldn't be able to talk to people about hope if it wasn't for my Christian faith.'

He also finds spiritual solace in the wilds – Hluhluwe is very close to his heart. He is a committed member of the International Wildlife Society and he was invited to address their conference in San Antonio (Texas) in 1971. His colleagues in the legislative assembly and Inkatha members collectively ensure a ring of maximum security around the *Mtwana* (infanta or Prince as he is often called). 'My responsibilities inhibit my freedom of movement,' he says. The only reasonably quick way of getting in and out of the Ulundi is in a small plane. Aides insist that their leader always flies with two pilots in a twin-engined craft. Like many leaders, he takes a wad of paperwork with him wherever he goes and uses every spare second to work on it. He goes through his colossal postbag personally and chivvies his clerical staff to get the answers out promptly. He has a terrific mind for detail so everyone must keep on his toes. One of his officers tells a delightful story of how a Tasmanian welfare organisation wrote to say that as a fundraising exercise, they were compiling a recipe book of the favourite dishes of leading politicians from all over the world.

'See to it, please,' said the Chief Minister to an aide who obviously didn't feel the job merited priority action. Weeks later, Buthelezi asked out of the blue: 'Which recipe did you send to those Tasmanians?' There was an instant scramble and the instructions for making steamed mealiebread were zapped into the post double quick! As befits a black leader, Buthelezi is a man of Olympian passions. When he loses his temper, he shows it: an openness which has disconcerted many a white journalist accustomed to more reptilian political emotions.

The lion of KwaZulu might roar, but his anger passes cleanly and he soon returns to his normal jocular mood.

'I was probably happiest during my university days.'

He attended Fort Hare in its heyday. Learning was an exciting business then.

'Even at school we had such a hunger for knowledge we'd pick up any scrap of paper in the mud to read. I am very concerned about the situation in out schools now. It will take generations to make up the time that is being lost. Our people had an educational backing even before things were disrupted.'

He is justifiably proud of KwaZulu's Mangosuthu Technikon but says he would dearly love to see the University of Zululand become the fertile institution Fort Hare used to be. He says sometimes when he contemplates the human intransigence that unnecessarily impedes progress, he feels: 'I wish I had another life. I have not enjoyed a private life.'

Even while he was in mourning for the mother he was so devoted to, there was no respite. Two days after her funeral he addressed a mass rally in Johannesburg. A meeting with President Botha in Stellenbosch followed shortly afterwards.

'I can never really take a holiday,' he says, 'and the family has suffered as a consequence. Sometimes I feel that my children hardly know me.'

There are seven young Buthelezis – three girls and four boys.

'I am always busy, always away. My children have been picked on at school because they are my children.'

But the lament is mild. He was born and bred for the work he is doing. While he was growing up, his mother went down on her knees every day to pray for the growth of his wisdom. He was the light of her life – the son for whom she had waited many years.

Two of Mangosuthu Buthelezi's children, Princess Mandisi Sibukakonke and son, Prince Nelisuzulu Benedict Buthelezi, died from AIDS-related illnesses in 2004. He is the only high-profile national political leader to speak openly and honestly about HIV and AIDS. The Inkatha Freedom Party lost the KwaZulu-Natal Province to the ANC in 2004.

The Inheritance of Zinzi Mandela

Denis Beckett

Fairlady 16 October 1985

'There is much expected of me, and people want me to be a mini Mandela. They tend to overlook that fact that I might have a personality of my own.' When we asked Denis Beckett, editor of *Frontline* to interview Zinzi he anticipated a clash with that personality but emerged somewhat disarmed.

For three reasons I was not looking forward to meeting Zinzi Mandela. I anticipated a lecture on the evils of the system and my complicity. I know whites are ostriches, fascists, and so on. It's all true, as our grandchildren will recognise. But I get tired of hearing it all the time. Zinzi's father, Nelson Mandela, has been jailed for a quarter of a century, her mother endlessly banned, herself deprived of a passport. Warmth is not to be expected.

I suspected she would suffer from The Princess Complex, with all its lousy effects. Many ordinary people who'd be better off as housewives or schoolteachers are thrust into prominence by accident of birth and put on ridiculous airs of self-importance.

So when the appointed time arrives and Zinzi does not, there is little sorrow. An hour later, she appears. She is unflurriedly apologetic – a missed bus, a misunderstood message – so that the prejudices begin to thaw.

Zinzi Mandela plans to follow in her father's footsteps and enter the legal profession. She is a first-year student at the University of Cape Town – a belated enrolment, as she matriculated at Waterford eight years ago.

She chose UCT specifically because she thought she would be less identifiable there than at Wits. It didn't work.

'I had hardly arrived when people were coming for interviews. People nudge each other and point and whisper. You feel like a curiosity. It's so uncomfortable when people are friendly, especially when strangers are friendly. It's terrible.

'I never know whether they are accepting me or whether what they're accepting is Mandela's daughter, the talking point.'

I ask the inevitable: Is a political career on the cards?

'I get thrust into the forefront whether I like it or not. I don't see myself as belonging at the head, by instinct or by inclination. But I do obviously want to play a role. Partly of course I feel myself to be the spokesman of my

'No, no, no, no. My father is not like that. He is not a bitter man; he does not know bitterness. Read his reply to Botha. Where is the bitterness? There is anger of course, but there is no bitterness ...'

silenced family, and also because as a black female in South Africa I have to speak up.

Zinzi always speaks her mind. Sometimes unexpectedly.

'Do you mind if I cut my toenails?' she asks suddenly.

Mind? Well no, or at least that's what you say. But it jolts your Anglo-Saxon sensibilities to find your office turned into a stranger's bathroom. She whips out a pair of scissors and clips away, gathering the shearings in her hand – chatting casually as if she were smoking a cigarette. Done, she wraps the clippings into a tissue and packs them away in her bag. Less invasion (of all but convention) than the stubbing of a butt.

Why is it Zinzi who bears the family flag?

There are two elder sisters, and one brother. The brother and one sister are technically half-siblings – children of Nelson's first marriage – but Zinzi does not employ the distinction.

'People must find their own directions. My sister Zeni married into the Swazi royal family. *That* cuts you out of politics all right – whew.'

The other two are both in the Transkei – one a sociologist, one running a family shop.

'They are royalty down there after all. There are ties and links, people can't all be expected to just cut away from everything else because of political pressures ...'

Does it still mean much then, the royalty story?

'Not in urban areas, of course; nobody gives two hoots. But in the Transkei, it's all very la-di-dah. People who don't give a fig about the big political issues take it really seriously. It's fading away now among the younger generation, but even around Umtata a young man will have to put on at least a pretence of respect for noble families, or the elders will give him an earful. It's very embarrassing actually. People humble themselves. You

visit some remote area where they can hardly keep body and soul together, and they slaughter for you. Imagine it.'

Suddenly, the pensive expression gives way to a peal of laughter. 'And there are the honorifics ... my family has about thirty surnames. You can be dying of thirst, stop at a little village after a long trip, and an old granny offers you tea. You're standing there with your tongue hanging out and she's holding the tray out to you but you have to hold back while she intones the whole list. 'Oh yes, it has its perils. But it's still important to the people there. From the old people you hear much more muttering and discontent about KD (Matanzima, Transkei's president and Zinzi's cousin) tampering with tradition than you hear about him accepting a government-created post or dismembering the country, and the things that count in national politics.'

The more I talk to Zinzi the less she comes across as the kind of person who gets beaten up in a domestic tiff (an incident in her private life which made newspaper headlines).

Hesitantly, I venture: *I wonder if you'd mind if I asked you about something very personal ...?*

'Aha,' says Zinzi, swinging her fist in a mock sock of her own eye. 'You mean the punch? Yes, that was very meaningful to me. I learnt a lot during that business. I learnt there are no support structures for one thing. You read about women being battered and so on, but you don't pay any attention really. It's the kind of thing that always happens to "other people" but then it happens to you and you find out where society falls down. People just don't know how to handle this sort of thing.

'I'm not complaining about my case. As it happened I had quite a lot of informal support. Of course some of that was because of the publicity. Back to that old "Mandela's daughter" thing. In fact that was irritating

Zinzi Mandela – 'I feel myself to be the spokesman
of my silenced family.'

(*Photo:* Ingrid Hudson)

in all sorts of ways on this occasion. I was very upset about people assuming that I couldn't really be hurt by a couple of little punches, that the media blew it up because it was me. Actually I was badly injured.

'I'm okay now. I'm not emotionally wounded, scarred on my psyche, and all that. But I did realise quite how little we have in the way of preparation to be able to handle that sort of experience. I wondered if you'd bring this up? I do think it's an area that needs to be tackled.

'I was also annoyed by the constant references to "my husband". I am not married and never have been. Would you point out that it is not necessary to be married in order to have a child? He gave me a beautiful son and for that I'll always thank him. I now have one ex-boyfriend, no ex-husbands and a wonderful child, Kalantsho Zondwa.'

Zinzi's first visit frightened her stiff. It was not like not having a father at all. She'd always been conscious of this. At two years old, at three, at four, people were saying 'Mandela's daughter'.

The name is thoroughly traditional. As is the custom, the first name is picked by the paternal grandfather who lives in Pietersburg. It is the Pedi word for a black branch found in a certain rare tree in the area. Zinzi is not sure of the detail. The second name is chosen, also traditionally, by the maternal grandfather. It means 'to be hated'.

Or 'the hated one'.

After a moment I ask whether it is reasonable to see in this a certain degree of embitterment on the part of the maternal grandfather.

Zinzi is horrified. I've already seen many human emotions on her volatile features. Now I see distress.

'No, no, no, no. My father is not like that. He is not a bitter man; he does not know bitterness. Read his reply to Botha. Where is the bitterness? There is anger of course, but there is no bitterness … In any case Zondwa is one of our surnames, it's just traditional, it doesn't really mean anything at all any more, like white people are called Brown, or Smith, or Carpenter. They're just names.'

Zinzi pauses. 'Still,' she says, 'I'm always having people saying "how dare you name a child that?"...'

A move to safer ground seems in order. How often does she see her father? It brings the next surprise, and an enormous grin, a huge embracing beam.

'Aah, it's so wonderful they allow contact visits now. Since July last year. It was so wonderful to touch him. The first visit I actually sat on his lap, like a tiny child.'

What do you mean, touch him?

'You know, *touch* him.'

Do you mean to tell me that you did not touch your father until July last year?

'Yes, that's right.'

Matter-of-fact.

'Not since he went to jail, when I was 18 months old. I wasn't allowed to visit him in fact until I was 16.'

Perhaps one isn't entitled to get upset about this. Rules ... law and order ... prisons aren't holiday camps. But we all have our blind spots. I can imagine few things harder than being told I may not touch my kids for 25 years.

Zinzi's first visit frightened her stiff. It was not like not having a father at all. She'd always been conscious of this. At two years old, at three, at four, people were saying 'Mandela's daughter'. There was a pride in it, but a distance. She had been able to correspond, yes, but her concept of him was more of a god than a father.

That first visit she was shivering, trembling, but as soon as it began she actually fell in love with him as a father. He realised what she was going through, drew her into his personality, the grille fell away from her eyes, the glass between them disappeared, the listening warders vanished and she became a daughter.

'From then on I have known him, there are no problems at all.' Silence for a moment, and then: 'But I still don't know how to live with him, when he comes out ...'

July last year was a high point.

It isn't only touch; it's also sight, full sight. Hitherto he'd been a shape through the grille, head and shoulders only. Now he is a complete man. She can show him what she's wearing. They can see each other's gestures and body language. There's a whole new dimension.

When he comes out ... is that a when or is that an if?

To Zinzi it's a when.

What does she think of the State President's offer of freedom on condition that her father renounce violence?

'It doesn't mean anything to me. I dismissed it from the beginning. So did everybody else who knows even the slightest bit about him or has any understanding at all of what the struggle is about. That was just rubbish from beginning to end and it really surprised me that the newspapers made such a fuss.'

But Zinzi must have been torn, her emotions as a daughter must have at least in some part wanted him again as a present, accessible, father – all right, not 'free' in the full sense, but available? Sharing the supper table, like other fathers, whatever the broader level of freedom?

Not at all. Zinzi thinks it's a very stupid question – and it's a great tragedy the whites remain so ignorant of what freedom is about. Not for one second was she even tempted. She hadn't thought of it as anything to take seriously at all.

Zinzi tires of the topic. This non-talk about non-freedom. She turns to a different side of the coin.

'My greatest fortune is that my mother has always had enough love for two parents. Not that I'm boasting,' she trills in a sing-song of mocking a cliché – 'but I do think I am mentally healthy and I have a mother to thank. She's wonderful. You probably see her as a political figure, but you must look further. She is really wonderful.

'How many grandmothers do you know who roll on the lawn with their grandchildren? He lives with her, my son. She treats him like as her son. She says all the children I have will be hers. I am just the biological passage to give her more children.'

Zinzi's mother is Winnie, Nelson's second wife, a wife for four years and a prison widow for 25 and a public figure in her own right. In 1977 the government evidently decided that various banning orders were not having quite the isolationist effect desired, and she was shifted from her Soweto home to the docile Free State dorp of Brandfort. Why Brandfort? No-one knew, no-one explained. It didn't even have the supposed logic, in government terms, of tying in with her nominal ethnic identity. She knew nothing of the local language – South Sotho. There was an outcry at the cruelty of this form of punishment, and much suggestion that the

'People want equal rights, they want equal opportunities, they don't want crumbs and charity.'

object of the exercise was to knock the stuffing out of Winnie.

I ask about Brandfort, expecting at least a show of sadness.

But Zinzi is full of surprises: 'She's got so much going for her there. She'll find it really hard to leave, when the time comes.' (When, not if.)

'She's got a clinic there, and a crèche. There's an Operation Hunger committee. She's grown into the community; they've grown into her. It built her, being there. The people were apathetic and hopeless. They'd given up. The yards were barren. There was no idea of self-help, no expression of constructive energy. She's mobilised that place. The people grow vegetables now; there are sewing groups, it's a different community altogether. There's excitement. It's vibrant. She speaks Sotho like a native now; the whole experience just shows what can be done. All it needed was a spur, just something to bring out people's realisation of their own worth.'

(In August, two petrol bombs were thrown at Winnie Mandela's house, partially destroying it and her adjoining clinic. A collection for their rebuilding was taken up in the US Senate, and the US Government undertook to make up any shortfalls.)

What of Zinzi's own political outlook?

Not surprisingly she has been identified with the 'progressive' movement in the current black political conflict – the faction which in line with ANC tradition and UDF practice stresses non-racialism, in contrast with the Black Consciousness segment.

I suggested that all the conflict between the two approaches seems sad; a lot of sound and fury to cover up that neither is making any progress towards its stated goal.

All we're getting is much frantic governmental fluttering around the edges of apartheid while society as a whole drifts deeper and deeper into a belief in the inevitability of a coming conflagration.

Zinzi bridles.

'That's half their mistake. It's only the whites who talk about "coming". They want to deny that it is already here; that implies that the situation is reasonable and tolerable now. It is not. That is an offensive and racist belief.'

Well how do we get out of it?

'We have tried. We have tried to explain it peacefully, but we are always answered by violence.'

The government is scared that if it does not command the violence it will become its victim.

'That is such nonsense, such nonsense. Botha must only look at Mandela's answer to his offer. It shows how easy peaceful transition can be.'

How do you envisage the government coming to see that, bearing in mind that they are answerable to the white population and the whites on the whole believe the abolition of apartheid means a black domination and Idi Amins and a fate worse than death?

'Botha must recognise that his power is illegal. He must come to terms with the fact that he is not a true leader of South Africa.'

Can you really expect him to pay attention to that sort of demand?

'He should not be there.'

Can you try to put yourself in his shoes, trying to feel the imperatives working on him, and see what you would do in his position?

'No way, I won't do that. That is useless. I can't see why anyone should think the way he does.'

What you're wanting is a free and non-racial political process where the majority is free to choose leaders who espouse socialist principles. Is that right?

'Yes, that's right, that's exactly right.'

What if a democratic majority should freely elect a conservative government to power, perhaps a government composed largely of white people?

Zinzi is nonplussed, in common with everyone else who comes across this thought for the first time. She is clearly more used to the argument that the blacks aren't ready, and takes it that this is what I am getting at.

'There is this image of majority rule being like Ethiopia. So what? It will be our Ethiopia; it has to end up in a socialist economic structure. That is our value, our desire …'

Whose desire?

'Blacks' desire.'

How can you claim to know what 'blacks' want?

'People want equal rights, they want equal opportunities, they don't want crumbs and charity.'

But they might use their equal rights to choose to vote for PW Botha or to work for Harry Oppenheimer?

'What they want is betterment. Most people don't understand theories; they're not interested in theories. If a conservative system gave people what they want, they would probably support it. The trouble is, it *can't* give them what they want; only a socialist system can.'

In the society you foresee, what changes are there to the lives of the whites?

'There are no drastic changes, there are no squatter camps of anything like that. What they got too easily because of the advantages apartheid gave them will be taken away. They must work genuinely for the common society, like all of us.'

If a white man wants his children educated in the company of other white children, is that okay?

'No, it's not. There has to be real mixing. We are all here and everything we have belongs to all of us. You must accept the society you are part of.'

Nobody insists that Jewish kids aren't allowed to go to Jewish schools. If you have a completely democratic base, then you've solved apartheid. Why do you have to interfere with people's personal liberty?

'If that sort of thing should turn out to be fully democratically acceptable … then maybe … if no offence is caused …'

The words are coming slower, then there is a sudden recoup:

'But that's just silly hypothesis. Of course that sort of thing would not be democratically acceptable.'

Well, I wonder. I wonder too quite how inoffensive people like Zinzi might find various of the practices which now seem inextricably linked with apartheid. If only apartheid were removed from the equation.

As Zinzi leaves she tells me she'll think around those issues.

'I'll agree with you this far,' she says. 'There's too much complaining now. We get onto platforms, we push our fists in the air, we say that we are oppressed. By now, we all know that we are oppressed. There's too much of that. We need something new. We need to find a real way out.'

And so it came to pass that Nelson Mandela was released in 1990. The rest is history. Zinzi Mandela is a managing trustee of the Nelson Mandela Children's Fund.

The Afrikaners: On the Lip of the Volcano

JM Coetzee

Fairlady 28 May 1986

While violence simmered in the Cape townships, acclaimed South African novelist JM Coetzee journeyed into the calmer reaches of the minds of four fellow Afrikaners, to interview them for the *New York Times* magazine. These are the impressions he conveyed to American readers: he describes them simply as 'fragments of the text of national discourse'.

Some 40 miles from Cape Town, on the fringe of the wine-farming region of the Cape Province, lies Stellenbosch, the second-oldest town in South Africa. Though it is the seat of a major university, Stellenbosch is not a notably liberal place. Its students are well behaved; its white voters have always stood firmly behind the National Party, which has held power since 1948. Liberals have gained no footing here, but then neither has the ultra-right.

A few months ago, the highway between Cape Town and Stellenbosch was effectively closed: bands of black and coloured youths hung about the verges or waited on the overpasses to stone cars; burning barricades sometimes blocked the road; on bad days even the airport, which lies along this route, could be reached only under police escort.

Today, as I drive out to Stellenbosch, the highway is reputed to be safe. I pass an armoured troop carrier parked under a tree. A soldier, crouched on the embankment, stares at something through binoculars. From the vicinity of the Crossroads squatter camp, the scene of recent violence, a pillar of yellow smoke rises into the air. The sun blazes down. All is quiet on the southern front, by South African standards.

I am on my way to meet some citizens of Stellenbosch, strangers as yet to me, to hear how they feel about what is going on in our country. My mind is open; I am ready to be surprised.

A week ago, in the village of Greyton, I overheard a farmer, a fat, apoplectic-looking man in khakis, everyone's notion of a brutal slavemaster.

'PW Botha and his promises!' he growled. 'If he won't put up, he should shut up!' (The idiom he used in Afrikaans was a good deal cruder than the English version.) If, even in the somnolent remoter valleys, Afrikaners were irritated by the snail's pace of change, the gap between talk and action, how much bolder might they not be nearer the big city?

As I will discover, the people I interview do not confirm to the reigning

As I will discover, the people I interview do not confirm to the reigning stereotype of the Afrikaner. They do not speak contemptuously of blacks. They are not notably intolerant in their attitudes, heartless in their conduct or indolent in their daily life.

stereotype of the Afrikaner. They do not speak contemptuously of blacks. They are not notably intolerant in their attitudes, heartless in their conduct or indolent in their daily life. They seem not to bear the worst marks of apartheid, a doctrine and a set of social practices that scars the moral being of whites as it degrades and demeans blacks. Whether they can be said to be representative of their three million compatriots – in other words, of 60 percent of South Africa's whites – I do not know. They all identify themselves as Afrikaners, but their allegiances seem to lie as much with the broad South African middle class as with the Afrikaner tribe. In this respect they are typical of the generation born after 1948, a generation that, having grown up under Afrikaner hegemony, can afford to be more self-assured, less belligerently nationalistic than its fathers.

Indeed, I am struck above all by the *calm* of those I interview. They do not talk like people perched on the lip of a volcano. All of them believe the world around them is changing (and should be changing faster), but nowhere do they seem to envisage an eruption of change that might sweep them and their children away. Yet they live in a country seething with black anger, and

at war on its borders. Have the ring of steel around the black townships and the clampdown on news coverage fostered in them an unreal sense of security, a culpable ignorance, a foolish calm? Or do they in truth have darker fears, more dire visions of the future, than they are ready to divulge? Are they telling the truth, the whole truth, or have they chosen to engage in acts of self-presentation for an audience of strangers?

I put the question, yet it seems to me falsely put. How often in our lives does the truth of ourselves, the whole truth and unmixed truth, emerge? Are we not routinely engaged in acts of self-presentation, acts which it would be excessively puritanical to condemn as insincere? Surely, in getting to know the truth of another person, we neither accept nor reject his self-presentations, but *read them*, as best we can, in whatever context we can summon up. A few hours of conversation will not give us privileged access to 'the Afrikaner': It would be naïve to expect that. What we have below are excerpts from the texts of four lives, uttered (I believe) with due deliberation, for the record, at particular moments in four life histories – fragments of the text of a national discourse, to be read and weighed alongside whatever other

fragments we come to possess.

In one of the pleasanter white suburbs, I meet, Kaffie Pretorius, an attractive, matronly woman in her thirties. Brought up in Lambert's Bay, on South Africa's west coast, where her father kept a store, she married an academic, settled in Stellenbosch, paints in her spare time, but still hankers for the desolate west-coast landscape: When she goes there on vacation, she takes her children on long rambles in the veld to teach them the plant-lore she learnt as a child.

We speak in Afrikaans, the common language in most of rural South Africa. Like everyone else I speak to, Kaffie Pretorius is depressed about the failing economy, about accelerated inflation and the collapse of the South African currency, which has led in only a few months to a doubling in prices of imported goods, including petrol. Yet, to my surprise, she observes that these economic woes might not be such a bad thing: 'For the first time whites are truly affected – for the first time they must think seriously about the future.'

And then, after a pause: 'How did we think we could hold on to all of this?' She waves a hand to embrace her spacious home, the prosperous neighbourhood, and beyond it the town of Stellenbosch, surrounded by thousands of acres of farmland. 'How did we think we could ever hold on to it?'

I have no reply. I am touched by her words, by their suddenness, by the feeling behind them. Perhaps one can be so naked only with strangers. Yet afterwards, I wonder whether I would not be have been equally touched, thought about it in a different way, had she lamented: 'How can they take all this away from us?'

And is it a good idea to indulge, in oneself or anyone else, these fits of voluptuous self-recrimination?

'Things go in phases,' she resumes. 'We are the generation that will

I am struck, as we talk, by how vague and shifting her fears are, and by how typical she is of most whites in this respect. At one moment, she envisages a future social order, much like the present one, though without the racial laws. At other moments, she seems to have a grimmer picture before her eyes: a hand-to-mouth existence as an unwelcome guest in the land of her birth. It is one of the bitterest consequences of the decades-long suppression of black dissent that ordinary whites now not only have no one with whom to imagine their future, but have not the vaguest idea of what blacks might be prepared to settle for.

At one moment, she envisages a future social order, much like the present one, though without the racial laws. At other moments, she seems to have a grimmer picture before her eyes: a hand-to-mouth existence as an unwelcome guest in the land of her birth.

have to make the adjustment. Our children will find it easier. Already children find it easier to relate to coloured friends than we ever did.'

In what spheres of life, I ask, are whites going to find it hardest to adjust?

'First, education. When schools are integrated, standards drop. It's unfortunate, but it's a fact. Look at Zimbabwe. Second, neighbours.'

Would she personally mind black or coloured neighbours?

'Not at all,' she replies. 'If a black family can afford to move in next door, I would welcome them.'

'Our women are the worst,' Kaffie Pretorius remarks. 'It is because domestic help is so easy to get. Utter idleness. They get into their cars in the morning and drive around aimlessly all day. If they are the most conservative, it is because they have the most to lose.'

Does she herself have a servant, and how have interpersonal relations been during the present unrest?

'Martha is going to have a baby soon, which has led us to talk to each other more openly. It strikes me how hard we find it to think our way into the life our servants lead. I wonder how I would feel, in this awful summer heat, living in a corrugated steel house in Ida's Valley.'

After lunch, some teenage friends of the family stop by. They have just written their school-leaving examinations. For the boys, the choice is whether to enrol in college and postpone military service or to go into the army. I ask whether they have any doubts about serving in Namibia (still called South West Africa by most white South Africans), or patrolling South Africa's black townships. No, they reply: One must be prepared to make sacrifices for one's country.

All the same, they are cynical about South Africa's occupation of Namibia and its professed aims there (to protect the right of the territory to self-determination). As for the strife at home, they agree that blacks should be given more freedom.

But then, says one of them, Dawid, whites should have freedom too – freedom to found a state in which they will be their own masters. I ask where this state should be, thinking he will propose some tiny Spartan colony on the Orange River.

'The Transvaal, the Orange Free State and northern Natal,' he replies, naming the vast area containing perhaps three quarters of South Africa's economic resources.

'Our forefathers shed enough blood for those parts of the country to justify our claim to them.'

He speaks the language, arrogantly, possessive, of the enduring right-wing dream of a national

homeland where the Afrikaner will be left to run his affairs without interference, and where black people will face a clear and simple choice: to stay on as rightless, wage-earning sojourners, or to pack their bags and seek salvation elsewhere.

Dawid's friends shake their heads and smile. Clearly they don't take him seriously. As for Dawid, his face is inscrutable.

Does he believe in what he says, or is he trying to shock me? I know the streak of sly humour behind the Afrikaner's mask of dourness. Is Dawid a joker?

'What are your ambitions?' I ask him.

'To qualify as a clinical psychologist and then go into a career in politics,' he replies.

'I travel widely, I talk to many people,' says Michiel le Roux. 'I would say that, down in the smallest town in South Africa, there is a perception that things have changed, totally and drastically; 1985 has left a mark on everyone.'

There is an awareness that the country is in a crisis situation, and this cuts across all of age, class, language.

'No-one thinks we need only take a few deep breaths for things to go back to normal, as they did in 1977,' he says, referring to the 1976-77 uprisings in Soweto that shook the country for 18 months.

'For this reason it has become possible for a strong leader to take South Africa in a direction that would have been unthinkable in 1984, provided that the leadership is strong enough.'

Le Roux, a graduate in law, is, at the age of 36, the managing director of a Stellenbosch-based liquor company. We meet in his spacious office overlooking the courtyard in which stands an old wooden wine press, tall as a house, preserved for prosperity.

Does the strong leadership he refers to exist?

'No, clearly it doesn't. President Botha gave strong leadership – stronger than one expected – up to a certain point. Then he faltered. The issue on which he faltered was residential segregation. The feeling that we were directionless is widespread. People have no feeling of being on the road anywhere, or of knowing where we are on the road to.'

If last year has been a year of crisis, how has the crisis manifested itself in this quiet, civilised town with its oak-lined streets and painstakingly restored houses?

Race relations are good, or seem to be, Michiel replies. He is conscious of no hostility when he visits coloured areas; calls for a boycott of white business have met with little success. Yet, he concedes, it is quite possible he is deluded. A coloured school principal warned him of a 'tremendous level of aggression' just beneath the surface. What more can he say? One can report only what one sees.

Where we go from here, neither of us is sure. I remember the soldiers I passed on the highway, the smoke over the shantytowns.

Which is the true face of South Africa – Crossroads, burning, or Stellenbosch, on the surface so

> Like me, he was born in the twilight of a centuries-old feudal order in which the rights and duties of masters and servants seem to be a matter of unspoken convention, and in which a mixture of personal intimacy and social distance – a mixture characteristic of societies with a slaveholding past – pervaded all dealings.

placid? Months ago, I remember, on a quiet Sunday afternoon, I cycled through this town. 'Amandla! (Power),' shouted a voice behind me. I glanced around. A man, not black, but coloured, waved a fist at me from the sidewalk. 'Amandla!' he shouted again, in case I had misunderstood him. Was his the true hidden face of Stellenbosch?

My next stop is at the farm of Jan Boland Coetzee. I have seen him scores of times, from the sidelines, in his rugby-playing heyday, and can make a fair guess at his approach to life: hard work, no nonsense. Within minutes we have compared genealogies, as is the custom in our country, and established that, like so many Afrikaners, we are probably distant relatives – fourth or fifth or tenth cousins.

For our interview he conducts me into the cavernous cellars of his wine farm, which are lined with huge oak casks imported from France (the craft of cooping has died out in South Africa, he tells me). In a subterranean hush, we sit down and talk.

'How is apartheid faring in the countryside?' I ask.

'Apartheid has never been a word in my book,' he replies, establishing his footing at once; and he proceeds to reminisce about the farm on which he grew up, where his grandfather drove to town to do the shopping for everyone, black and white alike.

'It was only later when I left the farm, that I first experienced apartheid.' For a while he muses: 'Apartheid has created a gulf between

people. We no longer know each other. Also, we whites have simply appropriated things for ourselves, leaving the blacks and coloureds to do the producing. It is not just. It is not a healthy state of affairs'.

He is not, strictly speaking, answering my question, and knows it. I understand the difficulty he is having. Like me, he was born in the twilight of a centuries-old feudal order in which the rights and duties of masters and servants seem to be a matter of unspoken convention, and in which a mixture of personal intimacy and social distance – a mixture characteristic of societies with a slaveholding past – pervaded all dealings. To whites brought up in this old order, the codification of social relations into the system of racial laws known as apartheid always seemed gross and unnecessary, the brainchild of academic ideologies and upstart politicians. So, for Jan Boland Coetzee to shake his head over apartheid, yet look back nostalgically to an age when everyone knew his place, by no means proves him a hypocrite, though I suspect he forgets the iron hand needed to keep the old order running.

He is known not only as a winemaker, but also for his part in the movement among progressive farmers to improve labour relations in the countryside. The age of the average farm labourer in South Africa, he tells me, is 52 years. Two generations of workers have quit white farms to seek their fortunes in the cities. In another generation, there will be no-one left to till the soil. Therefore he has striven to create an exemplary environment on his own farm that will draw younger coloured men back to the land: decent wages, productivity incentives, comfortable housing, health care, recreational opportunities.

'During the present unrest we have found many younger coloured people wanting to come back to the farm simply in order to be part of an ordered little community with civilised standards and regular routine. For years we farmers were preoccupied with land and capital. Now we have begun to pay attention to people again, and the result is a change in attitudes that cannot be described – it truly has to be experienced.'

There is a certain Utopianism in the vision he projects of a rural order based on small, rationally organised labouring communities. Utopian less because his brand of upliftment does not work – it clearly does, here and now within it's self-imposed limits – than because it draws much of it's attractiveness from somewhat sentimentalised memories of a feudal past. Farmers like Coetzee reject such vast, centralised blueprints for the future as Hendrik Verwoerd's

'grand apartheid' in favour of small-scale, independent, pragmatic local solutions. As long as the politicians (and perhaps the police too) will leave us alone, Coetzee seems to be saying, we country folk can find ways to live harmoniously together.

In much of the talk rife among more progressive whites today, the same spirit is to be detected: loss of faith in large-scale national policies, impatience with red tape, readiness for ad hoc approaches to local problems. The irony is that this is precisely the moment in history when black South Africans are grouping together in larger and larger political blocks, and black leaders prepared to limit discussion to merely local issues, are proving harder and harder to find.

Only the darkest cynic would claim that the effort Jan Boland Coetzee and his wife have put into the social upliftment of their workforce has not been sincerely intended. While their workers are well housed, the Coetzees themselves live in a cramped bungalow – renovation of the old farmstead is barely under way. Nevertheless, looking towards the future, one may ask

whether marriage will ever be possible between the kind of enlightened paternalism they stand for and the egalitarian black nationalism sweeping across the land.

When I ask Jan Boland what he thinks the effect will be on this part of the country, once restrictions on black mobility ('influx control') have been lifted, he is dismissive: 'There is no tradition of blacks living in the Western Cape,' he says. True; but only because the full force of the law has been brought to bear to keep blacks out. Can a farm remain an island of tranquility in a country of turmoil? Can the Western Cape, this tiny tip of the continent, declare itself independent of Africa?

Can Jan Boland imagine circumstances that would make him give up his farm and quit South Africa? Vehemently, he shakes his head.

'Never. I say, I have enough faith in my countrymen, black, white and coloured, to believe that South Africans are not such bad people as the Americans and the rest say.'

The Afrikaners – On the Lip of the Volcano
© *JM Coetzee*, The New York Times

Gcina Mhlope – Another Alice

Are you Gcina? *'Ye bo! Who are you?'* The voice is bluesy, deep, melodic. It is a voice that speaks for silent generations of black women who 'haven't even started to tell their side of the story', a voice that, like Alice Walker's, is defining a culture.

Ellen Fitzpatrick

Fairlady 11 June 1986

She made me cry. But my tears were not shed at the footlights where she easily moves people to laughter, too. No, it was her story.

At only 27, Gcina has established herself as a poet, playwright, writer and actress of note. Director Barney Simon calls her 'an extraordinary talent, a very important person for her place and time'.

Slim and casual, she lopes across the room and relaxes her rangy suppleness into contours of a large armchair. In that deep, sensitive voice she tells her story …

Her childhood was spent with her adored grandmother in Hammersdale, Natal. While the old lady was occupied with household chores she entertained little Gcina for hours with traditional folk tales. 'I loved her very much, she spoilt me rotten and I had a lovely childhood.'

Then, at the age of 10, Gcina was taken from her grandmother's care and had to start a new life in the Transkei with her mother, whom she hardly knew.

'I missed my grandmother terribly, and longed to go back to her and the other family.'

Gcina never saw her grandmother again.

'I was not allowed to go and see her while I was at school, and when I finally made it back to Hammersdale in 1977, I discovered she had died three months before. She had left a huge suitcase for me – one of those big, old-fashioned wooden ones – filled with presents for all the years she hadn't seen me. Ribbons for my hair, dresses with stiff petticoats and tight sashes that tied in bows at the back that I liked, bobby socks, nice little toys and books and dolls.'

She pauses, then continues, her voice even deeper.

'But everything was for a 10-year-old. In her mind I never grew up. That suitcase made me cry so much. Yes … I miss my grandmother still, and yet I feel she's always with me. I feel her presence. There's a lot of her in me. Everything I do I know she'd love.'

Gcina Mhlope – 'Black women haven't said enough, they haven't even started, in fact, to tell their side of the story.'

'One day I discovered a toilet in Twelfth Avenue. It was quite nice and clean and I watched it for a while to see if it was busy. I started to use that toilet as my study. I would sit on the closed toilet seat and read and write for hours. Most of my published stories and poetry were written on that toilet.'

Gcina cherishes her grandmother's memory, the legacy which secures her traditional bonds. Ever present in her conversation is the inevitable conflict between tradition and contemporary reality, best illustrated in her relationship with her mother, who died two years ago. Gcina took her death very badly.

'Although we had never been close I was always hoping that one day we could be mother and daughter. She died while there was still unfinished business between us.'

But she must have been very proud of Gcina?

'No, not at all. She was very traditional, very conservative. All my sisters were married. I am the only one who was not. I travel up and down in planes. I don't want to work; I'm only acting. I'm so thin. I don't look like a woman. Her attitude never changed. My sisters are learning to like and accept the work I do now – she never did.'

Gcina's appreciation of her past is reflected in her love of praise poetry and the richness and beauty of the Xhosa language; and in her preservation of folk tales. But on the other hand is her wholehearted rejection of traditional attitudes to women.

'In the Transkei I really got into my schooling. But,' she adds ironically, 'Transkei women must get married, they've got no business being well educated. When I was about 14, friends were being forced to marry men they didn't know. These men, you see, had a lot of lobola. I hated the system,' she says vehemently.

'It could have been my turn any day; I had nightmares about it.'

Gcina went to boarding school to escape an arranged marriage, and it was there that her writing career began. She was inspired after hearing a praise poet for the first time.

'A praise poet sings the praises of his chief and tribe, its history and achievements. He does it poetically, using beautiful phrases and language, wearing bright attire and performing and dancing and jumping. I was so impressed and I knew then what I wanted to be.' But women praise poets were unheard of, which is why Gcina started writing secretly.

Her first short story was published in *Bona* when she was only 16. Her face lights up as she recalls: 'I'll never forget the day it came out. I was so excited. I kept reading it, picking it up and putting it down, going to the toilet and coming back and picking it up again!'

From then on there was no stopping her. When Gcina left school she was staying with her sister, a domestic worker in Orange Grove. Her sister's employers objected to Gcina being on the premises 'but there was nowhere else to stay' so at 5.30 every morning she would sneak out and wander around the streets.

'One day I discovered a toilet in Twelfth Avenue. It was quite nice and clean and I watched it for a while to see if it was busy. I started to use that toilet as my study. I would sit on the closed toilet seat and read and write for hours. Most of my published stories and poetry were written on that toilet.'

Eventually Gcina moved into a women's hostel in Alexandra township and, to make ends meet, was forced into domestic work. At first she tried to hit it off with her difficult 'madam'.

'But then I couldn't pretend any longer and we quarrelled. She told me that if I was a "good girl" she would take me overseas with her where I could marry a "negro"!' Gcina grins.

In the final confrontation, 'she told me "What you must understand is that you are a black person and you belong to a lower class. Don't ever forget that you will die with a broom in your hands."'

She shrugs and smiles.

'I said: "Ye-es Medem".'

> 'What you must understand is that you are a black person and you belong to a lower class. Don't ever forget that you will die with a broom in your hands.'

Gcina goes into a paroxysm of shoulder-shaking laughter that clears the air like a cool breeze on a hot day.

Nevertheless, Gcina has strong views on the status of black women: 'Apart from racial tyranny, sexual domination has gone too far now, and it is only women who can rectify this. It's up to us now. There is a lot that hasn't been said that should have been. Black women haven't said enough, they haven't even started, in fact, to tell their side of the story. It's long overdue.'

Gcina has started. Perhaps her greatest talent is vision, her translation of her experiences into her poems and writing. She treats all that life offers as opportunity and inspiration. She wrote about her disastrous domestic experiment in *Reconstruction*, and her short story *Nokulunga's Wedding* (published in *Lip*) is based on her sister's arranged marriage. She still contributes to *Upbeat* and writes for *Learn and Teach*, a (now) politicised literacy magazine.

In between jobs Gcina was a nanny to four children.

'I grew to love those children very much. I'd invent stories for them, and when I ran out I started telling them my grandmother's stories. At first I thought, how can white children understand African folk tales? But they loved them. That's when I discovered the universal appeal of storytelling' – an art Gcina is determined to preserve.

'When we talk of change in South Africa we don't speak of a huge force, we speak of little things that can change people. Storytelling is one of those things. It can bridge gaps.'

She pauses, formulating her argument: 'The weapon of this government is ignorance. The whites don't know the blacks and are scared that black people may do something – like kill their children. And the blacks don't know the whites. They only know the white man as the oppressor. South Africa is such a rich, cosmopoli-

tan country. If only we could have storytelling bringing people together.'

Idealistic? Maybe. But her sincerity is genuine and her message clear: Let's get to know each other.

Gcina's book, *The Stories of Nolali*, a collection of her own tales and traditional stories from her childhood, is soon to be published by Ravan Press.

'It's lovely to have written that book; it is a link with my grandmother.'

Have you seen Zandile?, Gcina's play based on her own life, is another link. This two-woman production ran for five weeks to packed houses at the Market Theatre in Johannesburg.

How did she start acting?

'I just got up on stage at a writer's gathering one day and started performing my poetry. After that people used to invite me.'

People like award-winning playwright Maishe Maponya asked her to act in *Umongikazi*, which played at the Market and in the townships before touring Britain and Europe for six months. And people like Barney Simon who cast her in *Black Dog inj'emnyama* (which also played locally and overseas at the Edinburgh Festival and in London) and *Born in the RSA*.

At 27, with no formal training to smooth her path, Gcina has accomplished more than many do in a lifetime. How? She goes into another shoulder-shaking paroxysm.

'I just jump into anything. Like journalism – I just hijacked it!'

What about rejection? Failure? The thought doesn't seem to have occurred to her.

'What would I do? I don't know – I'd just do something else.'

Gcina Mhlope has gone on to become one of the country's foremost storytellers and authors.

Finding Common Ground

In August 1986, as
violence engulfed
townships and whites
began to arm themselves,
a historic gathering
of women took place
in Johannesburg. The
National Assembly of
Women, organised by five
leading black women's
groups aimed to unite
South Africans on the
fundamental issues of
education, family life,
employment, health and
food production.

Sue Grant

Fairlady 23 July 1986

It's a knuckle-cracking, freezing winter's evening as we hustle into the opulent offices of a swish Parktown public relations company. We're there to attend a press conference about the proposed National Assembly and the chill outside is not that different from the cool atmosphere inside.

The five-member planning committee sits at a table bisecting the room and the mostly white press faces them. We're uncomfortable. We're there by invitation but we feel oddly obtrusive. Our questions are handled with suspicion. There are silences.

A question is asked: 'Is the National Assembly likely to produce political statements?'

The effect is electric. The answers in the affirmative come rapidly. There is no anger, merely an effort to educate us about the realities of life for black people. The bottom line is that everything is political, even toilets – particularly toilets.

The cross-fire questioning turns to chatter. The five women at the table begin to relax. By the end of the meeting, there is some degree of understanding. We sip steaming cups of tea and percolated coffee, crunch potato chips and wonder if the National Assembly will have the same wintry beginnings.

After a while you wonder if you imagined the initial chill. In the days ahead and many, many hours of interviews later, your original instincts are confirmed by members of the planning committee. Most of them did not know most of us. There was a sense of mistrust. We were a true reflection of our divided society.

Deborah Mabiletsa has played a vital role in women's organisations and is one of the members of the planning committee.

She says: 'At the End of the Decade Conference in Nairobi, the spotlight was on apartheid all right. There was a committee, Women Under Apartheid,

> 'Freedom is indivisible. As long as blacks are not free, neither will whites be. A white friend invited me to tea in Johannesburg and then the waiter said: "This is not an international restaurant." I can't forget the look of disappointment on my white friend's face. She thought she was free – free to invite me to tea.'

that organised several forums. At one of these there were 4 000 people in the hall and 3 000 outside. About 100 women from South Africa were at Nairobi and on our return we decided to keep the momentum.

'It's important for the National Assembly to include as many women as possible. So many of us are feeling helpless in our little divided camps. Let's use the common bond of motherhood to break the polarising effect on the unrest. This poses a tremendous challenge for women of all colours to work together.

'In this togetherness we will find the strength we need to support each other. I was tremendously impressed when white women came to Soweto to show their solidarity and when they went to Alexandra Township to mourn and put flowers on graves.

'The National Assembly could highlight this movement. In Africa, women have worked for the betterment of their country. In Ghana, women in the informal sector are improving their country's economy. In Kenya, women work together for the abolition of polygamy. And in this country, in 1956, women of all races marched to Pretoria. That was a landmark which could be a point of reference for this Assembly.

'Freedom is indivisible. As long as blacks are not free, neither will whites be. A white friend invited me to tea in Johannesburg and then the waiter said: "This is not an international restaurant." I can't forget the look of disappointment on my white friend's face. She thought she was free – free to invite me to tea.

'I am not prepared to think of a future in which black and white don't get together. I'm a prisoner of hope. I will hope as long as there's a tomorrow. But if the tomorrows are too long in coming, we could exhaust out possibilities.

'There must be fundamental change within the next five years. Blacks must sit in parliament.

'At this Assembly, black and white women could decide to work together on community projects. Our children seldom leave Soweto to go to the zoo or museums. I know organisations such as Women for Peace do this, but it's a drop in the ocean. Our problems are so broad, so complex, we must all do something now. Every day, we all see injustice. Speak up, do something.'

Deborah Mabiletsa is president of the Women's Informal Training Institute (WITI) which is one of the five convening organisations of the Assembly. (The other four are: The YWCA, the National Council for African Women, the Black Housewives' League and the Christian Women's Movement.) Deborah is also chairperson of the United States of South Africa Leader Exchange Programme in South Africa.

The logistics of placing a phone call to *Malikolo Motumi* in Soweto are awesome, even for South Africa. You dial and dial. First the silence, then the clicks, the burrs, the wrong numbers. She's a little on edge when the call finally breaks through the telephonic logjam. An hour later we are talking with a capital T.

'I have three children. One of them is already out of the country because of the crisis. Basically all mothers have the same nightmare of receiving a call at the office: Hey, things are bad at home. I worry about my daughter at Wits University. I worry my son at school might be caught in crossfire. Sometimes I can sympathise with white mothers whose sons are on the border or doing duty in the townships, because they never know when they'll be hit. Black youths say, don't sympathise, they have the vote, they didn't use it. I have no sympathy for mothers who are doing nothing. At the same time I acknowledge there are lots of whites who are genuinely concerned.

'White women should speak to other white women about the necessity for change. I have the constraint of being very bitter.'

In view of that comment, it's surprising to hear Malikolo exclaim: 'Oh yes, we do want white women to come to our conference. We need each other. For instance, there are networks I would like to join. Say we need to do something in the food industry and we can't get through to the relevant Minister – a white contact might help. It's for that reason that I belong to the Women's Bureau. Suspicion about each other's motives will continue. But as we work together we will get to know and understand each other.

women of my age group are still saying, we have empathy. If you are living in a corner somewhere, and you haven't heard what's going on, we'll tell you. You don't have any other chance; it's now or never.

'Someday things will have to get better. The painful part will be over. But in the meantime, if sanctions come and poverty, then we'll survive on pap and water for much longer than the white woman. We have a track record of knowing how to suffer. But will the white woman? We are saying, let's get together, let's talk about it.

We are the last generation of black women that is prepared to talk. My daughter is not going to talk to anyone. Right now, women of my age group are still saying, we have empathy. If you are living in a corner somewhere, and you haven't heard what's going on, we'll tell you. You don't have any other chance; it's now or never.

'The saying goes, the time for talking is over. But for chrissakes, we need to talk to each other on this continent. We're not seen as collaborators by other blacks and we are not compromising ourselves because we are saying to our white fellow women, your time is up, your attitudes are outdated.

'The future if we don't talk is the worst you can imagine. The Sally Motlanas, the older generation, are bitter. We in our 30s and 40s are even more bitter. But we are the last generation of black women that is prepared to talk. My daughter is not going to talk to anyone. Right now,

'In five years' time there will be blacks in parliament. There will be an equal and uniform system of education. It will be common for us to share toilets. In the past two years, it has been my goal to be arrested for using the "wrong" loo. I have been all over the platteland and nothing has happened. I don't even ask permission. I see "Female" and in I go. When I see raised eyebrows, I say, you are living in the last century. One woman called the garage proprietor and he ignored her. After all, I pay the same price for my petrol.'

We discuss the mistrust prevailing at the press conference.

'This extends to black women too. There is an inability among us to co-operate. I find it amazing that all these different organisations are going to work together. The fact that people like me and Pearl Luthuli (editor of *True Love*) are involved in the same initiative is one hell of a breakthrough.

'Initially the Assembly started as a black effort. We didn't say we were excluding other race groups but we felt we had enough problems of our own to sort out.

'Now we appeal to all women, of all races, all age groups, both individuals and those belonging to organisations: come, let's talk.'

But won't that be difficult in view of her self-ascribed bitterness?

A rich chuckle from this big and friendly woman sweeps the question aside. 'I have a lot of white friends, we meet in each other's homes, we understand each other.'

Malikolo Motumi, like so many of her community leader colleagues, works in many organisations. She is development advisor for SANCA (South African National Council for Alcoholism). She is also vice chairperson of the Transvaal Family Planning Association; she's a member of PRISA (Public Relations Institute of South Africa) and a member of the SA Black Social Workers' Association.

Sally Motlana is fast asleep in her Soweto store when I phone her at 9 pm on a Saturday night. She did not make our interview that morning and she explains to me in a voice heavy with exhaustion that she has spent the day in one of Bishop Desmond Tutu's last meetings in his Johannesburg diocese. (Sally is a devoted member of the church; she is also life vice president of the South African Council of Churches.) Someone has just arrived to discuss a problem, and she must talk to him, so sadly there is no time left now for an interview before she flies off to Canada. No, not even 20 minutes.

At the press conference it was Sally who replied to the question about the Assembly making political statements.

'I can't see any meeting in South Africa which includes mothers of all races not being political. Black people are submerged in politics. So there will be strong political statements. We hope that white mothers will be prepared to discuss these issues openly so we can look forward to the year 2000.

'If the white mother has the illusion that she will be free and others not, she's wrong. White mothers and fathers sleep with guns under their pillows for fear they will be attacked. That's why I say that unless I am free, no white person in South Africa will be.

'It's a pity that only the converted will come to the Assembly. But I can't blame them really. White women who live in the suburbs don't meet people like us. When they do, they get a fright. They say, that's a very cheeky girl. Now I am 60. Biologically I am the same as you. My pigmentation doesn't make me a girl. Even the dogs and cats of whites have names but I'm a girl. If we don't change things like this now, the crisis will worsen.'

Sally Motlana is president of the Black Housewives' League and a well-known black community leader.

Joyce Siwani is a research evaluator at the Centre for Continuing Education at the University of the Witwatersrand, and has travelled the world extensively, attending church, women's, family life and children's conferences.

'We're getting together from a recognition that even the oppressor is oppressed. We're extending our hands in desperation, in the hope that white women will recognise they are not comfortable. We want them to understand the sense of crisis.

'If we don't meet, if we continue to live in our isolated pockets, then the agony will continue. South Africa is already in a state of war, although the battle lines have not yet been drawn. One of my children has been tear-gassed. My daughter was nearly shot.

Fairlady has been forced to censor certain statements and sentiments in view of the State of Emergency declared as we went to press.

'One of the things that makes me sad about whites is that they don't listen to us; they hear us, but they don't listen. They have built a wall of arrogance between us. They know everything about blacks. I imagine it would be difficult for them to understand why I can feel sorry for their kids.

'There is great fear on both sides, that is why we must meet. And it's white women who need to learn how we live in the townships. In a country of great opulence, some of us have no running water. I am always amazed that we are supposed to be clean without the necessary facilities.

'How can blacks be clean when we live in townships designed to be filthy? I often wonder how a day-old baby survives in our fog (from the coal fires). A friend of mine went to a doctor who asked if she smoked heavily (she doesn't smoke) because her lungs were so coated.

'I think this Assembly will initiate a momentum for change. I'm not advocating we all belong to one organisation; that would be impossible. But we need to identify ourselves with a mainstream that is trying to do something about the situation.

'There is so much that needs to be done, starting with the education policy. Even whites admit it's not as good as it could be. We need a universal education to recognise the human potential in us all. Then we begin to sow the seeds of unity in a country which should be competing with world powers, if only because of its vast mineral resources.

'I urge all women to take the responsibility of shaping this country. We have every right to do so.'

Joyce, who once worked as a reporter for the Rand Daily Mail, *has also been a literacy tutor for Anglo American. She is widowed with five children.*

Virginia Gcabashe, national president of the South African World Alliance YWCA, lives in Clermont, Durban. She's so incredibly busy that she often wishes she worked

for economic gain so she could tell people to go away. There are cocks crowing and children laughing in the background as we talk.

'I'm not bitter but I get angry. I grew up in the Orange Free State and whenever I went into town, I knew I had to prepare for a fight. I knew that whites were going to humiliate me and I have never allowed that. If someone in a shop said: "Yes, nanny?" I would exchange words with them. That took courage.

'One ruthless white detective insisted on questioning me about a township fight about which I knew nothing. Finally, he said: "Do you know anything?" And I said: "Don't you talk to me like that." The tension was terrible. We glared at each other. Then he shrugged his shoulders and drove off. I think he was immobilised by being stood up to by a black person.

'To understand why mothers cannot order their children to stop the violence in the township, you have to go back years. Our children are bitter because they have seen how their parents have been treated as workers and humiliated. Parents haven't lived up to their children's expectations and by the time we realised this, it was too late. We now have a band of young people who understand each other.

'White women can't understand what black women are going through because our daily experience of life, our perceptions are so different.

'They ask: Why are children destroying their own schools? They can't understand those schools are symbols of oppression. If I had to

die in crossfire, I couldn't be bitter about it because in violent situations there are victims on all sides. Whites say blacks are killing blacks. But in the final analysis your enemy is not necessarily a white person but someone who's standing in your way. I'm not condoning this, I am saying I understand it.

'Women can make an impact. In Argentina, I had the privilege of marching with the mothers of the Plaza de Mayo. Whatever the weather they marched once a week around that square to remind everyone of their missing loved ones. They watched their men folk disappear in the most traumatic circumstances but their courage kept them marching. Their success is that the world knows of their plight.

'One of the things I hope will emerge from this Assembly is that women will see that political liberation goes hand in hand with the liberation of women. We must try and get women into decision-making positions in this country.

'I hope this Assembly will come up with a strong plan for solidarity. This has been impossible in the past because each women's organisation worked on its own. We will retain our own organisations but together we will work for equality, development and peace.'

Virginia Gcabashe is convener of the organising committee of the Christian Women's Movement; a member of the SA Council of Churches Executive; a founder member of Women for Peaceful Change Now; and president of the Clermont Child and Family Welfare society.

Women of Resistance

A few months after the historic National Assembly of Women activists met to try and revive the spirit of resistance.

Wilna Botha

Fairlady 29 October 1986

9 August 1956, Union Buildings, Pretoria

From all over South Africa, 20 000 women of all races converged, wave upon wave, surging up through the gardens and engulfing the amphitheatre. Some carried parcels of food, others had babies on their backs. They came to protest against the proposed extension of the pass laws to women and the effect this would have on family life.

They delivered a petition to the office of Prime Minister Strydom, who chose not to be there. Then all 20 000 women stood in silent salute for 30 minutes.

Their mission completed, they started to move down through the gardens again, going as peacefully as they had come.

The march had little effect. In 1958, the pass laws were extended to women. In December 1956, only four months after the historic march, practically every one of its leaders was arrested and charged with high treason. By 1961 they had all been acquitted, but were silenced through bannings, banishment and detention.

The Federation of South African Women (Fedsaw), which had organised the march on the Union Buildings, was never banned but its leaders were: Ray Alexander, Hilda Bernstein, Lilian Ngoyi, Francis Baard, Helen Joseph, Dorothy Nyembe, Amina Cachalia and Albertina Sisulu – and so were the federation's largest affiliated organisations, including the ANC Women's League and the women's branch of the Congress of Democrats. Silenced, the Federation of South African Women disappeared almost completely until the '80s.

9 August 1986, St Mary's Cathedral, Johannesburg

One week after the National Assembly of Women conference, and once again women congregate in Johannesburg. This time the occasion is a prayer service to commemorate the march to the Union Buildings 30 years before.

Albertina Sisulu alone was detained for 90 days in 1963 (when her youngest child was six); was under consecutive banning orders, including ten years of house arrest from 1964 to 1981; was banned for another year in 1982; was arrested under the Criminal Procedure Act in 1983 for singing ANC songs, distributing pamphlets and displaying the ANC flag at a funeral; and sentenced to four years' imprisonment, two years of which were suspended for five years.

In itself, this prayer service is almost a non-event. But in terms of its historical significance, the powerful process of women's dissent that it commemorates matters. High hopes for a revival of the spirit of the '50s had inspired the Federation of Transvaal Women (Fedtraw) and others to organise a massive conference representing women of all races. They hoped to revive Fedsaw, and believed it would be stronger now than the old 'Fed' ever was: Grassroots women's organisations have begun to flourish since the late '70s

But the state of emergency crushed these hopes as the bannings had obliterated the Federation before. Albertina Sisulu alone was detained for 90 days in 1963 (when her youngest child was six); was under consecutive banning orders, including ten years of house arrest from 1964 to 1981; was banned for another year in 1982; was arrested under the Criminal Procedure Act in 1983 for singing ANC songs, distributing pamphlets and displaying the ANC flag at a funeral; and sentenced to four years' imprisonment, two years of which were suspended for five years.

At 3 pm on this Saturday afternoon, the section of Johannesburg surrounding the cathedral has shrugged off any pretension of being a white city. Card games are in progress on the paving outside the cathedral; rows of carrier bags hold the wares of insistent street vendors; a woman is begging on the cathedral steps; papers and plastic flutter around in the August breeze.

There is nothing glamorous about the women who file into the cathedral, picking up programmes and small candles in holders made from egg containers as they go in. Black and white women look ordinary, subdued, working class, the white women perhaps more deliberately dressed down in their jeans, dungarees and ethnic prints. Writer Nadine Gordimer arrives quietly and on her own; a group of coloured women from Eldorado Park arrive together, with community worker Ellen Lambert in the lead. Most striking are a number of women dressed in the black and green uniforms of the old Fedsaw.

No more than 300 women in all fill up the front third of the cathedral. Dominating the scene are the dozens of newsmen who have noisily installed themselves and their large cameras in the front of the cathedral, making it difficult for the congregated women to see either Helen Joseph or Albertina Sisulu in the pulpit on the one side, or the Dean of the Cathedral and newly-elected Bishop of Johannesburg, the Reverend Duncan Buchanan, across from them.

The bishop calls on the media to remember that this is a religious service – their behaviour is obviously annoying the organisers, who afterwards express the suspicion that the large media presence was prompted as much by the opportunity to see Johannesburg's new bishop in action in the cathedral for the first time as by the service itself.

Thirty years before, Helen Joseph, who spent nine years under house arrest in her red-roofed cottage set in an English garden in Norwood, had been one of the leaders and major organisers of the protest march. Now, despite her 81 years, she still seems to be doing all the work, bustling around beforehand to get everything organised. The programme says that she will open the service, but she steps down for Albertina Sisulu. Afterwards we hear that Albertina would have led a simultaneous service in Soweto, but that women there had been unable to organise a venue.

At three o'clock exactly, a glow of candles spreads from the back as women use their own candles to light their neighbours'. For 15 minutes, the women stand in total silence, recalling the past. Thirty years before to the hour, 20 000 women had stood in similar silence in the amphitheatre of the Union Buildings. Then, the only sounds had been occasional birdsong or the crying of a baby, quickly hushed. Now the stillness is disturbed by rapidly clicking cameras, the glare of flashlights and the milling about of pressmen.

At 3.15 pm the singing of *Wathint abafazi, Wathint imbokodo* ('Strydom, you have tampered with the women, you have struck against rock') gets off to a false start, as Albertina Sisulu struggles to get the other women to join in. The woman who had promised to lead the singing has not turned up.

The rest of the short service includes a welcome prayer by the Rev Duncan Buchanan, Helen Joseph's recollections of 9 August 1956, a prayer by Bishop Simeon Nkoane, the reading of two moving poems, and the reading of a prayer written by Pastor Dietrich Bonhoeffer before he was executed during the Second World War.

The repeal of the pass laws and women's new freedom to walk in the streets without fear of being arrested for lack of a pass are noted with gratitude to God, and a plea is made for God to preserve that piece of freedom.

When the service ends with the singing of *Nkosi Sikelel' iAfrika*, a group of black women towards the back comes alive to take a spirited lead, and continues to sing a second song with as much fire.

In many ways, the prayer service is an anticlimax. Plans for this day had been so different.

According to Fedsaw leaders, the call would have gone out to all South African women to join hands across the colour bar and to work for a just democracy that will make peace and the preservation of life possible.

Then came the state of emergency and Fedtraw's president, Sister Bernard Ncube, was detained; several of its members went into hiding, and the organisers decided to wait and see when the state of emergency would be lifted.

'We could not risk planning a large-scale meeting to form a women's political organisation during a state of emergency, and knew that many people would stay away out of fear,' they said.

The prayer meeting was organised hurriedly about a week before it took place. The pile of unclaimed candles that remained at the entrance to the cathedral proved that the attendance had been disappointing. Black women, who would normally have constituted the bulk of a gathering such as this, represented only about half of the people present. It had been hoped that the Sowetan women would come en masse when their own service did not materialise, but they did not. They were afraid, said the organisers. And, unless I happened to miss them, Indian women were conspicuously absent.

There is nothing glamorous about the women who file into the cathedral, picking up programmes and small candles in holders made from egg containers as they go in. Black and white women look ordinary, subdued, working class, the white women perhaps more deliberately dressed down in their jeans, dungarees and ethnic prints.

In view of the massive demonstration by 20 000 women being commemorated, the prayer service seemed dismally small and uninspired.

It seems that history has repeated itself. In the late '50s and early '60s, soon after the march to the Union Buildings that is still seen by many as the high point of women's resistance in this country, the Federation of South African Women was squashed. Now, when organisations throughout the country consider the time ripe for revival, it is again 'driven into non-viability', as Fedtraw women put it.

But only temporarily, they insist. They are adamant that they will have their big conference.

Will a new Federation of South African Women become the umbrella organisation for concerned women that some want it to be? Its power base would be large – the name of Fedsaw is already used arbitrarily to refer to all women's organisations that have sprung up in recent years and that have been pushing for the revival of the Federation: the UDF's women affiliates and organisations such as Fedsaw, Jodac (Johannesburg Democratic Action Committee) women's group, the Natal Organisation of Women (NOW), the United Women's Congress in Cape Town (UWC), the Port Elizabeth Women's Organisation, the East London Women's Organisation and the Border Women's Organisation.

The National Assembly of Women the previous week had indicated that many black women's affiliations lie elsewhere. Differences between the Assembly organisers and Fedsaw remain unresolved despite a visit from an Assembly 'peace mission' who met women like Helen Joseph, Fedsaw's Jessie Duarte and soft-spoken Fedtraw patron Amina Cachalia at the exquisitely furnished Burgersdorp home which bears witness to the many years Amina and Yusuf Cachalia spent under banning orders and house arrest.

The divisions in the house of ranks of the women seem to date back to the End of Women's Decade Nairobi conference last year, when the South African delegation, which included a group of Fedsaw women, was already divided.

The Fedsaw women's criticism of the National Assembly was that it was too elitist and intellectual, that grass-roots women could not afford the R50 that it eventually cost to attend, and that the total cost of the conference could not have been justified in these difficult times.

Perhaps the National Assembly group were on the whole more moderate, and more free- market orientated, or at least economically neutral. Fedsaw women stress that their organisation is certainly not communist, that it is non-violent, that it will always operate above board and out in the open, and that an allegiance to socialist doctrines is no requirement for membership. The new Fedsaw will be the same, they say. Yet the Federation's historical links with the ANC and now the UDF indicate its allegiance. It operates within a community that sees capitalism as an enemy and espouses socialist goals. Its ideal is a people's government that will redistribute wealth; its aim a new order, not reform of the present one, and its stand is confrontational. If the Federation of South African Women is revived, women who consider joining it will have to make peace with these aims first.

District Six: Christmas 1960

Richard Rive

Fairlady 24 December 1986

Richard Rive remembers the Big Day when the men wore Waynick's hire purchase suits, the young women wore Passion at Midnight, the adolescents sneaked dizzying cigarettes and Pretoria moved closer.

We prepared for Christmas from the day or maybe the week before. Some say that people in the District prepared for Christmas from the Boxing Day before. I remember the air of expectation on Christmas Eve and then the reality of Christmas in District Six during the days before we were shifted to Hanover Park and Bonteheuwel and Manenberg.

Sometimes today, especially during those big days, our eyes still travel over the mounds of rubble, beyond the man-made craters and the piles of dead soil to the celebration of Christmas past. We still remember.

My Christmas Day, when I was sweet 15 and rapidly growing up, when I was at high school and wore long trousers for the first time, when I was in love and carefully cultivated my first moustache and practised making my voice deeper, always started the evening before. Elvis was king and we all wore curls on our foreheads in imitation of Tony Curtis. As the first bells of St Mark's rang out an hour before midnight, we began dressing in order to attend mass. I tried hard to feel grown up but was already sleepy, and the tolling reverberated through my drowsy head. The dark had rolled down Table Mountain and covered the streets and lanes and stoeps and houses. There was also the smell of rain in the air.

The second tolling, half an hour later, was the signal for lamps to be blown out or lights to be switched off and keys turned to lock houses, as we began to mince our holier-than-thou way up Caledon Street to the incense-warm stone church on windy Clifton Hill. We smelt of Waynick's hire purchase suits and pungent Christmas present deodorants. My older brothers also smelt of cigarette smoke, and my one unmarried sister of a sweet and sickly eau-de-cologne called Passion at Midnight.

We solemnly made our way up the street avoiding puddles and ignoring invectives hurled at us by less holy Christmas Eve drunks. While dressing at home, my eldest brother and I had been alone in the boy's room. He winked

On our way to morning service we stopped at Moodley's shop, which was open since he was not a Christian. Neither for that matter was Armien but he was our friend and went wherever we went even though he was a Muslim.

an eye at me and slipped over half a glass of whisky. He said it was only once a year and after all I had just written the Junior Certificate examination. I downed it in one gulp and felt my inside set on fire.

Once in church, I felt dizzy and nauseous. The drowsy atmosphere, the thick smell of incense, the roll of the organ music, all turned my stomach. Fortunately I was supported on either side by two grownup brothers in their new, stiff, navy blue suits.

I was not able to listen to the long, soporific sermon but did pick up the preacher's references to the joy of Christmas. I realised that this was not intended for me. Half dreaming, I agonised about the wickedness of boys of 15, still at school, who drank whisky and then had the audacity to attend a church service. My stomach gave an extra turn. I was afraid of getting sick right there over my brother's new navy blue suit. When they went up to take Holy Communion I was too miserable and ill to accompany them. By the end of the service I was recovering rapidly. When we came out into the night it had rained slightly, a playful wind was gusting and mercifully blew the last fumes of whisky out of my head. Fatigue was now rapidly setting in and I walked back almost asleep,

hooked into the arm of my sister who was supporting me.

I crept into bed and was soon astride my cowboy stallion riding the range. It was springtime in the Rockies and my six-guns exploded between strums from my guitar. I was oblivious of the low hum of discussion around our dining room table, of my mother and sister speaking in the kitchen while cooking, of the gossip about who was in church and who not and why.

Christmas morning blazed bright and apricot yellow. The wind had dropped and the sun had chased the dark and drizzle back over Table Mountain. The streets were still mirror-wet. Christmas Eve drunks were evaporating with the water puddles. But in our home the family slept on as if dead, their new clothes neat on hangers in wardrobes or suspended against doors. I was the only one awake, feeling wonderfully refreshed as I breathed in the cool, robust air.

The blare of a Christmas choir band burst into the morning and I rushed onto the stoep to watch. It was the Young Stars of the East who trumpeted and strummed *Christians Awake* as if they meant it. The bandsmen wore white Panama hats, white flannels and bright red blazers with formidable badges on

We solemnly made our way up the street avoiding puddles and ignoring invectives hurled at us by less holy Christmas Eve drunks.

the breast pockets. Two men, one of whom was Last Knight, our barber, proudly bore the banner aloft depicting a nativity scene under an enormous star of the east, which proclaimed for all the world to read that the band was established in 1934 and had as its motto *Per Ardua ad Astra*, which made it seem like a local chapter of the Royal Air Force. Mr Joseph Knight, the barber's correct name, was very dark-skinned and soon after he moved into the District, received the nickname Last Knight. His elder and even darker brother, Henry, helped out in the shop when it was full of customers or Joseph was away from work. On one such occasion when his brother was ill, Henry was running the shop. Alfie du Plooy had not had a haircut for three months and resembled a very shaggy St Bernard dog. His mother, who had a reputation as a shrew, sent him to have his hair cut. Mr Henry Knight took one look at his shaggy mane and sent him home with the cryptic message that if his mother thought that any decent barber would plough through that jungle of hair for one shilling, she had other guests coming. Mrs du Plooy marched on the shop with a howling Alfie in tow. Arms akimbo, she stood in the doorway and, not finding Last Knight there as she had

expected, addressed his brother.

'If you don't cut my boy's hair right now for one shilling, I'll hit you that you'll look like the night before last.'

The name stuck and the brothers were known from then onwards as Last Knight and Knight Before Last. Now Last Knight proudly bore the banner of the Young Stars of the East behind a much older and less hirsute Alfie du Plooy as drum major.

My family had by now woken up. I wished my mother and sister a merry Christmas and then my brothers, who seemed to be anything but merry. They had started their celebration immediately after the church service and were now suffering from massive hangovers. I cleaned my teeth and washed my arms and face in water my sister had warmed for me on the primus stove. When we were all ready we sat down to a breakfast of hot, egg-rich bread dotted with sesame seeds which my mother could bake to perfection. These slices were smothered in thick layers of melting butter and slabs of sweet milk cheese. My brothers merely pecked at them.

Then the presents. We had no Christmas tree so the presents were stacked up on the sideboard. I gave my mother a string of imitation pearls I had spent weeks select-

ing and months saving up for. My sister received a bottle of pungent perfume (not Passion at Midnight), and my brothers deodorants, the same brand. Then I received my presents. My brother, I think spitefully, also gave me deodorant of the same brand. The men in our family seemed obsessed with deodorants, and the air smelt sweet and sickly as we all tested ours.

From aunts and uncles who believed in my scholastic potential, I received books about schoolboys in England, Tom Merry, Bob Cherry and the Boys of Greyfriars, as well as *Beano* and *Dandy* annuals. And a pocket knife which sprouted a multiplicity of blades and gadgets with a multiplicity of uses, even one for taking stones out of horses' hooves, if only we in District Six had horses with hooves out of which I could take stones. And from my sister, a new wallet containing a crispy, new £5 note. My mother always gave me something useful that you can share with the family. It could be a kettle or a wardrobe or a piece of linoleum. The family kept up the pretence for at least a few days and made a great play of saying in my presence, 'Boil some water in Richard's kettle,' or 'Hang it in Richard's wardrobe,' or 'Doesn't Richard's lino match the curtains nicely?'

Then I carefully removed my new clothes from their hangers – the shirt, tie and suit, which was navy blue. Maybe one could only get suits at Waynick's on hire purchase if one chose navy blue. Maybe every clothes shop in the District had a sale at the same time of navy blue suits.

I put on my new shoes, which were pinching, and feeling decidedly uncomfortable went out into the street to team up with Ronnie, Norman and Armien who were all wearing new navy blue suits. On our way to morning service we stopped at Moodley's shop, which was open since he was not a Christian. Neither for that matter was Armien but he was our friend and went wherever we went even though he was a Muslim.

Moodley's shop was dark inside and smelt of curry powder and turmeric. At the entrance one negotiated hessian bags rolled down at the top and filled to the brim with beans, peas and lentils. We fervently believed, and it formed the basis for much discussion among ourselves, that in spite of his advanced age, and frail and desiccated appearance, he still had enough energy for his three wives, all of whom he had bought in India.

Two of them we had never seen and it was rumoured that he kept them in the storeroom at the back with the masala. The third served behind the counter. She was a pale, ghostlike creature with a dot painted on her forehead, her teeth stained brown from chewing betel. We could just make her out in the permanent twilight of the shop. In a fit of extravagance we bought twisty ice creams, Turkish Delight and blackballs that stained our mouths when we sucked them.

The crowded congregation at morning service was stiff and starched. We sat stiff in our starched rows sucking discreetly and loosening the laces of our over-tight shoes. Armien was with us. I usually sat in the front row, where I could see the porcelain effigies displaying the nativity scene. My mind would wander back to the Christmas plays at primary school, where I was usually cast as a sheep which shepherds watched. My sister and brothers had also in their time always been cast as sheep and my mother had fatalistically accepted that with our limited acting ability she would have to alter the sheep's costume for the new incumbent. Then after one glorious audition I broke with mediocrity and was promoted to being a shepherd watching his flocks by night. I watched either too enthusiastically or maybe too unenthusiastically, for the following year I was demoted to rejoin the flock. Fortunately my mother had kept the costume. Now at 15 I was long past such childish things as nativity plays. When the collection plate came round I generously took sixpence out of my stiff new wallet and dropped it in loudly so that those around me could hear.

Then out into the sunlight to do the wishing rounds. First to wish my married sister and her husband in Bruce Street, where I received a present and cake and ginger beer. Then to wish my aunt in Coronation Road, where I received a pound note and cake and ginger beer. Then to wish my Standard Two teacher, with whom I still maintained contact, in Lavender Hill, where I received cake and ginger beer. And then, because I could not face another slice of cake or glass of ginger beer, I went home to the midday meal for which by now I had no appetite.

Everyone enjoyed the feast except me. The whole family was present. We wore paper caps and looked silly. We pulled paper crackers and looked even sillier. We found cheap trinkets inside them and pretended they were pieces of treasure. We read the platitudes on the strips of paper in the crackers and discussed them as gems of wisdom. Then, with the sun shining warm outside, we started with hot mutton curry, then the *pièce de résistance*, a huge, roast leg of lamb done to a turn, crunchy sweet potatoes, green peas and yellow rice with raisins and cinnamon. Over the meat we poured thick, spicy gravy. Then, exhausted with eating and the heat, we still had a choice of fruit salad, which we called 'angels' food', rice pudding and trifle. The adults had wine and spirits with their meals and although I was offered a glass I wisely declined.

While the grown-ups took an afternoon nap, Ronnie, Norman, Armien and I decided to take a joy-ride by train to Kalk Bay and back. We walked down empty streets to the semi-deserted station. Everyone seemed to be sleeping off heavy Christmas lunches. Although we bought first-class tickets (we had

> District Six rested from the hurry and bustle of yet another Christmas. Here and there the sounds of a band still wafted faintly in the tired night air. Somewhere Bing Crosby was singing *I'm Dreaming of a White Christmas*.

so much money) we still had to occupy coaches set apart for 'non-whites'. The sheer exuberance of speed as we flashed and rattled past houses, trees and stations like Har-field, Wittebome and Retreat. The surly white conductor resented our shouting and laughing. Maybe he resented having to work on Christmas Day. Glaring at us he demanded our tickets as if he hoped to catch us out. I slowly drew my new wallet out of the jacket pocket on my new suit and extracted the ticket, which I presented with studied *sang-froid*.

We took off our shoes and socks, rolled up our trousers and walked along the dirty beach. Even the sand had long given up being white and was now a dirty grey. The beach was almost deserted, waiting for the hordes that would descend upon it on Boxing Day. A few families were camping under blankets that acted as makeshift tents. Others sat under the arches over which the train rattled on its way to Simonstown. Some people were lying in the sun eating watermelon. A few men sat in the shade drinking wine. Two were already so drunk that they were gambolling in the dirty green water fully clothed. By the time we returned home it was getting dark. Christmas bands were marching along the streets playing spirited hymns

and carols. Older people came out of their houses to sit on benches, gossip or just sit the evening away. From a high stoep we ogled girls on the opposite stoep, who pretended to ignore us.

Ronnie produced a silver case filled with cigarettes and at a signal we all strolled nonchalantly to the field behind the church where, out of sight, we lit up, drew the blue smoke into our lungs, coughed and felt bilious. We smoked until our heads were turning, lighting one cigarette from another. Then we returned to the stoep feeling grown-up and sick. Dusk changed to dark, and dark was accompanied by the quiet of exhaustion.

District Six rested from the hurry and bustle of yet another Christmas. Here and there the sounds of a band still wafted faintly in the tired night air. Somewhere Bing Crosby was singing *I'm Dreaming of a White Christmas*. Many of the older people were happy that one of the Big Days was over. Now only Boxing Day and New Year remained. Others were too tired to care and just went on sitting breathing in the mountain air, fanning themselves and speculating softly about how many more Christmases they would be allowed to remain in District Six before someone in Pretoria ordered them to move.

The late Richard Rive, one of South Africa's leading literary voices.
(*Photo:* New Africa Books)

From 'Buckingham Palace', District Six by Richard Rive, published by David Philip, Cape Town.

The murder of Dr Richard Rive by two young men in his home in Retreat, Cape Town, in June 1989 robbed South Africa of one of its leading literary voices.

Killed in Action

In a week when there were eight reported deaths of SADF troops fighting in Angola, we mourned the death of two comrades in arms, Rifleman Pieter Heinrich Groenewald and Rifleman André Schalk Groenewald, both of whom leave families whose lives will never be quite the same again.

Lin Sampson

Fairlady 27 April 1988

Today is Tuesday, 23 February, a shiny South African day that sinks easily into contented materialism. Here, within the shifting shadows of the Outeniqua mountains of the eastern Cape, two funerals will take place later in the day.

Pieter Heinrich Groenewald of George and André Schalk Groenewald of Oudtshoorn will be buried, each in their hometown. This is an area of South Africa that consists of a series of softly pleated plains slung between a stagger of mountain ranges.

These two young men were friends. They shared the same surname; lived in the same part of the world; fought in the same battalion; and died in the same armoured vehicle called a Ratel on the same day, 14 February, St Valentine's Day.

One was a gentle, conservative boy, deeply religious, duty-bound, fond of music. The other was outgoing, fond of jokes, and the centre of all the summer fun in the district.

Both leave many people – but mothers in particular – who are anguished by their deaths.

The funeral of Pieter Heinrich Groenewald is held in the Nederduitse Gereformeerde Moederkerk in George. Set in that particular South African landscape of blue mountain, green grass and white steeple there is a tribal coherency about the town. The church appears to have been designed to withstand adversity and now that George has grown around it, it no longer seems too big for the town.

People start arriving early for the funeral and stand around in slightly ambushed-looking groups like dancers waiting for direction. The farm workers arrive in the back of a bakkie, their black Sunday suits restored with careful pressing that has left them shiny and worn. There are a lot of pretty young girls, one of whom leans her head against an older woman and sobs loudly.

> The ten bearers, soldiers of the same rank as the dead man, lift the coffin onto the gun carriage and the band strikes up the stirring and prayerful sounds of the death march. Slowly the procession moves on, the long beat of the slow march drubbing through the heat of the day.

Inside the church the dim sanctuary of Christianity seems subdued with a whispered misery linked to the thin rustle of prayer-book pages. Through a half-open window the mountains, a row of blue agapanthus, and the white gable of a house can be seen. The woman next to me, who has on bright red shoes, opens her bag and methodically lays out tissues in a row across her knees.

On the pulpit *God is Liefde* is written in gold on a purple background.

A platoon of young soldiers marches down the aisle followed by members of the close family – mother and father, sisters, younger brother, uncles, aunts, cousins. Their eyes seem fearless but the backs of their necks look smooth and vulnerable and very young, and perhaps it is the recognition that these soldiers are no more than boys that makes the whole congregation heave with a collective half sob.

The military chaplain *Dominee* Hattingh stands on the carved stinkwood pulpit buttressed with a pattern of flowers and reads: 'We mourn the death of a beloved son, brother and friend at the age of 19. It was a privilege to walk with him on life's path where he left deep footprints of tender love, caring and friendship. Those were lovely years, which is why we will miss his sweet presence but his valued memory will always live on.'

The woman beside me picks up her row of tissues, chooses one, blows her nose, rubs energetically under her glasses.

Coming out of the gothic gleam of the cathedral, the bright sunlight lends a harrowing shine to the phalanx of the army. The 22-piece military band stands by in polished splendour, and the coffin, draped with the South African flag, is topped with a small green beret.

The ten bearers, soldiers of the same rank as the dead man, lift the coffin onto the gun carriage and the band strikes up the stirring and prayerful sounds of the death

march. Slowly the procession moves on, the long beat of the slow march drubbing through the heat of the day. We wind along the road to the cemetery past the familiar litany of a small South African town: Spur Steakhouse, Pick 'n Pay, Foschini, the old school, The Outeniqua Technical College, where all the pupils have lined up outside to pay their last respects. The head boy and girl, looking absurdly young, stand to attention. It is not their first ex-pupil to die in the South African defence forces, nor will it be the last.

The leading detachment of 12 troops led by an infantry school colonel, medals bristling on his chest, form a guard of honour outside the graveyard. The bugler breaks away from the main body of the band and makes his solitary way to the graveside where the midday sun beats down on the red earth and bright green artificial grass. Two spades with blue handles rest under an orange tree.

The mourners gather, men and women from this small farming community, showing something of the stoicism that marks all Afrikaner death scenes, something of that scorched-earth endurance that has marked their history. The words of the funeral service splutter in the intense heat and join other words rattling in my head, said by, I think, Hendrik Prinsloo before Spioenkop: 'We are now going in to attack the enemy and we shan't all be coming back. Do your duty and trust in the Lord.'

The command 'present arms' strikes out across the desolate scene and the bugler sounds the general salute. But it is the plangent sound of the last post, nudging mortally, that directs the hearts and eyes of the people towards one woman, Pieter's mother, Julia Groenewald, a grey-haired little figure in a black suit, whose face crumples like a small white handkerchief.

All the officers, dressed today in Dress 18, medals, mourning bands and brown leather gloves, draw their hands up in a salute as the sergeant shouts: 'shoulder arms' and the bugler plays the reveille.

As I drive through the countryside to interview Julia Groenewald, I wonder how many times her son must have driven this road, past the modern Dutch Reformed Church with its needle-sharp steeple that stands out in the sweet green fields like an exposed nerve, to the south the sea, to the north the mountains. The farm *Uitkyk* is situated in flatland that spreads between two rivers. The old farmhouse has been abandoned and the newer house in textured half-bricks and '50s spangles stands beside it. Inside the house smells of sweet roasting meat, pumpkin, potatoes and polish. It is easy to understand the joy of returning here.

Julia Groenewald is a warm, friendly woman, who fingers her two strings of pearls as she talks. Her small childish face which so much resembles the picture of her son – surrounded by a nimbus of grey curls, puckers with concentration.

'Oh my dear, it is *bitter swaar* to give up a child. Some-how one can give up anything, a sister or a brother or a father or even a husband, but a child, no a child is too terrible. I'll never forget the night the *dominee* came here. For me it was so terrible to get that news at night. It was Monday 15 February.

'I had just written to him and I heard someone at the door. Right out here on the farm it is strange to have visi-tors so late at night. My husband came to me and said: "*Jong*, the *dominee* is here. It looks like trouble."

'When he said "the *dominee* is here", I didn't think of my other three children. I thought of Pieter. Everything went very fast. There were two other people from the army, and as soon as I saw them, I knew.

'Oh yes, he couldn't wait to come back here. He loved this place, this old farm. This was his home, the place he loved the most in the world. He would write about it from the border. He wanted to know whether the rains had come. He asked about food all the time. He couldn't wait to get back for a *lekker bordjie kos*, a good plate of food. He loved steak and chips and those little caramel cakes and Hertzog cookies and salad. *Hy was mal oor* tossed salad, and biltong. I made him up a parcel last year before Christmas. It cost R30 to send, just for postage.

'When his friends came here for the summer he was always at the centre and he loved *meisies*. When he was in the army he only had one girlfriend, that's why we have so few pictures of him. He was always giving them to girls. But he was humble and kind-hearted, he never wanted anything. I always said he wasn't for this world. I would say to him: "Can't I buy you something like a pair of takkies?"

'He always said: "No, ma, it's not really necessary." He asked so little from us. He was such a *fluks* person – what is that in English? – energetic and enthusiastic, he was always a leader, wasn't he, Henrie?'

Henrie is her younger, 17-year-old son. To him Pieter was a hero. He draws his chair close up to mine and tells me, 'Pieter and I had such *lekker sports* together. We did everything when he was home on pass. Last pass he just rang from George and we didn't even expect him, and I sprang in the bakkie and went to meet him and there he was, right out of the blue. When he was here life was always exciting. He would say: "*Jong*, lets take our *meisies* and go for a braai beside the river Montagu." Does *tannie* know Montagu pass?

'And you know, *tannie*, when we were small years ago my father gave us two pigs. Every day we would feed them together but when he wasn't around I would go back and give my pig a lot of extra food. My pig got bigger and bigger and he couldn't understand why his pig didn't grow. He told my father that he had given him a *vrot* pig. Then one day he discovered me feeding my pig on the quiet, *skelmpies, tannie*. He was so angry but on his last pass he was telling my girlfriend and we laughed like mad.'

'You know what was the worst part for me?' Julia Groenewald rubs her fingers free from crumbs after eating a piece of cake, wipes the crumbs from her mouth, 'the worst part. A month before he died he sent me one of those little tracts. Have you seen such things? *Ag*, so beautiful. You dream that you are walking with God in the sand. Later you see there are two lines of footsteps, that you are not alone.

'When Pieter died I felt so alone. I felt I had been forsaken. Every day I prayed for his safe return. And I didn't only pray for him, I prayed for all those other *outjies* on the border. I was so *hartseer* that after praying so faithfully, God had let me down.

'He died on the Sunday at about 4.30 in the afternoon. A letter came from him the following Wednesday. In the letter he said I must read Psalm 142. That letter really shook me because the psalm told me he was in need. Perhaps he was frightened. It is written there in the words.

'That very morning I had prayed to God for an answer and then when I got the letter I really felt that God had worked through Pieter, and I felt comforted. Yesterday I went to his grave and saw how it had been made up with flowers and wreaths, *tog so pragtig,* and I talked to him there and prayed that he would come to me in a dream.

'You know, I often think of how it happened. There were ten of them in a Ratel and it was one of those new bombs, a missile, something like that. They say it was the most modern thing out of Russia. He was in a convoy of Ratels and it was the only one that was bombed. Can you believe that? Isn't it terrible that it should be my son? Personally, I feel our children should not be fighting in that war. It is our duty to give our sons to the army – nobody really wants to go, but it is our duty to send them. But we feel they are there to guard the borders. We are not told that our children are being sent into Angola. We think they are in South West Africa. Since Pieter died I have had a lot of phone calls. People are unhappy that their children are being sent into Angola.

'The big thing is that you can never bring your child back. Your child is dead. You are the one who suffers.'

Later in the day, driving up the slow steep curve of the Outeniqua pass, with scenery falling away to the south in a long low line of pink-tinged mountain peaks, I see the gun carriage bumping along in front of me. Drawn by a large army truck, from funeral to funeral, it bumps away on its sinister mission. So frequently in South Africa, life and death seem to stumble along hand in hand.

The funeral of André Schalk Groenewald born 25 February, died 14 February, is held at the Dutch Reformed Church at Zeelandsnek in Oudtshoorn. The church is modern with opaque orange glass and lots of blond wood. A vase of proteas stands on a pedestal draped in green cloth; it has the vague look of a dressmaker's dummy. At the back of the church the organist pumps and sways, the pattern on her dress subsiding and reasserting as she plays with that energetic concentration demanded by an organ.

And so André Schalk Groenewald is remembered just as Pieter Heinrich Groenewald was remembered through verse and psalm, Job 1 verse 21: 'The Lord gives and the Lord takes away. Praise the name of the Lord.' The *dominee* reads a poem by Totius.

'Jou kind is dood met 'n vreeslike dood en ek gryp my bors van die pyn.' (Your child has died a terrible death and I clutch my breast with the pain.)

Like other mothers in her position it is the details she remembers. Dates light up like neon in her head, sayings are recalled, even gestures still form an energetic pattern in her head. Her mind is filled with thoughts of her dead son, and his image is recalled by a stereotype army picture of him standing next to an armoured vehicle, a tall honey-toned boy with a gentle face.

His mother Louisa Groenewald sits in the front pew. Beside her is her daughter, Elzane (11) and her son Nordus (16). Both watch her anxiously throughout the service; she remains a slightly tear-stained but strong figure.

Night has already fallen across the Oudtshoorn suburb of Zeelandsnek and through the windows of the small houses families can be seen preparing meals. A half-moon hovers above the scarred *koppie* that marks the northern boundary of this township.

André's mother is a staff sergeant who works as a nurse in the army headquarters in Oudtshoorn. As the divorced mother of a family, she has had to work hard to bring up two children on her own. During the last 14 months in which André had been in the army, her life has been filled with pass-outs, *min dae, sterkte* and food parcels, the mythology that surrounds boys on the border.

Now, sitting surrounded by bowls filled with triangles of yellow chrysanthemums, she speaks in a small voice and betrays her misery only occasionally with neck muscle spasms that pull her face into a fleeting grimace. She says her whole body aches. Like other mothers in her position it is the details she remembers. Dates light up like neon in her head, sayings are recalled, even gestures still form an energetic pattern in her head. Her mind is filled with thoughts of her dead son, and his image is recalled by a stereotype army picture of him standing next to an armoured vehicle, a tall honey-toned boy with a gentle face.

'It was last Monday night, 15 February at 9 o'clock.

I'd just been visiting a friend and said to her, "Do you know what? I've just received a letter from the Colonel in Bloemfontein. He said André can come home for a holiday and then after that he'll have to go to Tsumeb or Middelburg."

'I complained a bit about it. I kept saying, "*Ag*, when he has a pass how will he ever get home? It's such a long way."

'But he never minded that part. He always said: "*Ag ma,* that's part of the fun."

'Now I wish I hadn't moaned. If I knew what was going to happen, I wouldn't have made such a fuss.

'You know he always liked to surprise me. I remember the last pass. He didn't phone. One day I just opened the door and there he was. *Ag* yes, last Monday. That's a day I'll never forget. When I saw the *dominee* I knew immediately. I think a mother knows immediately. When you've got a son on the border and you see those three people together, you know. Last year I was reading a book about a woman who had lost her son and how the priest came and told her her son was dead. I remember thinking, "That will never happen to me." I must say I never thought of death but I did worry that he would get hurt.

'You know, he was such a loving child; everyone loved him. When it happened, his teacher from Bethlehem in the Free State wrote and said she could still remember his voice. No, he didn't have a girlfriend. You know he was not yet 19. He was only a boy. We are such a big family and there are so many grandchildren and we have never even had a serious illness in the family and then this. It seems so strange. It is my other son who will miss him most. He says nothing – he will not speak of it – but he is suffering.

'All I can think of now is how it happened. I wasn't allowed to see his body. I can understand that but somehow unless you see someone dead you find it so difficult to believe. All the time I hope and pray that he did not suffer. A friend who was with him when he died came and told me about it. He said Pieter was standing up in the Ratel and the moment they were shot at he fell back inside. They couldn't see anything. Everything was dark and there was smoke everywhere. He said he thought it happened very quickly. He didn't see Pieter, but he's sure he didn't suffer.

'You think you've worked so hard to bring up your child correctly. Then you think, "Did I bring him up correctly? Do I get full marks? Has he got the right approach?" You know, when we were divorced he was already in Standard 9. He was very protective towards me and the younger children. When we went to bed at night he would always go downstairs and see that all the doors were shut. "*Ag ma,*" he'd say, "don't you want some tea before you go to sleep?" He would be the one who would come and ask at the end of the month when we were going to pay the accounts. He always felt he was the man in the family.

'When the *dominee* told me, I thought: "Why him?" He never hurt anyone. He worked very hard. For instance I moved in here early one morning and that night when we went to bed he stayed up and hung the curtains and arranged the furniture so that when I went to work at 6.30 the next morning everything was ready. When I came home at midday he had cooked the lunch and everything was laid out ready.

'Every pass he brought me a little present. Once he brought me a shell from Pietersburg and we laughed because I said: "There's no sea in Pietersburg." Then he brought me an empty bottle with a label that said: "This is full of my love. Do not open." He would always bring the other children something, even if it was just a tin of condensed milk from his ratpack.

'In his letters he was always moaning about the rat-packs (ration packs) they get. Really, they're not so bad but they get sick of the food. In his last letter he said he'd made some beef with cheese sauce. "*Ag,*" he said, "it's not so bad if you use your imagination." We had this agreement that every week we would write letters. Then he went to the border and he didn't have time but I continued writing every week. When you're in the army letters and parcels are everything. He always wanted to know what was going on, even the littlest things like: "Do you still talk at night-time before you go to sleep?" He always talked about food. At Christmas time when we went down to my mom's place in Cape Town, he wrote: "I just had banana for pudding. I thought all day about the trifle at home."

'He loved music so much. When he was unhappy he would play the piano for hours. This year it was my aim to try to save up and buy new curtains, new duvets and a hi-fi set for him. I plan my life like that, saving up for little luxuries. I wanted it to be a surprise so that he would come home and there it would be.

'I think what saves me is knowing that he was happy. I spoke to a friend who said that André was very positive, very motivated. He was always singing. He was a very religious boy, you know, and I think that helped. In my family there were eight children, three were boys and I was brought up with the idea that boys have to go to the army. If you have a son, I think you have to keep that in mind. I think it helps if a mother is positive about the army. André always used to say: "*Ag ma*, don't worry. I'm doing it for my country. I'm not doing it for me."

After André Groenewald's funeral I stopped a minute on that red gravelly hillside where he was buried and watched the green artificial grass being rolled up in the noon light and heard the first thudding spadeful of earth hitting the coffin. I picked up a few stray petals of frangipani and threw them into the grave. 'That,' I said to myself, 'is for all mothers who have sons who are in – or will one day go to – the army.'

Lin Sampson's beautiful and intimate portrait of two mothers' grief at the death of their sons during the former government's illegal invasion into Angola is a tribute to all mothers, on both sides, who lost beloved young sons in this war. Many of the stories of young MK soldiers who were killed have yet to be told. A collection of Lin's work, Now You've Gone and Killed Me, *is published by Oshun.*

In Whitest Africa

What do your average, young, normal, peace-loving, white South Africans do about the racial problems destroying the country? The two-word answer: they drink, says American reporter PJ O'Rourke.

PJ O'Rourke

Fairlady 14 September 1988

'd been told South Africa looks like California, and it does look like California – the same tan-to-cancer beaches, the same granulated mountains' majesty, the same developed desert scrub. Johannesburg looks like LA. It was all built after 1900, like LA. It's ringed and crisscrossed with expressways, like LA. And its best suburb, Hyde Park, looks like Beverly Hills. All the people who live in Hyde Park are white, just like Beverly Hills. And all the people who work there – who cook, sweep and clean the swimming pools – are not white, just like Beverly Hills. The only difference is that the lady who does the laundry carries it on her head.

I was prepared for South Africa to be terrible. But I wasn't prepared for it to be normal. Signs of 'No dogs' or 'Non-Europeans' are rare, almost tourist attractions now. There's no colour bar in the big international hotels, restaurants or nightclubs. Downtown shopping districts are integrated. You see as many black people in coats and ties as you do in an American city. If I'd really tried, I could have spent my month in South Africa without noticing any hint of trouble, except for the soldiers all over the place. South Africa is terribly normal. And this is why I think we get so emotional about it.

Everywhere you go in the world, somebody's raping women, expelling ethnic Chinese, enslaving Stone Age tribesmen, shooting communists, rounding up Jews, kidnapping Americans, setting fire to Sikhs, keeping Catholics out of country clubs and hunting peasants from helicopters with automatic weapons. The world is built on discrimination of the most horrible kind. The problem with South Africans is that they admit it. They don't say, like the French, 'Algerians have a legal right to live in the 16th *arrondissement* but they can't afford to.'

They don't say like the Israelis, 'Arabs have a legal right to live in West Jerusalem, but they're afraid to.' They don't say like the Americans, 'Indians have a legal right to live in Ohio but oops, we killed them all.'

The South Africans just say, 'Stuff you.' I believe it's right there in their

> The Voortrekker Monument is to Afrikaners – the controlling majority of South African whites – what Salt Lake City Tabernacle is to Mormons.

constitution: 'Article IV: Stuff you. We're bigots'.

We hate them for this. And we're going to hold indignant demonstrations and make our universities sell all their Kruger Rands until the South Africans learn to stand up and lie like white men.

Sixty-five kilometres from Joburg is Pretoria, the administrative capital of South Africa. It looks like Sacramento with soldiers, like Sacramento will if Chicanos ever revolt. And on the tallest hill in Pretoria stands the Voortrekker Monument, a 37-metre tower of granite visible for 32 kilometres in every direction. The Voortrekker Monument is to Afrikaners – the controlling majority of South African whites – what Salt Lake City Tabernacle is to Mormons. It commemorates the Great Trek of 1834-54, when the Boers escaped such annoyances of British colonial rule as the abolition of slavery and pushed north into the interior of Africa to arrange things their own way. The Voortrekker Monument's rotunda is decorated with an immense, heroic-scale bas-relief depicting the entire course of the Great Trek, from Bible-kissing send offs in Cape Town to the Battle of Blood River in 1838 when 3 000 Zulus were killed, versus 0 dead Boers.

Therefore, my heart sank when I saw the Great Trek sculpture. Every single give-me-a-home-where-the-buffalo-roam bromide was there except the buffalo were zebras and at that inevitable point where a billion natives attack, it was Zulus with spears and shields instead of Apaches with bows and arrows. The Zulus were doing everything the Apaches were always depicted as doing before we discovered they were noble ecologists – skewering babies, clobbering women and getting shot in massive numbers. South Africa's Boers turn out to be North America's revered pioneer forefathers. And there I was, a good American descendant of same, covered with gore from the slaughter of Indians and belly stuffed to bursting from the labour of kidnapped slaves, ready to wash up, have a burp and criticise the Afrikaners.

Now if the Afrikaners resemble us, what about the English-speaking white South Africans? They're possibly better educated than the Afrikaners, richer, more cosmopolitan. They dress and act the same as Americans and, forgiving them their Crumbled Empire accent, speak the same language.

I'd heard about the suffering blacks in South Africa. I'd heard plenty about the intransigent racists in South Africa. And I'd heard plenty more than enough about the conscientious whites who go to South Africa and feel bad about the suffering blacks and intransigent racists there. But I'd never heard much about the middling sort of ordinary white people, with Mazdas to keep Turtle Waxed and child-support payments to avoid, the ones who so resemble what most of us see when we brush our teeth. What are they like? What's the response to the quagmire of apartheid? How do they cope with the violence and hatred around them? Are they worried? Frightened? Guilty? Bitter? Full of conflicting emotions?

I stayed one month in South Africa, travelled 5 000 kilometres, talked to hundreds of people and came back with a two-word answer: They're drunk.

The South Africans drink and open their arms to the world. Before I left the States, I phoned a lawyer in Joburg, Tom Mills, a friend of a friend. I called him to see about doing some bird hunting. And when I called him back to tell him what hotel I'd be staying in, Tom said, 'The hell you are! We've got a guesthouse and a swimming pool. You're staying with us.'

This was a sixth-generation white African, no radical or pal of the African National Congress. He knew I was an American reporter and would do to South Africa what American reporters always do – what I'm doing here. And he didn't otherwise know me from Adam. But Tom insisted. I was his guest.

'It isn't like you thought it would be, is it?' said Tom, as we walked around his lawn with enormous whiskies in our hands. 'It's like California, isn't it?'

Except the sparrows are chartreuse and the maid calls you master.

'That doesn't mean anything,' said Tom. 'It's just like saying boss or whatever. Mind your step,' he added. 'This is where the garden boy got a cobra in the power mower.'

The South Africans drink and make plans to change the country. Tom's plan was to put a property qualification on the vote. 'Do away with apartheid and the Group Areas Act,' he said. 'Let anybody have whatever he can afford. If he can afford political power, let him afford that too. That's about how you do it in the States, isn't it? It doesn't change things much.'

Tom's friend, Bill Fletcher, had a plan for splitting up the whole country into little cantons, like Switzerland's, and federating it all back together again – togetherheid.

We watched the TV news and mixed more drinks. Down in the black townships the 'comrades', the young radicals, were 'necklacing', putting flaming car tyres around people's necks (actually down over their shoulders to pin their arms to their sides). But this wasn't on the news. The government had issued new regulations forbidding media coverage of civil disturbances. The lead story was about sick racehorses.

The South Africans drink and go on the offensive. Tom, Bill and I and some other birdhunters went to Jim Elliot's house for drinks. Jim was a dentist with a den decorated with animal heads and other parts. The bar stools were elephant feet.

'A man can live like a king in this country,' said Jim, petting a Labrador retriever named Soweto. 'Like a king! I've got my practice, a house, a couple of cars, a shack down on the beach and the best hunting and fishing in the world. Where else could I live like this?' He filled my glass to the brim with Scotch.

'The blacks live better than they do in the rest of Africa. I'll tell you that,' said Bill.

'We like the blacks,' said Tom.

'They don't deserve to be treated the way they are.'

'We all like the blacks,' said Jim.

'Though they are a bit childish,' said someone who then told a story about how the new maid tried to make tea in the steam iron.

'But they don't deserve to be treated the way they are,' said Tom. And told how last year he'd seen a white motorist run into a black man and knock him across the road. The motorist stopped but wouldn't get out of his car. Tom called the ambulance and tried to get the white man to help, but the man just drove away.

'He was a British tourist,' said Tom with satisfaction.

Later Jim said, 'We fought alongside everybody else in the First World War and the Second World War. Now they all turn their backs on us. The minute we're in trouble, where are our friends?'

And a good many drinks later, somebody said, 'Thirty days to Cairo', by which he meant the South African army could fight its way up the length of Africa in 30 days. It's probably true. And it would have the advantage of putting the South African army 30 days away from where it's getting into trouble now. But I didn't point that out.

The South Africans drink and get serious. Tom and I were shooting doves and drinking beer with a Greek car dealer named Connie. Connie had lived in the Belgian Congo, had been trapped there with his wife and children in 1960-61. Connie recalled angry blacks mutilating each other, recalled the rape of nuns 'by

I'd heard about the suffering blacks in South Africa. I'd heard plenty about the intransigent racists in South Africa. And I'd heard plenty more than enough about the conscientious whites who go to South Africa and feel bad about the suffering blacks and intransigent racists there. But I'd never heard much about the middling sort of ordinary white people, with Mazdas to keep Turtle Waxed and child-support payments to avoid, the ones who so resemble what most of us see when we brush our teeth.

the very ones they were ministering', recalled cattle with their legs cut off at the hock.

'It makes me shake when I think of what I saw.'

That night Tom and I also drank with Gianni, who as a teenager from a little village in Sicily, had to come to Africa in 1962, carrying his mother's entire savings: one English pound and fifty pence. He'd made his way to Angola.

'So rich,' he said. 'So beautiful. You put a dead stick in the ground it would grow.' He'd prospected for minerals, gotten rich, started a big-game-hunting operation that had 18 camps. Then in 1975 the Portuguese left. He talked about corpses hanging in the trees, about men castrated and foetuses hanging out of the slit bellies of women and, like the Greek, about cattle with their legs cut off. He abandoned all his mineral claims, dynamited his hunting camps – 'not even the stones were left in one piece', he said – and came to South Africa to start over.

I wondered what I'd think if I were South African and looked at the rest of Africa and saw nothing but oppression, murder, chaos, poverty, famine and corruption – whereas in South Africa there was just some oppression, murder and poverty.

'You think the blacks can't govern themselves?' I said to Gianni.

He shrugged and said, 'It was the East Germans and the Cubans who did the worst things I saw.'

The South Africans drink and get nostalgic. I spent the Christmas holidays on the Indian Ocean in Scottburgh – a sort of Southampton or Hilton Head whose peak season is South Africa's midsummer yuletide. There were a lot of old people there, members of the 'Whenwe' tribe, so called because most of their sentences begin with 'When we were in Nyasaland ...'; 'When we were in Bechuanaland ...'; 'When we were in Rhodesia ...' It seems Africa was a paradise then, before 1960, and the more they drink, the more paradisiacal it becomes. Though it must be an odd kind of Eden for some of its residents.

'You can see why the blacks steal,' said one old man, a former settler of Rhodesia. He'd been captured by the Germans at Tobruk. In the POW camp of Breslau, we worked in the post office – stole everything in sight. Only natural under the circumstances.' He flipped his cigarette out on the lawn, the way everyone does in South Africa. There's always someone to pick up the butts.

'The only reason blacks have bones in their skulls is to keep their ears apart,' said a startling, ugly old lady, just as the maid was serving the cocktail weenies.

'Now wait a minute,' I said.

'Well, of course, *your* blacks have white blood,' said the ugly woman, shaking her head. 'I've never understood how any man can be attracted to a black girl.' She helped herself to several miniature frankfurters and looked right through the very pretty maid.

'That kinky hair, those fat noses, great big lips.'

I would be drummed out of the Subtle Fiction Writer's League if I invented this scene. The old woman was not only ugly with the ugliness age brings to us all but also showed signs of congenital hideousness – pickle-jar chin and a nose like a trigonometry problem. What's more, she had deep frown-and-snit wrinkles that come from a lifetime of bad character. That day I'd driven through the Valley of a Thousand Hills, in the Natal outback. I'd passed through the little villages where Zulu girls, bare-chested to show their unmarried status, were bringing goods to market. Burnished skin and sweet features and sturdy little bodies. I had fallen eternally in love 30 or 40 times.

The South Africans drink and grow resigned to their fate. At a dinner party full of junior business executives, the talk was about the olive-coloured South African passport, which most countries won't accept as a travel document.

'We call it the green mamba,' said an accountant, 'because you can't take it anywhere.'

The dinner guests talked about foreign countries the way people in Manhattan discuss distant neighbour-hoods where they might be able to find a decent apartment.

'We're thinking Australia,' said the real estate agent.

'Oh, hell, England, I guess,' said a law clerk from Tom's office. 'My grandmother is English.'

'The Florida option is what most people are thinking about,' said an assistant hotel manager. 'Same weather, strong economy and that's where everyone else goes when their government's fall apart.'

They don't talk about money or careers. They don't even talk about apartheid as much as we do.

'If the United States were serious about fixing the situation here,' said the law clerk, 'all they'd have to do is give every young professional in South Africa a green card. Nobody would be left.' At least, nobody they knew very well.

'When you don't work with people and you don't live with people, you don't know them,' said the accountant. 'Just the servants.'

And the domestic staff's attitude lately has been, as they put it, 'shifting'.

'Who can blame them?' said the law clerk.

The real estate agent said, 'They say it's those of us who've been moderates who'll have our throats cut.'

'Do you blame the Afrikaners?' I asked.

Helpless shrugs all around. 'A lot of us are part Afrikaans,' said the assistant hotel manager.

The Afrikaners drink a lot too. I spent an evening in a dirty little bar in a farm town called Humansdorp, in the Cape Province. At first I didn't think the locals even noticed me. Then I realised that they had been speaking Afrikaans when I came in but, after they'd heard me ask for more ice in my whisky, had switched their conversation to English – still not saying a word to me.

The bartender regaled one customer with some details of a practical joke he'd played, putting cayenne pepper in somebody's snuff. The rest of the bar was trading stories about bad and foolish black behaviour.

A kid who'd just gotten back from his two-year army hitch was saying that Namibian girls smear blood mixed with mud all over their bodies. (For all I know, it's true, it's no weirder than some of the ingredients I've noticed in my girlfriend's shampoo.) There was concerned clucking over the neighbourhood black teens. After they're circumcised, they're supposed to spend a month alone in the bush, but instead they spend it begging beside the highway. Finally one of the Afrikaners turned to me and asked about sheep farming in the United States. By that time I'd had enough drinks to tell him. Although I don't believe I know which end of the sheep you're supposed to feed.

Then everyone wanted to chat. 'Was it difficult figuring out the South African money?' 'Do people try to deal (cheat) you around here?' 'Does America have a lot of blacks?'

'I want to go to America,' said the young ex-soldier. 'To see how you do it.'

'Do what?'

'Get along with the blacks.' What a strange place America must be to South Africans – a sanctuary for all beleaguered oppressors, a land of simple money and end-less sheep-farming opportunities, where blacks behave because they've got white blood. Mike Boettcher, the NBC correspondent in Joburg, told me that his baby's nurse, a beautiful girl of 19, wanted to go to Harlem

> I was prepared for South Africa to be terrible. But I wasn't prepared for it to be normal.

'because everybody is young and rich there' and because no-one in Soweto had enough cows to pay her bride price. Mike said he tried in vain to tell her most guys in Harlem don't have many cows. And in the Transkei 'homeland' I talked to a black divinity student who'd visited America. 'The most wonderful place,' he said. 'So wealthy and beautiful and with perfect racial harmony.'

'What part of America did you visit?' I asked.

'The south side of Chicago.'

I was pretty drunk myself by the time I'd been in South Africa for three or four weeks. Not that I'm not usually, but there was something 'heart of whiteness' about this bender. I was fuddled. My head boiled with clichés. I was getting used to being confused. I was getting used to hearing the most extraordinary things. From this Irish couple who'd been living in South Africa for three decades, for instance.

'There hasn't been apartheid here for years,' said the wife.

'One problem is that the word was invented,' said the husband.

I was becoming South African, growing accustomed to having people all around me all the time doing everything for me and not doing it well. I went to dinner at my resort hotel in Mosselbaai, along the Big Sur-like coast between Port Elizabeth and Cape Town. I'd had my six or eight whiskies with the Irish couple in the lounge and was ready for one of those elaborate, big, bland and indifferently cooked meals that constitute South African cuisine. The restaurant was turned out in red plush and crisp linen. Candles glittered in cut-glass sconces. But when I sat down at my table, there were three spoons, two water glasses, one dirty wine glass, no fork, no knife and no napkin.

'I need a dinner fork, a salad fork, a knife and a napkin,' I said to the waiter, who stared at me in dull surprise before retreating across the dining room at the speed of a change in seasons. His feet were sockless below his tuxedo pants and he was standing on the backs on his unlaced Oxfords.

He returned with another spoon.

'I need a knife, a fork and a napkin!' I said.

He came back 20 minutes later with a water pitcher

and filled my wine glass.

'Look here,' I said. 'Do you speak English?'

He thought for a long time. 'Oh yes,' he said. He disappeared and came back in half an hour with one more water glass. 'Is the master ready to order?'

He was voteless, impoverished, unpropertied, not a legal citizen in his own nation, and he had me reduced to a paroxysm of impotent drunken rage. I left him a huge tip and ate my chicken with a spoon.

It's always hard to see hope through a hangover, particularly when you're at the butt end of this benighted continent, in a country that's like a nightmare laundry-detergent commercial – makes whites whiter, coloureds brighter. South Africans have built themselves a big-screen, Technicolor version of Northern Ireland. The troubles in Ireland have been going on since 1169. I think we can expect the same swift and decisive resolution here.

Disinvestment and sanctions – I guess those are the solutions of choice in the States. Well, economic sanctions sure nipped the Russian revolution in the bud, made Khomeini's Iran fold like a hideaway bed and put Chiang Kai-shek right back in power of the mainland. The whole time I was in South Africa, I talked to only one person who was in favour of sanctions, and that was the divinity student in Transkei who'd been so taken with the south side of Chicago.

Of course there were a lot of people I didn't talk to. The comrades were too busy necklacing. And I never bumped into Bishop Tutu. Most of the blacks I did talk to would be considered, by South African standards, middle class, even sellouts – Uncle Bantus. They told me, 'Political power grows from economic power.' They saw sanctions as hurting blacks' chances of getting a leg up the ladder.

I have no idea whether they were right or wrong. But when I was drinking beer and talking to people in Ulundi, the administrative capital of the Zulu tribal lands, a young political organiser leant over to me and said, 'It's very simple why we are against sanctions. If we have money, we can buy *guns*.'

We should factor that into our next US-out-of-South Africa rally.

The South African government's own solution, the homelands, is a hideous joke. I travelled through the Tswana tribal homeland, Bophuthatswana, in the north; the Zulu homeland, Kwazulu, in Natal; and the two Xhosa homelands, Transkei and Ciskei, along the Indian Ocean. They're all the same. Every place is littered with windowless huts that you couldn't tell from latrines if there were latrines to tell them from. The garden plots look like a Deadhead's beard. People are dumped into these rural wastes, far more people than the land can support. So the men have no choice but to go off to the rest of South Africa and work as 'foreigners'. The homelands are on the worst land in the country, scorched foothills and prairies on the verge of desertification. Raw trenches of the red African soil have eroded in webs across the pastures. Every metre of ground is overgrazed.

The tribal economic system, like ancient Europe's, is based on cattle. So the cows, don't often get eaten or sold or even milked. They are the bank account, the measure of a family's wealth. They're also an ecological nightmare in these cramped precincts.

I used to have eight head of Hereford beef cattle at my place back in New Hampshire. I asked some people in Ulundi what kind of wife these would get me.

'Oh,' said one, 'probably a girl who's lived in the city for a while and has a couple of kids.'

'But,' I said, 'these are purebred polled Herefords, going for 1 000 pounds or more.'

'No, no. It's the number of cows that counts.'

I did see one homeland that worked. It was beautiful and severe bushveld taken back from Boer farms and restored back to its natural state with blesbok and gemsbok and springbok bokking around and herds of zebras – Art Deco on the hoof – packs or gaggles or whatever they're called of giraffes. This was, however, a homeland for the animals, the Botsalano Game Park in Bophuthatswana.

Later, driving with Tom Mills in his Mercedes sedan through the empty Sunday streets of Joburg, I put it to him about South Africa: 'There aren't that many Afrikaners,' I said. 'What, three million, versus two million English and other real Europeans? And you guys control the money, almost all the major industries, right?'

'Mostly, yes.'

'You've got the money. You've got 40 percent of the white vote. And you've got 24 million blacks, coloureds and Indians who'd back you up. What's keeping you from taking the Afrikaner National Party and snapping its spine like a chopstick?'

'That's just not how the English are, you know,' said Tom. 'Most of us just aren't very political.'

'A couple of Chicago ward bosses and you'd have this country in your pocket.'

'I suppose people think it wouldn't be cricket.'

We'd pulled onto the N3 freeway. Joburg's office towers shone behind us. Flat-topped artificial hills from the

'If you look over there,' said Tom, 'you can see Alexandra. It's one of our older black townships.'

Maybe he hadn't noticed it was on fire. 'Isn't it on fire or something?' I said.

'That's from the stoves,' said Tom. 'They don't have electricity.'

Tom had a client named Gilead, a man of 60 or so who'd started out selling coal from a sack in the black townships and was now one of the richest men in Soweto. Save for a bit of melanin, Gilly was the image of my Irish grandfather – close-

I'd been in South Africa for a month and had not met one white person who'd been there. Soweto is just outside Joburg, a city in itself, taking up the whole southwestern quadrant of the city's outskirts. But I hadn't talked to any white who'd even seen Soweto.

gold-mine tips rose in the distance. I was staring out of the window at South Africa's admirable highway beautification when we came over a rise and I caught a glimpse of what was beyond the screen of trees.

Thousands of tiny, scattered huts were pressed together in a jumble stretching for kilometres. And every one of those hovels seemed to be on fire. Smoke drifted in an ominous smudge across the highway.

'Riots!' I thought, trying to fasten my seat belt for the high-speed evasive driving we'd have to do through hordes of angry comrades who would, no doubt, come roiling across the freeway at any moment, with stones and fire bombs in hand.

cropped hair, a build like a washing machine and fingers thick as wrists. He even had some of the same gestures as my grandfather, pulling on the old-fashioned pointy lapels of his banker's striped suit and then planting his thumbs in the pockets of his vest. Gilly's skull bore four or five large hatchet scars from the gang quarrels of his youth. When I first met him, in Tom's office, he was telling how one of the stores he owned was 'offloaded' by the comrades.

'The gangs, they set up at either end of the street,' Gilly said. 'They are just boys, some no more than ten years old. Some of the boys come into your store and buy a Coke. Then they throw the bottles around to create a diversion and empty the shelves. You just stay quiet if you don't want to be necklaced.'

'Yes, but you weren't in the store when that happened,' said Tom.

Gilly began to laugh. 'No, I was not there the first two times it happened.'

'Well, he was there the third time,' Tom said, 'and he chased them down the street with his pistol.'

'You know what we have to do,' said Tom after Gilly had left. 'We have to get Gilly to come out to our house for dinner and bring his wife and some of his friends. It would be interesting for you to talk to them.

But the riots in Soweto kept anyone from getting in or out after dark, and even in the daytime there were too many barricades and stonings to bring the women along. So Gilly and three friends from Soweto, young men in their 20s, came to an afternoon braai at Tom and Sally's house. A Christmas-week strike had begun in Soweto that day and Gilly, Bob, Carswell and Nick arrived in a rusted Datsun, although Gilly owns a BMW.

We sat on the patio for a stiff 20 minutes while the Mills' maid peeked around the door post with an expression of intrigued disapproval. But then a few beers were had and the steaks and the boerewors began to spatter on the grill, and one more of the hundreds of thousands of endless discussions of South Africa's 'situation' started in earnest.

The strange thing is that when I look at my notes now, if I cover the names, I can't tell who said what or if the speaker was black or white.

Carswell and Bob (and me, I guess) favoured one man, one vote. Gilly, Nick, Tom and Sally felt Tom's idea about property qualification had merit. There was a general denunciation which dictates where what race can live, and of US sanctions, too. 'Politics is dirty,' said Carswell.

And there was unanimous disparagement of both President Botha and Winnie Mandela. Everyone agreed that moderates would come to the fore if they had a chance. Bob described with considerable anger how the riots and strikes in Soweto were managed by anonymous pamphlets and unsigned ads in *The Sowetan*. He blamed outside agitators, just as the Reagan White House does.

Nick, Bob and Carswell had small children and were furious about the black school boycott, which had been going on for nearly a year. They said the ANC leaders were pushing a government school strike while the leaders' own children were being educated in private schools. They feared, they said, 'the intentional creation of a black underclass'. Of course there's one of those already.

Everyone praised capitalism for a while, and Bob made a poetic appeal for whites to stay in South Africa. Although perhaps he was just being polite in response to the hospitality. Then Nick said something that I could see surprised Tom and Sally. 'I'm angry that South Africa is singled out,' he said. 'Why should Senator Kennedy come here and tell us our troubles? We're not the only country in the world where bad things happen.'

'I have just this one fear – attack

from the outside,' said Carswell. 'South Africa has no friends.'

'What are you guys going to do?' I asked Gilly's friends. 'How are you going to get rid of apartheid?'

'Such meetings as this are valuable,' said Carswell, as though something had been accomplished that afternoon.

'That was a real eye-opener,' said Tom after Gilly and his friends had left.

'Incredibly interesting,' said Sally. 'We've got to do that again.'

And it dawned on me: They'd never had black people as guests in their house before.

'We've seen Gilly and his wife at office parties,' said Sally. 'And there are black and Indian students at the kids' schools. We've seen the parents at school functions.'

We were going to the Fletchers' house that night for dinner. 'Let's not say anything about this,' said Tom. 'I'm not sure how Bill and Margaret would feel about it. They're a little old-fashioned about some things.'

On my last day in South Africa, I drove through Soweto in a shiny red rental car – probably not a good idea for a person as putty-coloured as me. Also, it was illegal. No white person can go there without permission. [*Ed's note: He was misinformed. Since the Pass Laws were abolished in 1986, a permit is no longer needed.*] I'd been in South Africa for a month and had not met one white person who'd been there. Soweto is just outside Joburg, a city in itself, taking up the whole southwestern quadrant of the city's outskirts. But I hadn't talked to any white who'd even seen Soweto.

And then I couldn't find the place. A city of two million people, and when I looked at the car-rental map, it wasn't there. I drove around the N1 beltway, and there were no signs, no exits marked 'Soweto'. I got off the southwest and headed in what I thought might be the right direction. I took a couple of gravel roads, navigating by the sun. Finally I saw a 'Soweto' sign, the size that says, 'Picnic area, 1.5 km'. And on the other side of a hill was Soweto, as big as the San Fernando Valley, a huge expanse of little homes. It was not such a terrible looking place, by Third World standards. It was littered and scruffy and crowded, but most of the houses looked like what you'd see on an American Indian reservation. Each modest dwelling was set on a small plot of land. There was electricity and no raw sewage stink.

Soweto was almost rich, as riches are measured in black Africa. And there was plenty of economic power here for political power to grow out of, if things worked that way in South Africa. But South Africa is one of the few places I've ever been where things are not a matter of dollars and cents. It wouldn't have mattered if each of those houses had been Graceland. People would be just as trapped.

I locked my car doors, adjusted my necktie and drove through the place in a sweat. Soweto is like discovering arithmetic. It is an epiphany about what '83 percent of the population' means. Until then I hadn't seen the blacks in South Africa, not even in the overpopulated homelands. Now they pressed in on every side in the slow jam of bicycles, trucks and foot traffic. I hoped I had something in my wallet, some leftover USSR press card or some damn thing to save my white skin when the comrades got to me. Everyone was staring at my pale, stupid face.

And then I saw that they were smiling. And here and there was a happy wave. There was laughter from the little kids. I drove through Soweto for nearly an hour without so much as a bad look tossed in my direction, let alone rocks or firebombs.

Maybe I'd caught them by surprise and they didn't know what to make of me. Maybe they thought I was so crazy to be there that it was funny. I didn't know.

Months after I got back, I was giving a lecture on journalism at some little college in the middle of Pennsylvania, and I told the students about driving through Soweto. One of them came up to the lectern afterwards. She was from Soweto, an exchange student.

'Don't you know why people were smiling and waving at you?' she asked. 'They thought you were great.'

'But why?'

'It's illegal for you to be there. How did you get in?'

'I was lost. I came through some back roads.'

'The government isn't letting anyone in there, and when people saw you, that you had managed to get in some way, they figured you must be somebody good, an organiser or from some international group.'

'Even though I was white?'

'Because you were white.'

So maybe there is some hope for South Africa, some hope for the people there, for their souls anyway.

'In Whitest Africa' – extracted from Holidays in Hell *by PJ O'Rourke, published by Macmillan, London, UK.*

Mama Courage

Albertina Sisulu is a woman of character, courage and conviction whose story of hardship and suffering is the stuff shocking fiction is made of.

Amy Thornton

Fairlady 11 April 1990

Soweto lies on 'the other side' of Johannesburg. It takes more than an hour to drive there from the airport and we did not have the exact address. But this was no handicap. The first person we asked explained where to go.

'You will recognise the house – there is a big flag flying from the roof.' And sure enough there it was on a corner, surrounded by a high concrete black wall, the entrance guarded by a security gate. Above us, the ANC flag flapped in the wind.

This house had been Albertina Sisulu's home for 42 years. The gate is unlocked by a young man.

'Mama' (a term of endearment and respect) greets us with a warm smile, a big hug and a kiss.

'Before we start, my children, what will you drink … you must eat something,' she says as she ushers us inside the small freshly-painted house. It is spotless. New curtains frame the windows and healthy pot plants decorate the rooms. On the wall hang two Sue Williamson portraits – one of veteran anti-apartheid campaigner Helen Joseph and one of Albertina. A framed portrait of Nelson Mandela has prominence in a display cabinet. So too does a plaque inscribed with 'Newsmaker of the Year 1986-1987' which was awarded to her son Zwelakhe, editor of *New Nation* and former Nieman fellow at America's Harvard University.

'We cleaned and prepared the house for Walter,' she says offering us biscuits and cool drink served in tall glasses. My eye is drawn to an exercise bike standing in one corner of the lounge. Nodding towards it Mama says, 'The old man uses it.'

'How old are you, Mama?' I ask her.

'Seventy-two,' she replies.

'And you call your husband "the old man"?'

She laughs, crinkle lines at the corners of her mouth, her face belying her years.

Albertina Sisulu – 'A powerful force within me would not allow me to rest while all around I saw others suffering.'

(*Photo:* Omar Badsha)

'When I was at work Walter, who was also restricted, did the housework, the washing and the bathing of the children. Ideas of feminism are not new to us.'

'Yes, he gets up at 5 am and pedals away on his exercise bike, whistling as he goes.'

Albertina was born in the Transkei district of Tsomo and orphaned in her teens.

'I lost my mother when I was 15 and my father when I was 17. My mother died of diabetes and my father got double pneumonia. I must say that when I think of their unnecessary deaths I feel bitter. If we had had access to medical facilities in the Transkei both of them would have lived.'

Brought up by her grandparents, Albertina was educated by Catholic nuns who made arrangements for her to train as a nurse. Her starting salary was £1 a month. Even after she qualified she only earned £15 compared with white nurses who, after the same training and the same examinations, earned three times that amount.

'The Afrikaans nurses used to come to the exams with pictures of their mothers which they put in front of them for inspiration – we thought they were crazy.'

Albertina first worked in the Johannesburg Native Hospital and then Baragwanath, where she became a senior nurse. Her active political involvement led to banning orders and subsequent house arrest. The police wanted to impose a 24-hour house arrest but the Nursing Council made representations on her behalf and she was allowed to leave the house between 7 am and 7 pm. These restrictions prevented her from becoming a matron at Baragwanath Hospital even though she was in line for the promotion. She could not be considered as the post required the incumbent to work day and night duties.

How did she cope with such a strenuous job, and reporting to the police every day of her life?

'When I was at work Walter, who was also restricted, did the housework, the washing and the bathing of the children. Ideas of feminism are not new to us.'

Albertina retired from Baragwanath and was later asked by Dr Abu Baker Asvat, an anti-apartheid activist and health secretary of the Azanian Peoples' Organisation, to come and work for him at a surgery he had opened in the township.

It was there that she experienced the horror of seeing him murdered before her eyes. It still gives her nightmares.

'He was such a good man,' she says. 'He never could turn a patient away if they could not afford to pay him. Hundreds of people in Soweto still owe him fees.'

Yet he was murdered for money. Giving evidence in the subsequent murder trial added to Albertina's trauma. It was but one of the many crises that dogged her life.

Albertina met Walter when she was 25.

'I was staying in a nurses' hostel. Walter's cousin, Evelyn, who was Nelson Mandela's first wife, was also training there. Walter would come and visit. I had refused all offers of marriage from "home boys" because I didn't consider myself to be marriage material. My aim was to work and help educate my brothers and sisters and eventually provide a home for them all. A powerful force within me would not allow me to rest while all around I saw others suffering.

'I noticed that Evelyn was forever making excuses to leave me alone with Walter. It didn't take me long to realise he was as strongly motivated as myself.'

There were objections from family and friends to a proposed marriage as Walter was 'coloured', the son of a Xhosa woman and a white road-building foreman who, soon after Walter's birth, abandoned his black family. But when Albertina was 27 they were married in Soweto's Holy Cross Anglican Church and have been practising Anglicans ever since. After her marriage Albertina, the good daughter-in-law, insisted Walter's mother stay on in the house.

'I loved her very much. She lived with us until her death in 1962.'

The Sisulus have five children of their own and have adopted another three, the children of Albertina's brother who was disabled and unable to support them. Of these children two are in exile and one is serving a five-year sentence on Robben Island. Another is studying at the University of the Western Cape and her eldest daughter, Unda, is completing a doctorate in literature in England. Zwelakhe, detained without trial for 720 days from late 1986, was released in 1989 and subjected to heavy restrictions which were only recently lifted. Added now to the large family are many grandchildren – two run in and out and greet us with big, curious eyes.

In 1964, after the Rivonia Treason Trial, Nelson Mandela, Walter Sisulu and other African National Congress leaders were sentenced to life imprisonment for plotting sabotage and planning to overthrow the government. But prison did nothing to dim the Sisulus' relationship. This despite the fact that during the first 18 years of Walter's incarceration their only contact was talking on the telephone through a glass panel. It was only from 1982, during visits to Pollsmoor Prison, that Albertina was able to touch her husband. The separation only served to strengthen their love.

'Walter is a very sweet person,' says Albertina.

'He will be returning from Lusaka soon and I will be there to greet him. This is the first time we have been separated since he was released.'

Albertina feels she can't make up for the years that have been lost; she can only treasure the time they now have together. But that doesn't change who she is.

'I was always very independent and the breadwinner in our family. Even now I sometimes find myself walking out of the house without saying anything, to go to a meeting, and Walter will softly inquire,

'I was always very independent and the breadwinner in our family. Even now I sometimes find myself walking out of the house without saying anything, to go to a meeting, and Walter will softly inquire, "Are you going out, my dear?"'

As far as Albertina is concerned, she and Walter are at the disposal of the people. When asked whether she had ever entertained the possibility of one day living in a ministerial mansion, she laughs loudly. 'No, darling, I will stay in Soweto. My roots are here and my inspiration comes from this place.'

"Are you going out, my dear?"'

The publicity and media hype that surrounds her and Walter hasn't changed her. She has never lost touch with her roots. And she is unawed by the powerful political leaders she and Walter have met overseas.

About Margaret Thatcher she says, 'The Iron Lady! We tamed her. I think she wanted to tell us how to run the struggle! But when we left she said she had been looking forward to meeting us.'

Albertina related better to President Bush. 'I felt he was really friendly and wanted to know about our struggles. He was shocked when I told him of my own life. But what really horrified him was what I told him about my daughter, Unda.'

Unda was caught up in the 1976 Soweto uprising, which revolved around the compulsory use of Afrikaans as a medium of instruction in the schools.

'It started right here in this district,' says Albertina.

'Unda was arrested. The police refused to tell us where she was. I was under house arrest, so my son went to Pretoria Prison, as we had been told she might be there. He stood at the wall and shouted her name. For that he was arrested and sent to solitary confinement for 90 days. After 11 months Unda was released, but in all that time we never knew where she was. She had been thoroughly tortured and was severely mentally disturbed. She would wake in the middle of the night, screaming to me to save her from the police. Later we had to send her out of the country for treatment. President Bush asked me how old she was at the time and was really shocked when I told him 16.

'This was the worst time of my life. Walter was in prison, Unda and my son Max in detention.

Then I too was detained and my other children were left to fend for themselves. Eventually we had to send them to Waterford School in Swaziland because it was impossible for them to study.'

Despite the upheavals that had turned Albertina's life upside down, she found the strength to carry on. She never lost sight of why this was happening to her and was driven by her conviction that she was struggling for a better society.

'This is the price I've had to pay for freedom. Remember: Others have paid with their lives.'

Do her children resent having to live in exile?

'No, I don't think so. All the children are politically involved.'

But Albertina did find the separation particularly painful, especially coming from a culture that values the extended family. Letters and phone calls had kept family ties intact, but what really helped the Sisulu children survive was the strong foundation of love and security, which had been laid down during their formative years when the family were still together. It was only recently that Albertina was reunited with two of her children.

'Do you know that until recently, I had not seen Max [an economist with the ANC] since 1967. And it was only a few months ago, on my way to America, that I saw Unda for the first time since '76.'

Despite her age, Albertina is still active as president of the UDF, in the Soweto Civic Association and as the coordinator of several community projects which include four sewing co-ops, 17 crèches and eight pre-primary schools. But what does tire her these days is all the travelling which is now part of her leadership role. Among her most recent engagements have been trips to Lusaka, Sweden and Norway, and last month's Namibian independence celebrations. Her schedule is so hectic that she does not know when she and Walter will get time for that second honeymoon!

As far as Albertina is concerned, she and Walter are at the disposal of the people. When asked whether she had ever entertained the possibility of one day living in a ministerial mansion, she laughs loudly. 'No, darling, I will stay in Soweto. My roots are here and my inspiration comes from this place.'

Despite necessary safety precautions consisting of bullet-proof windows and guards who live in the house (there have been death threats against Walter recently), she doesn't feel cut off from the community. She has a spontaneous empathy and you know that when she calls you 'sister', 'child', 'mama' or 'sweetheart', that she means it.

Does she feel, or has she felt, bitterness towards whites?

'No, I don't feel bitter. As children in the Transkei we never hated white people, but we were scared of them. From the time I became politically involved, however, I met whites who were supportive of our cause. Helen Joseph has stayed in my home. My white sisters have nothing to fear from us blacks. We are Christians and we will not take revenge for all the wrongs that have been done to us. Now is the time to bridge the gap, not widen it. We must all work together to overcome the barriers of apartheid so that our children can grow up together as one big South African family.'

The biggest problem Albertina sees in post-apartheid society is the restructuring of the economy so as to provide jobs and a better standard of living for all. She expresses anger at some white women who pay domestic workers low wages.

'Don't they stop to think,' she says, 'that it is not possible to feed and clothe a family with R150?'

Mama Sisulu is working to help people find a way of earning a better living. Taking us to see one of the sewing groups she has help organise, a co-op for unemployed women, she explains that the group specialises in dresses, shirts and bags. Key people are sent for training as cutters and designers, sales are advertised and goods sold from tables in the local shopping centre.

'Everything sells like hot cakes,' says Albertina. 'Prices range from R40 for a hand-woven bag to R80 for a dress. We make enough money to pay rent, buy material and pay the members of the co-op a modest salary.'

Albertina is unhesitant when asked about her happiest moment.

'We were consulting with Nelson at his prison house,' she recalls, a smile lighting up her face, 'when he said there would be some interesting news on the TV that night.

'We all gathered in his lounge and soon heard the announcement that Walter and the others were to be released. That was the happiest moment of my life. We were too excited to continue the conference. I wanted to go home right then to prepare for Walter's homecoming. 'We drove straight to the airport but we could not get a flight. So there and then we hired a car and drove through the night to Soweto. It was sad to leave Nelson behind, but I was comforted that if the others were released, he too would soon be out.'

Walter's release was a joyous occasion. And although since then they have not been together as much as they would have liked, their relationship is typical of a long-married couple. They both display a closeness which belies a quarter of a century of separation. As daughter-in-law Sheila Sisulu remarked at their reunion, 'They're like a honeymoon couple.'

Walter Sisulu died at the age of 90 in May 2003.

Aggrey Klaaste – 'a man of vision'.

(*Photo:* Antonio Muchave/*Sowetan*)

In the News

When he's not sharing his vision of a new, improved South Africa, he's enjoying a laugh with his three live-wire sons. Margaret McAllister meets Aggrey Klaaste, the editor of SA's biggest daily newspaper.

Margaret McAllister

Fairlady 25 August 1993

'Freedom is necessary but with it comes tremendous responsibility,' says newspaper editor Aggrey Klaaste, leaning chummily across his desk in *The Sowetan*'s bustling offices.

With a journalist's love of words, Aggrey delivers his opinions in neatly parcelled phrases. His most famous is the 'nation-building' concept that calls for nothing less than social reconstruction.

As editor of the country's biggest newspaper, with its staggering 1,6 million readership, Aggrey's words carry weight. But he's careful not to spread any gospels.

'The newspaper stands for good. We don't beat the drum for any particular organisation. I like the fact that the paper is part of the furniture of black urban life. It has integrity; it's not just sex and sport. And it's a paper with strong community links because both I and the journalists who work here live in Soweto.'

Home for Aggrey is a modest house in upmarket Diepkloof. It's a retreat from the world where he enjoys unwinding with his wife of 17 years, Valetta, and his sons Moeketsi (19), Nthato (18) and Langa (8).

Aggrey is clearly much entertained by his sons who, despite his denials, appear to be chips off the old block.

'They are three superb boys. The two teenagers are very different thinkers. One is a capitalist, the other more of a radical,' he says, roaring with laughter.

'Interestingly, the capitalist gets things done. He can fix a car and even bake, which tends to make the radical look rather bad. The *laatlammetjie* is called Langa, which means sun. I know I'm biased but when he's ill it's as if the clouds have passed in front of the sun. He's so full of life.'

Valetta, who devotes her time to running the male-dominated Klaaste household, describes her life as 'chaotic'.

'But I wouldn't change it for anything. We have a lot of fun together.'

'We can make it. We have no choice but to make things work. The responsibility is awesome, of course. But all of us, white and black, could be saviours of the African continent. We have the skills and infrastructure to be of assistance to other African countries in the fields of medicine and technology, for example.'

'Family is important,' says Aggrey, who believes one of South Africa's greatest tragedies is the tearing apart of black family life.

'This is where the nation-building concept comes in. Nation building is not Red Nose Day. It's an ongoing process, a way of rebuilding the elements of black culture that have been destroyed, like the extended family and the schooling system.

'As the Afrikaners sorted out their poor-white problem earlier this century, despite their "broedertwis", so we black people must build ourselves up as a nation. We must stop acting like peasants in revolt.

'The happier and more viable people are, the better the country will be. People don't need the "isms" of socialism or capitalism. They need the practical elements that make up a nation, like a job and a house.'

'*Ubuntu*' – a word meaning humaneness – is another concept Aggrey believes in: 'It's a terrific ethos of mutual respect and civilised behaviour, with a history in most black communities. Unfortunately, the word has been turned on its head now and we are in danger of losing our humanity.'

Despite Aggrey's sometimes hard-hitting words, he's positive that South Africa will pull through all the rough patches.

'We can make it. We have no choice but to make things work. The responsibility is awesome, of course. But all of us, white and black, could be saviours of the African continent. We have the skills and infrastructure to be of assistance to other African countries in the fields of medicine and technology, for example.'

When Aggrey is not speaking at conferences, taking part in television debates and wrestling with words, he likes watching other people expend their energy – on the sports field.

'I support a certain football club, which I will not name, and enjoy boxing and rugby. I also love listening to good jazz. My father was a musician and my brother studied music so I come from a pretty musical background,' he says.

And when he really feels the need to escape life's hustle, Aggrey puts his feet up and takes his mind for a stroll through other landscapes – as far afield as South America and the poetry of Pablo Neruda.

Aggrey Klaaste died in June 2004 aged 64. He edited the Sowetan *from 1988 to 2002. In the meantime the* Sowetan *has repositioned itself as a tabloid.*

'Call me Tokyo'

Mike Behr

Fairlady 26 January 1994

Tokyo Sexwale, self-proclaimed political gladiator, opens his home to Mike Behr and talks candidly about the people who matter in his life.

The night before my interview with Tokyo Sexwale at his new Lower Houghton home, I kvetch a little over what to wear for our 8.30 am appointment.

The chairperson of the ANC's PWV region (some say the most powerful man of the north), has a reputation in business-lunch circles for being a dashing dresser. The last thing I want is to arrive inappropriately dressed.

But, judging by Tokyo's attire this morning, I needn't have worried. As he walks in, on time, from an early-morning meeting in the family room across the hall into his curiously minimalistic sitting room where the *Fairlady* team is waiting, appearances seem to be furthest from his mind.

In fact, it's hard to believe that this 40-year-old in a baggy tracksuit and a pair of sockless brown Docksiders with laces left deliberately undone, was not so long ago voted South Africa's sexiest politician by housewives from Joburg and Pretoria.

'Hello, I'm Tokyo,' he says softly, offering a strong handshake. No fanfare.

Ten minutes later, after an impromptu amble through the outrageously green dew-drenched garden and a few informal photographs with his wife Judy, two-year-old daughter Gabriella and baby Chris, we're relaxing in the sun on a bench facing the house.

For the second time that morning he remarks on the loveliness of his surroundings and wonders, almost wistfully, why he doesn't spend more family time here among the sweetly-scented fruit trees, the lush vegetation and a resident symphony of loud finches.

The reason is, quite simply, a demanding job – 13 hours a day, often seven days a week.

Since moving from the conservative Boksburg suburb of Dawn Park four months ago, Tokyo has cut down on travelling time to and from his Jeppe Street offices to give him more precious hours at home. But, he says, he's for-

Tokyo Sexwale – 'My job is fighting for the
hungry and the poor; for the
people who are degraded because of the
colour of their skin.'

(*Photo*: Corrie Hansen)

'My job is fighting for the hungry and the poor; for the people who are degraded because of the colour of their skin. Ordinary people who were never given a chance. That's why I'm a gladiator.'

tunate if he gets more than one uninterrupted weekend a month away from the demands of his sprawling PWV constituency, which embraces the combustible East Rand. As he is quick to point out, thousands of people depend on Tokyo Sexwale. Sometimes for a meal, sometimes for their lives.

'I'm a gladiator for the people,' he informs me. If it weren't for the deadly seriousness of Tokyo's tone (and an imposing presence), the way he defines himself would warrant a chuckle. I wonder whether what I'm hearing is ego or supreme self-confidence.

'My job is fighting for the hungry and the poor; for the people who are degraded because of the colour of their skin. Ordinary people who were never given a chance. That's why I'm a gladiator.'

And in case I misconstrue that Tokyo Sexwale may still be thinking with his MK cap he qualifies his gladiatorial role. 'I fight with passion,' he says, 'but with kindness and compassion as well.'

The battle for peace, he declares, is a relentless one.

'You fight for it every day. You articulate it whether you're talking to the business community, workers or the unemployed in a squatter camp who have almost no hope.'

Describing a typical working day, Tokyo says it's 'rough and tough. It's calls in the morning. Calls to say that people have been killed. It's cancelling my diary to attend to problems. It's defusing explosive situations. It's giving solace, covering the wounds of people. It's attending endless meetings to strategise, to hear complaints, to debate. It's coming home fatigued ...'

In Houghton, gladiators bring home the bacon, but not in the Sexwale household. The three-bedroomed double-storey house is rented. (From a landlord who asked them not to pick the fruit from the trees – 'I told him to go jump in the lake,' chuckles Tokyo.)

And the lease is in Judy's name because Tokyo's board membership of the ANC-linked Thebe Investments is pro bono and his ANC salary doesn't stretch as far as rent.

'It goes to ordinary people in need,' he explains as if this is the most natural way of spending hard-earned money.

Some months that need is so great that Judy has to raid her savings. 'Judy liberates me from the burden of having to worry where the next meal is coming from, so that I can get on with my work,' says Tokyo with undisguised admiration. Years in exile and over a decade in prison

have eroded the need for guilt.

'He calls on me a lot,' Judy confirms later. 'But luckily I've got a couple of things up my sleeve to support the family. There's my small fast-food business in town and I sell clothes that I buy on consignment from my father and brother-in-law's factory in Cape Town. And I also have some property that I rent out. It's enough to keep us alive.'

But not enough for an interior decorator or any of the other trappings that come with an upper northern suburbs home. Their bare sitting room, which contains nothing more than four black leather armchairs on a perfectly vacuumed turquoise wall-to-wall carpet, could do with a healthy injection of capital. So too could most of the other rooms in the house, which have been curtained with Dawn Park hand-downs. And their double garage houses a blue Uno, and a white Toyota Sprinter that belongs to the ANC.

If, as rumoured, the ANC is doling out cash to the party hierarchy in expectation of an April 27 walkover, then the Boksburg post office has forgotten to re-route Tokyo's cheques.

A marriage like the Sexwales' obviously demands extraordinary commitment. But, as Tokyo points out, being a pillar of support comes

In fact, it's hard to believe that this 40-year-old in a baggy tracksuit and a pair of sockless brown Docksiders with laces left deliberately undone, was not so long ago voted South Africa's sexiest politician by housewives from Joburg and Pretoria.

naturally to 33-year-old Judy who was once 'the grandma of Robben Island'.

A legal secretary who, through hard work and plenty of initiative, later became a para-legal in the human rights department of a Cape Town law firm, Judy was, in the late '80s, the sustaining link between 200 political prisoners and their families.

By all accounts, the position demanded a social worker's heart and obligations far beyond the call of any job description. Her hours were so long and consuming that they cost Judy her marriage to a South African Navy officer.

'We just grew apart,' she recalls.

Judy spent three years commuting between Robben Island and her law firm before she met Tokyo. It wasn't love at first sight but she remembers that his powerful presence made an immediate and lasting impression.

'Even in that drab uniform he was sure of himself and what he wanted.'

In the years that followed, Judy and Tokyo grew to know each other and eventually to love each other. There were always plenty of excuses to meet because he was chairman of the island's recreational committee, she his appointed supply link to the mainland. But with vigilant warders

as constant chaperones, they were never alone. Theirs was an '80s relationship under Victorian conditions which, with hindsight, accounts for a marriage unwavering in its understanding and compromise.

As Tokyo remarks, when he says his wife supports him, it's no cliché.

'It's so real it's frightening. All the attention Judy focused on the island is now concentrated on me.'

During their meetings on the island, Tokyo and Judy used to hope that one day they would marry and have children. But after Tokyo's release in 1990, almost two years passed before that dream began to materialise. After 13 years' incarceration, Judy felt Tokyo needed time alone to see his family and to acclimatise to his new world and his new job as head of special projects. Moreover, Judy was committed to those clients who hadn't been released. But in February 1992, Gabriella was born and a year later Tokyo and Judy were married – in the offices of Home Affairs in Boksburg.

Their wedding present?

A baby boy named Chris born in June last year. (He was named after Chris Hani and Judy's brother.)

Their marriage is built on rock, but what sustains the woman who was born Van Vuuren on an Eastern Cape farm?

'I have a strong understanding of what Tokyo's doing and why he's doing it,' she says. 'I know it comes from the heart and that's what's important. Obviously I'd like more time with him, but at the moment the country comes first.'

It's hardly surprising that Tokyo labours with such zeal. Since his teenage years, when he was 'incensed by the wrongs in society' he has been 'at the forefront righting the wrongs'. At 17 he joined an underground ANC cell and operated across the border from Swaziland for several years before being trained in the Soviet Union as a military engineer. Returning to the country as an MK commander in 1976, he operated undercover for six months before his arrest and subsequent trial for terrorism. Narrowly escaping the death penalty, he was sentenced, at the age of 24, to 18 years on Robben Island.

On more than one occasion since his release Tokyo has told journalists that they have yet to catch up with the real Sexwale. I ask him what we will find when we do.

'A father who should be spending more time with his children,' he says frankly, without skipping a beat. 'This is the age when they need you most. There's also this person yearning for sleep. A man who yearns to go home and take a holiday. A person who would like to have a braai right now ...

'Behind the gladiator,' continues Tokyo, 'stands a person who has dreams and aspirations like everybody else. A man who loves and wants to be loved. A man who wants to hug his children and spend time with his wife.

'Most of us forget to be a father and a husband,' says Tokyo, continuing before I can pop the next question. As Judy later remarks, this is a man who loves to talk.

'We forget and we smash the family. So you must have that lone sentry in your subconscious who reminds you to go home. A sentry who says "*Don't* accept that additional meeting or that additional call. You've got an appointment with your children and your wife".'

Sometimes, admits Tokyo, that sentry nods off, but Judy steps in and with big black letters in his diary, reminds him that it's family time. And, before I can even begin to speculate that this may be a source of tension in his marriage, Tokyo adds, 'My sentry agrees with Judy.'

It's not that Tokyo doesn't enjoy rest and recreation. One look at the way he's sprawled out on the bench bears testimony to that. It's just that being a gladiator requires unwavering commitment.

'I can't relax here while people out there are suffering,' he says. 'When I do shut off, it's very pleasing. But is also makes me feel very guilty. It's like being a doctor. I've got patients out there with political ailments that need attention.'

I figure that Tokyo's trying to tell me that the move to Lower Houghton (his wife's idea, I later learn) does not mean he's deserted the people or the cause. I also wonder whether his sense of duty isn't perhaps a hangover from his Catholic schooling.

'People ask how I can live here,' he says later, making sure he has made his point. 'But our struggle for freedom and justice in this country has always been against the townships and matchbox houses. Our fight has never been *for* poverty, but one that aims to uplift the people. I may live here, but I *die* for Phola Park and Soweto. I don't forget where I come from. There's a difference between living in Lower Houghton and dying for the stock exchange.'

Like Tokyo's televised tears at the assassination last Easter of his friend Chris Hani and his subsequent heroic calming of young township hotheads bent on revenge, the Sexwale love story is a symbol of hope for the emerging non-racial order.

Tokyo's other great fear is that his people might fail 'to achieve true democracy in this country'.

But not everybody shares this belief. That's why the Sexwale house is guarded day and night and why Tokyo daren't leave the house without armed protection.

'This job is a severe health hazard,' is his apt summation. It restricts the family's recreation options. Simple pleasures like window shopping and walks with Chris and Gabriella down the wide, tree-lined neighbourhood avenues are out of the question. So too are spur-of-the-moment outings to the movies or a restaurant because Tokyo feels it's unfair to demand any more time from his already overworked bodyguards.

He confesses that one of his fears is 'my immediate death'. Not because he's scared of dying. That's part of being a gladiator. 'But to leave these children without a father ...'

Tokyo's other great fear is that his people might fail 'to achieve true democracy in this country'. And then, just in case I see this admission as a chink in his armour, he tells me that *personal* failure never fazes him.

'Look, I'm irrepressible,' he says. 'I always come back. I *never* say die. That's why I never respect a suicide. You have to realise that failure is part of life.

'But where there's failure there's also challenge. I like that. I psyche myself on "never say die". Not in the sense of being reckless, but in the sense of finding another way of dealing with a problem. That's my strength.'

Tokyo has talked a lot and, if I read him correctly, has revelled in this time away from his responsibilities. Were it a Sunday, I'm quite certain he'd light a braai.

But I cannot make up my mind whether I've caught up with the man Judy calls Masimo (his Sotho name which, significantly, means the sturdy central pillar of a hut). The gladiator who unwinds to Schumann and Handel 'or anything else that sounds good on the ear'. The missionary whose supreme confidence can sometimes be misinterpreted as self-flattery, but whose conversation never for a moment

dwells on personal political ambition. A politician who, on the eve of a momentous election, never once pitches the party manifesto.

So, as he rises to dress for work, I lob one last question in the hope it will reveal something more.

'Will I have to call you Mr or Minister Sexwale after 27 April?'

'No. After the election, you can still call me Tokyo.'

Ten years later Tokyo Sexwale is one of the richest men in the country described variously as 'a champagne communist', a 'mogul' and 'South Africa's very own Donald Trump'. In fact, in June 2005 Tokyo hosted a local version of Trump's reality TV show 'The Apprentice'. After the 1994 election Tokyo became the Premier of Gauteng before leaving public office for the private sector. In 2003 he reportedly paid R15 million for Oude Kelder, a wine farm in Franschhoek. He is currently head of the multi-million-Rand mining company, Mvelaphanda. He is still married to Judy.

Uys into Gear

For years, with outrageous humour as his weapon, our Rambo of the stage blasted away at the hypocrisy and complacency of the absurd old South Africa. Pieter-Dirk Uys is enthusiastic about the new emerging nation, but equally confident that there will be plenty for him (and Evita) to satirise.

Marianne van Kuik

Fairlady 6 April 1994

In the leafy, sleepy Cape Town suburb of Pinelands, there nestles a darling, thatched, shuttered house straight out of *Hansel and Gretel*, complete with huge gnarled trees and squirrels in the garden.

Inside, it's crammed from floor to wooden-panelled ceiling with books, magazines, mementos, gewgaws, and more books. Every available surface is silted up and only the windows have been begrudged any clearance for a little daylight to trickle in. The effect, though, of all this literary flotsam and jetsam is neither messy nor chaotic. It's like entering an old library used primarily by thoughtful, scholarly academics.

For Pieter-Dirk Uys, it is a centre that can hold, the house he grew up in and the place he has once again made his base.

'Pasop die Rottweiler,' he cautions me as his little poodly dog (called Kitty) skitters across to greet me. (He's such a randy *malgat*,' Pieter tells me later, 'forever shagging an old doll called Oom Hendrik.')

I'm ushered through the warren of rooms to the music room where Pieter-Dirk launches into the conversational equivalent of the two-step: serious, funny; serious, funny; serious, funny. Serious about why he's funny, and funny while being serious.

'Someone in Australia once asked me, if I'd been a black South African, would I still be wearing dresses and telling jokes? No, I wouldn't. I would have been a member of MK. But I hate violence with an absolute passion, and I find humour is a much stronger weapon. You cannot fight it, lock it up, or kill it. A sense of humour is a basic democratic right.

'That's why political correctness is so dangerous. People become scared of laughter, and laughter is opinion and without opinions you can't have democracy because democracy is an *orgy* of opinions.'

As he speaks his delivery speeds up and up until his voice is an express train of swift ideas and racing emotions.

'I have to know *why* I do things. I'm not just a Master of Ceremonies

'The fact that black people have actually accepted us is in itself unbelievable, it's an absolute miracle. And to watch the younger generation take all the changes of the past four years in their stride is just great. Dreams are being dreamt again and there's an enormous amount of compromise and goodwill. We just have to keep focusing on the good guys.'

but it's also dangerous to think you can change people's opinions. No satirist in the Weimar Republic stopped Hitler.

'But I can laugh at fear and prejudice and make others laugh at its absurdity. Laughter gives you strength and cheekiness and helps you handle things. I get so bloody angry, that the only way I can prevent myself from hanging myself from the nearest tree is to know that I must filter this anger through the various absurd structures and characters of my work so that it comes through entertainingly, so that you can bear it, but it's still clear and sharp enough to make you go, "Ooooooh, Eina!"

'If we don't keep that humour outlet, we'll go stark raving mad. We're going to eat Volkswagens in the street!'

Fortunately for all VW owners, Pieter-Dirk is hard at work keeping us on a saner diet with a countrywide tour of *One Man, One Volt*, his special election show, and the publication and recording on audiotape of *A Part Hate a Part Love*, the no-holds-barred biography of Evita Bezuidenhout.

It is actually the story of apartheid as seen through the eyes of the Bezuidenhout clan, beginning with Evita's *ouma-grootjie*, Sarie Marais.

Apartheid, says Pieter, with his small trademark smirk, will soon be simply the footnote in history: 'There once was a crazy tribe of relatively decent white people who went mad and had to be put down. Democratically, of course.'

Many people may be 'poeping themselves' as Pieter puts it succinctly, but he himself can barely contain his excitement at the imminent 'change of baggage'.

At last, after 48 years. *Fantastic!* It's wonderful; it's so exciting! Democracy, the new position we've never tried before, is going to be as much fun as sex – only safer.'

So you're full of optimism then? I say somewhat superfluously.

'Look, I'm full of enthusiasm. He qualifies. Optimism is a very relative thing. My definition of optimism is when I expect the worst to happen in the hope that the worst won't be as bad as I imagine.

'Stupidity in politics is unfortunately something we have a huge copyright on, but there are *so* many good, compassionate people in this country.

'The fact that black people have actually accepted us is in itself unbelievable, it's an absolute miracle. And to watch the younger generation take all the changes of the past four years in their stride is just great. Dreams are being dreamt again and there's an enormous amount of compromise and goodwill. We just have to keep focusing on the good guys.

'I think we've got a really good chance of having a relatively balanced democracy. Yes, the ice is thin, we could also sink in 24 minutes, but this is a country where relationships at grassroots level *can* make a difference.'

To the worried 'My-God-we're-going-to-lose-everything' brigade Pieter has this to say: 'Think of the future as a health farm. We all need to go on a strict diet and there's some pain as you get rid of your toxins and things, but then you suddenly emerge stronger and better for it. And ready to swim naked across the Rubicon.' He adds a little sadly, 'I just hope people won't carry on going away. I miss the kugels.'

Pieter-Dirk Uys recently returned home from an immensely successful performing tour abroad. It did a lot to restore his confidence which, he admits, suffered a knock during a wave of negative criticism which he 'nearly believed'.

He is inspired by Helen Suzman, Robin Williams and

Pieter Dirk Uys: 'This is a country
where relationships at grassroots
can make a difference.'

(*Photo:* Angie Lazaro)

'Apartheid, *liewe genade*,' she exclaims with high-pitched fervour, 'I don't know *anybody* who supported it. Goodness gracious, it was all so long ago. A silly experiment that didn't work. If we'd called it ethnic cleansing we might have got away with it.'

Shirley Maclaine, whom he loves for her wonderful eccentricity and brilliant talent and who says, 'Believe in yourself and it *will* happen.'

In May, Pieter will be off travelling again.

'To China in a train. I do try to do one absolutely crazy, exciting, different thing every year. It's the greatest to be crazy. Many of my contemporaries have just given up on adventure.'

In between the crazy times, Pieter is a hard and disciplined worker. At his desk by 6 am, with a rigid, tight schedule. When he needs a breather, he pops into a morning movie, or takes the dogs for a walk along Blouberg beach. He loves seeing loyal old friends, but hates dinner parties with people he doesn't know.

'Now Pieter, say something funny,' he says in a plummy whine of the southern suburbs socialite and shudders.

'And I can't sit around listening to people talking about money all the time.'

I ask him how Pieter the satirist would send up Pieter the person.

He is, for the first time this morning, silent and stumped.

But for a few moments only.

'He would have a chocolate in one hand, a glass of wine in the other, a faceless person staring at his Filofax.'

A far cry from the way the public perceives him. Say Pieter-Dirk Uys to any South African, and their mind's eye immediately conjures up the imposing, overdressed personage of the ex-ambassador of Bapetikosweti, Evita Bezuidenhout, his most famous impersonation.

Pieter is enormously proud and fond of his extraordinary creation, but has never fallen into the temptation of converting or whitewashing her. He's kept her as charming and callous as ever, as I discover when I turn up again a few days later to interview her in her full Pretoria powersuit regalia: fireman-red jacket and black skirt, blindingly accessorised.

With Pieter I'd felt quite at ease. In his slightly frayed jersey, he is just so informal, so free of pretentious crap. But Evita is intimidating. Intimidating the way John Vorster Square can be intimidating. She smiles her face-lifted smile at me as if she were just another kindly *tannie*, and she answers my questions with saccharine benevolence, but I am not fooled.

The granite cheekbones and the flinty eyes glittering beneath a canopy of mascara are the giveaway. A fascist can hire a Saatchi and Saatchi image consultant but can she change her soul?

'Apartheid, *liewe genade*,' she exclaims with high-pitched fervour, 'I don't know *anybody* who supported it. Goodness gracious, it was all so long ago. A silly experiment that didn't work. If we'd called it ethnic cleansing we might have got away with it.'

I noticed though that she's very gentle and affectionate with her 'grandchildren' (two little poppets posed by models for our photographic shoot).

How does she feel about them being black?

'I *love* my little grandchildren,' she says with genuine and perhaps unexpected sincerity. 'You know, all children are children until they grow up, then they become black or white. They're very sweet, they don't blame me for being white and a Nationalist and I certainly don't blame them for waving their colourful ANC flags all the time.

'There's Winnie Jean, Nelson Ignatius and the new one La Toya Ossewania. La Toya is, of course, named after one of those Jacksons. I get so mixed up with the Jacksons. The only one I really know is Jesse Jackson, because he's the only member of the Jackson family who doesn't look like Diana Ross.'

I ask about her son, De Kok.

'De Kok is very involved with gay liberation. It's a very important thing for South Africa. All our movements have been far too serious for far too long. We need a lot of gayness. If the ANC and the AWB all go gay, SA will be a much happier place.'

She won't discuss her sister Bambi.

'*Ek het niks meer oor haar te sê nie*. She married a Nazi, I married an Afrikaner. You can't compare the two. We succeeded, the Nazis didn't.'

What makes her really happy?

'Pik's jokes, Pik's potjiekos and Mandela's smile, a wonderful smile. And the realisation that black SA will now have to start taking responsibility for SA, they can't point a finger any more, they will have to rule the country, they will be watched by the civilised world and CNN, and they will have to be taxed. Democracy means everybody gets the chance to have an ulcer.'

Among her reading matter she includes the *Government Gazette*, several magazines, including *Fairlady* – 'it's always nice to know what black people are doing' – and Margaret Thatcher's biography on audiotape.

She's been much inspired by the Iron Lady – 'I used to bring her biltong. She didn't know what to do with it and so she planted it thinking it might grow, and it did! And now there's a biltong tree at Number 10. The sad thing is, she's not here any more and the happy thing is, I am.'

Bapetikosweti doesn't exist any more as a homeland but, says Evita, Bapetikosweti will always be there as a state of mind. Anyone can live there.'

Evita herself feels ready for the new South Africa and the 'first non-racist, non-sexist, non-sensical election', her confidence spurred on, no doubt, by a golden handshake, a Swiss bank account and her own inimitable resourcefulness.

I'm relieved when Evita disappears upstairs and Pieter returns, albeit with a blue smudge of forgotten shadow under his brow.

Impersonations – from Evita to Koornhof to Tutu to Winnie M – are something Pieter-Dirk Uys has turned into a fine, fine art. His technique, he says, is to pick up two mannerisms.

'Usually what the hands and the mouth do. And the same with the voice. It's an alphabet of muscles and gestures. I know where the muscles are that will make them work. You've just got to concentrate completely. It *is* difficult, thank God. I'd hate it to be easy.

'Nelson Mandela is difficult – he's such an icon and so dignified – but I'm working on him. There's nobody I won't do. If politicians don't like laughing at themselves, they must retire to the Wilderness or somewhere.'

Pieter-Dirk Uys now lives in Darling and performs regularly at his theatre, 'Evita se Perron', as well as on international stages across the globe. He has won countless awards for his work. Evita still performs at Pieter's theatre when she's in town and the government still writes Pieter's scripts.

Going Fishing

Author Rian Malan
contemplates
political changes in
South Africa.

Rian Malan

Fairlady 6 April 1994

I went to a dinner party the other night at the home of a socially prominent person who should probably remain nameless, given that he might
be your best friend, for all I know.

In any event, it was a hot night, so we sat on the stoep, ate lamb chops,
drank red wine and talked politics. The guest of honour was the foreign
editor of a British newspaper. The token Negro was Aubrey from Guguletu,
who wanted to know whether we rich white liberals were not feeling a bit
threatened by the impending changes.

'Not at all,' cried our host, scion of one of South Africa's oldest and richest
white liberal dynasties.

'On the contrary!' he cried, 'I'm ecstatic!'

This did not sit well with Aubrey. Indeed, it upset him to think that the
owner of a five-bedroomed mansion with several servants and a swimming
pool should be so cavalier about the coming triumph of the impoverished
masses, so much so that he was inspired to deliver a corrective.

'My brothers in the shacklands,' he said, 'are just relaxing at present, not
bothering to hustle for jobs or money because they figure these will fall from
the trees once Mandela comes to power. Some even believe they will be
entitled to come into the suburbs on 28 April,' he said, 'and pick any house
of their choosing.'

'Indeed,' he concluded, 'I should not be at all surprised if several don't
have their eye on this one.'

It was a very fine performance, I thought; a little rude, subtly malicious,
but entirely called for. Our host's jaw dropped, while I fought down an im-
pulse to applaud. There's too much woolly-minded thinking in the suburbs
these days, too much guff spoken about win/win situations and similar fig-
ments of the anxious white imagination. The time has come to face facts.
All struggles produce victors and vanquished, and ours is finally coming
to its end, to the bit where victors pop champagne corks and collect their

All struggles produce victors and vanquished, and ours is finally coming to its end, to the bit where victors pop champagne corks and collect their prizes while the rest of us slink off to sulk and feel sorry for ourselves.

prizes while the rest of us slink off to sulk and feel sorry for ourselves.

When the sun rises on 28 April, they will have won; we will have lost. (They being the ANC, we the NP or DP or whatever. I could say whites and blacks, but it comes to the same thing, considering that 98 percent of us will be voting the racial ticket, according to the polls.)

Nothing will ever be the same again.

After that our taxes will rise. Our standards of living will fall. Resources will be diverted into the townships, and our roads will develop potholes.

All the best government jobs and state contracts will go to Africans. Your daughter has little chance of becoming a SABC-TV personality, and your son will never be ambassador to the court of St James. You'll probably keep your mansion, but as for the bushveld game farm and the bungalow in Plett, I wouldn't bet on it.

And if this depresses the hell out of you, all I can say is lighten up, comrade! Uhuru is at hand, and it's going to be lekker for us too, in ways that are just now beginning to dawn on me … tktktk

Bear with me while I explain.

Okay … so let's go back to the beginning, back to the bad old days of forced removals, job reservation and petty apartheid, to the time when TV was forbidden, books and movies banned, and ANC detainees were constantly slipping on bars of soap or falling out of windows. Something was rotten in this country, but what did we do, we spoilt members of white bourgeoisie? Mostly, we just said tut-tut, and sat back to count our money.

That's why I couldn't bear the white suburbs when I was young, or the stench of moral hypertrophy that hung over them. The fumes addled me so badly that I became a socialist of some amorphous sort, cursed my parents, donned the hair shirt and embarked upon the path of asceticism, renunciation and virtuous eschewal.

Many of us took that particular road. Some went to Crown Mines or Woodstock, into community medicine or the trade unions. Some went all the way to Dar-es-Salaam and Moscow. Myself, I got off in Bertrams, a bleak reach of face-brick semis on the east-side of Joburg downtown.

Bertrams was drab. It was poor. It was grey, inhabited by an interesting mix of Chinese people, upwardly bound coloureds and university-educated whites, driven down into the lower depths by an enormous burden of guilt and complicity.

There were buttonheads on the doorstep and *bloutrein-ryers* across the way. Things went blam in the night, voices screamed, sirens wailed. Bertrams was so low it was almost level with the *grevel,* which is why people like me moved there.

The general idea was to dress down, drink Tassenberg, drive a battered old Volksie and otherwise blend with the proletariat. You did not hire servants in Bertrams. You did not go to the Caribbean or to Plettenberg Bay on holiday. If you had parents in Houghton or Constantia, you lied about them, and anyone with a weakness for single-malt Scotch kept this shameful secret to himself.

As for high-society dos, you wouldn't be seen dead. The white left did not don penguin suits and cocktail dresses and swan around the dance floor, sipping French champagne. The white left stayed at home, ate boy's meat and read Gramsci. It was all very depressing in retrospect.

I found myself thinking about Bertrams a few months ago, while waiting for the Miss World competition to get under way.

I was sitting in King Sol's Superbowl, spotting celebrities and marvelling at the astonishing transformation we have lived through since those bad old days. There were many changes of course, but for me, the one most

Rian Malan

(*Photo*: Jacques de Villiers)

Nelson Mandela donned a penguin suit and waltzed into the very most rarified reaches of high society, where he schmoozed with the Ruperts, the Mendells, the Searlls and the Venters.

shocking came in the aftermath of the Great Leap Forward, when the ANC's top leaders stepped on to centre stage and turned out to be affable chaps in three-piece suits with a taste for precisely the sort of bourgeois revelry I had once found so disgusting in white people.

Cyril Ramaphosa confessed a weakness for single-malt whiskies and fly fishing, Thabo Mbeki acquired a BMW, Jay Naidoo got married in a Rolls Royce, Tambo settled in Hyde Park, Boesak in Constantia, Sexwale in Houghton.

Nelson Mandela donned a penguin suit and waltzed into the very most rarified reaches of high society, where he schmoozed with the Ruperts, the Mendells, the Searlls and the Venters.

The nation's private schools were suddenly teeming with little Ramaphosas and Maharajas, and portly Adelaide Tambo became a regular at Hoogland Hydro.

None of these luminaries was present at the Superbowl, but I spotted several NGO heavyweights among the bejewelled and tuxedoed masses, and at least one former Bantustan director, now aligned with the ANC. The perfumed elite of Soweto was out in force to root for Jacqui Mofokeng and the ANC was represented by Wally Mongane Serote, widely regarded as Minister of Culture in waiting.

Twenty years ago, Serote was writing poems about pouring petrol on white children and setting them on fire, but look at him now, gliding through the crowd like a statesman, bussing cheeks, pressing flesh, allowing his ring to be kissed.

I thought, I love this. This is fascinating.

I mean, Peter Mokaba was there!!!

If you told me in my Bertrams days that the ultra-militant leader of the ANC Youth League would one day attend such a gathering I would have laughed at you, but there he was, in the flesh, living it up with the bourgeois

pigs and plotting (if the papers are to be believed) to seize control of the entire glittering extravaganza.

God, what an enormous relief, to discover that our most fearsome mainstream fanatic was actually riddled with ordinary frailties, and quiveringly eager for status, luxury and deals! It was, in a minor way, a Damascus Road experience.

I thought, hey, there it is: free at last, free at last. Free to turn my back on Bertrams, order a bottle of French champagne, and not feel in the least shit about it.

Which brings me, at last, to the point of this story, which is the hidden upside of uhuru. I mean, think about it, bru. Liberation from guilt! Redistribution of responsibility!

The freedom to sit back in an armchair and snigger while Nelson and them wrestle with the nation's monster problems. The joy of watching the ANC trying to collect rents in Soweto, or forcing its juvenile petrol-bombers and stone-throwers to siddown, shaddup and listen to teacher.

Sure, you might be less comfortable than you used to be, and screwed to boot by affirmative action, but you will no longer be to blame for everything. On 28 April, the burden of government will lift off the bowed shoulders of the baas class, and descend on the backs of our ANC brothers, and from that point on, whatever happens will be their fault. Within weeks, you'll probably be wondering why you wanted power in the first place and why you were so cruelly determined to keep it in white hands. In fact, you will probably be chanting a slogan borrowed from the ANC. Never again! Never again!

We can only speak for ourselves in this regard, of course, but these are the blessings I anticipate from my own private uhuru.

Never again will I have to argue with foreigners and leftists who think SA is a simple country, and democ-

> And never again will I bite my tongue and refrain from criticising blacks because I'm afraid of sounding like a racist, or on the more honourable grounds that it is unfair to criticise people whose lips are sealed by banning orders or prison doors.

racy the cure for all its tribulations. Never again will I give myself headaches trying to devise solutions for the problem of poverty in South Africa. Never again will I be called upon to stick knitting needles in my eyes in an orgy of guilt-stricken self-flagellation over, say, what the Boers did to Steve Biko, and the way it left Jimmy Kruger cold.

And never again will I bite my tongue and refrain from criticising blacks because I'm afraid of sounding like a racist, or on the more honourable grounds that it is unfair to criticise people whose lips are sealed by banning orders or prison doors.

Such restraint is no longer necessary. The ANC has become an elephant, as Nelson Mandela puts it, and we are mice, and thus free to squeak.

Here goes: What on earth is Winnie Mandela doing at number 31 on the ANC hit parade, and she a convicted felon? And why did Miriam Makeba praise Gabon's dictator for his contribution to democracy? Is this a question of low standards, or is Ms Makeba merely stupid?

See? It's easy. I've already freed myself. I can say nasty things about black people and not feel at all uncomfortable.

But I can say kinder things too. Such as this, for instance. I wish Mr Mandela the best of luck, but I would rather not stand in his shoes. Indeed, I often fear that the rigours of the job will be too much for the old man.

For a start, he'll have to clean up the mess we've left behind us – apartheid's appalling legacy of corruption, inefficiency and gross maladministration. Then he'll have to tackle a mess of the ANC's own creation: wild schools, bankrupt municipalities, chaos and criminality; the legacy of the ungovernability campaign. And, finally, he'll have to tackle the real problems – find food for the hungry, jobs for the wretched, and homes for the untold millions who sleep under rusting *sinkplaat*.

But how? If you raise wages, exports become uncompetitive. If you raise taxes too high, capital flees. If you turn the land back to the landless, food prices rocket because high-tech Afrikaner agri-businessmen are vastly more efficient than peasants with donkey ploughs. And if you do nothing, the poor start burning cars, throwing stones and shooting shopkeepers with AK47s.

I've been mulling over this conundrum since I was 12 years old, the same old what-ifs chasing the same old if-onlys around my brain and never really going anywhere. Something always had to be done, and I always felt that we had to do it – we being whites, the bosses, the baas class. This was an insufferable arrogance of course, and quite typical of the white supremacists, but as long as white rule persisted, it was more or less true. Everything was our fault, and had been since the day I was born. Come 28 April, that will cease to be the case.

I'm so tired of carrying the white man's burden. Indeed, I wish we'd never picked it up in the first place, back in 1652. We would have been poor but richer in spirit, and our black brothers might have been less bitter and angry. In fact, we might even have been friends by now.

Hey, bru! Do you really want this thing we've clutched so selfishly to our white bosoms for so many bitter generations? Take it. It's yours. I'll help if I can. But right now, I'm happy just to lay it down and go fishing.

Rian Malan has settled in Cape Town where he remains unsettled and continues to practise what Anton Harber, Caxton Professor of Journalism and Media Studies, has described as a 'carbuncular journalism – that kind of writing designed mostly to get under people's skin, produce pain and pus and possible infection'.

'In every piece Malan writes,' Professor Harber added, 'one is never quite sure if he is being searingly honest or just contrarian. Certainly, he finds a way to go against the grain time after time and has made a successful international writing career off it. Certainly, he is himself at the focal point of most of his own writing.'

In a predictably unpredictable turn, Rian penned a surprisingly reconciliatory piece for the Sunday Times in 2004 in which he apologised for having been so pessimistic about the country's future.

'The gift of 1994 was so huge that I choked on it and couldn't say thank you. But I am not too proud to say it now.'

President Thabo Mbeki was so taken by Rian's piece that he quoted parts of it during his State of the Nation speech that year.

Also in 2004 a piece Rian had written for the Spectator questioning AIDS statistics and suggesting that the AIDS 'industry' had inflated numbers to secure funding, provoked robust and vitriolic public debate.

Professor Harber's take on the issue was that there is: 'Nothing wrong with questioning statistics, one has to say; and it would be no great surprise if, given the fight to get HIV/AIDS on the global and South African health agendas, there had been some overexuberance in stating the problem. Malan was certainly noticed. He was noticed by the AIDS dissidents, who trumpeted his article. And by the AIDS activists, who are vilifying him. And by the president, who I suspect was responding in his parliamentary speech as much to the oxygen Malan gave to the AIDS dissident industry as to his mea culpa on the new SA.'

Rian Malan remains one of the most controversial and widely-read South African journalists.

A Show of Friendship

After the divorce of the decade Winnie Mandela was in no mood to talk to the press. But Hazel Crane, her best friend and self-appointed spokesperson, was. The question is, just how much of Winnie's life is she really privy to?

Mike Behr

Fairlady 12 June 1996

It was as if Winnie Mandela had disappeared off the face of the earth. The telephone in her million-rand Orlando West mansion rang and rang. So too did the direct line to her office at parliament. And Caroline, the polite secretary staffing the presidential office at the ANC Women's League, had no idea when next she would see her boss.

We were about to contact Mrs Madikizela-Mandela's lawyers at Seriti Mavundla in Pretoria when a colleague suggested we speak to Hazel Crane, jet-setting commodity broker, self-made millionaire, champagne-and-caviar socialite and, let's not forget, best friend of Winnie Mandela.

Yes, that cocky, carefully coiffured blonde. The one who went public about her Winnie connection in 1994 in a blaze of headlines that trailed a whiff of scandal over *that* house in Bishopscourt. You know, the luxury mansion that Hazel and her Israeli lover and business partner Shai Avissar bought for R675 000 for the use of the then Deputy Minister of Arts and Culture because they felt sorry for her over her financial plight.

The very same woman who was rumoured to have bankrolled large outstanding debts on Winnie's mansion as well as the R150 000 court-contested bill for Winnie's hire of a Lear jet used in a botched diamond-buying trip to Angola.

Hazel was also present at the closed meeting held at Winnie's home in 1994 when Pakistani President Benazir Bhutto presented a cheque to be distributed among a number of women's organisations. Winnie was later accused of depositing the cheque into her controversial Co-ordinated Anti Poverty Programmes (CAAP) account.

Fortunately, Hazel is easier to contact than Winnie. She's listed with Telkom's directory enquiries and she answers her own cellphone. Not just any old cell mind you, but a faux-wood-panelled status symbol.

During the public row that ensued from the purchase of *that* Bishopscourt house, Hazel told the *Sunday Times*, 'Don't poke your nose in my business.'

Hazel Crane – 'Call me the million-dollar kid.'

(*Photo:* Debbie Yazbek)

'Every person I've introduced to Mrs Mandela
has been stunned by her charm and her strong
personality. Those are qualities that a lot of people
fear. Which is wrong, because she's such a loving,
giving person.'

With the press baying at her and Winnie's doors for comment on the divorce, I half expected a similar response. But Hazel is not only polite, she is eager to talk – about Winnie. She begins with an analysis of Winnie's bad press.

'Every person I've introduced to Mrs Mandela has been stunned by her charm and her strong personality. Those are qualities that a lot of people fear. Which is wrong, because she's such a loving, giving person. If I have a crisis, the first person to arrive on my doorstep is Winnie. Even when she was under great stress during her divorce case she took the time to ask about my niece who was recently born prematurely. She considers my family her family.'

The following week, during a call to confirm our interview, Hazel offers a rather unusual affirmation of their friendship.

After a strenuous session of tennis with her Sunday lunch guests, Hazel, who loves to win on the court as much as she loves to make money, collapsed in a spasm of pain. She had to be hospitalised the next morning. While she was undergoing a series of medical tests that later revealed a kidney stone to be the cause of illness, Winnie arrived in a flush of concern.

'She told me that she'd been worried sick and that I looked terrible, which I did. While she was talking I suddenly said, "Winnie! I'm going to be sick ..." and she said, "Oh, my God!" and grabbed a bowl and held it while I was sick all over her, all over the examination table, all over the floor. Then she lifted me from the table and into a chair and held my head while I vomited again. I was very embarrassed, but she said, "Everybody gets sick, Hazel. I'm glad I'm here to help you."

'That is how compassionate Mrs Mandela is. You don't know that side of her, but that's what she does for her friends.'

Hazel Crane and Shai Avissar share a large, white, double-storey house in Abbotsford, a small, very exclusive pocket of leafy suburbia tucked in between Melrose and Houghton in Johannesburg. In keeping with the rest of Gauteng's moneyed class, prison-high walls guard the expensive acre of real estate. The house itself is as unremarkable from the outside as it is on the inside. It's expensively furnished and there are all the antiques that money can buy, including a magnificent 18th-century silver candelabra, heaps of other silverware and rare porcelain clown dolls from Russia (Hazel collects them). But the rooms are gloomy and the lack of a unifying design theme is reminiscent of a very up-market bric-a-brac shop. Although Hazel spends much time redecorating rooms, *Habitat* is unlikely to come knocking at her door.

After announcing my arrival through an intercom, I pass through the main gate watched by an imposing marble eagle perched on the arch above. On the other side I'm met by Hazel's assistant, Desire, who guides me across well-kept lawns dotted with bell-shaped bird cages containing parakeets, a green Amazon parrot called Scarlet, who can say 'Hello Winnie', and a pair of African Greys called Nelson and Winnie. (The latter have not been separated because, Hazel later assures me with a mischievous giggle, '*They* still love each other.')

The venue for the interview turns out to be Hazel's sunroom, a bright, glass-enclosed, rectangular balcony furnished with green upholstered cane furniture and a cane bar counter containing an assortment of soft drinks. One wall of the room is plastered with photographs of the rich and powerful. Most of them feature Hazel.

Hazel with Thabo Mbeki. Hazel with Winnie and Benazir Bhutto, Hazel with Peter Mokaba, Popo Molefe – and the odd one out, *The Bold and the Beautiful* heart-throb Ronn Moss, who plays Ridge Forrester. Each one is intriguing, but one is particularly revealing.

Taken at a dinner at Adelaide Tambo's home, it looks like the photographer set out to capture a beaming President Mandela alone. Until Shai popped into the frame at the last second, with opportunism so swift that it fuzzed his image.

Hazel enters a few minutes later in a businesslike flurry and a blaze of money; designer white jacket and matching skirt from Morgans of Knightsbridge, black Wolford stockings monogrammed in white up the back seam, and a pair of fashionable but precarious-looking Socrati high heels made in Greece. Boasting big, broad laces and six-centimetre heels that boost Hazel's height to just over five foot, they're part of a huge collection housed upstairs in four cupboards.

'If I show you my shoes, you will die. I've got as many as Imelda Marcos,' she brags with a naughty chuckle, remarking that that is the only thing she has in common with the late Philippine despot's wife.

'I haven't met her,' she then offers without being asked, 'but I've met Corazon Aquino.'

Remarkable as her wardrobe is, though, it pales into insignificance when compared with the exclamation mark behind Hazel's bold, and for this time of day, somewhat brash fashion statement: an obscene, glittering display of diamond, emerald and gold jewellery.

Apart from her large, round, black-and-gold Versace earrings and her diamond-studded gold watch, the other chunky items were a gift from Shai, who designed them.

Her watch hand is the most loaded, with a diamond and gold tennis bracelet and three rings; one diamond creation and two diamond and emerald designs (one containing a 6,26-carat diamond, according to Hazel). Her right hand is dominated by a whopping 6,22-carat Colombian emerald and diamond encrusted 'H'. (Shai wears an identical bracelet.)

A smaller but similarly paved 'H' hangs round Hazel's neck on another heavy gold-link chain.

'Call me the million-dollar kid,' she teases when I remark on her jewels.

The last time I saw so many carats in one place was on a sorting table at Harry Oppenheimer House in Kimberley. Although Hazel is coaxed into volunteering their approximate worth, her call the next day persuades us not to print the amount.

'I discussed it with Winnie and Shai, and they both said it wouldn't be safe. Somebody would probably rip my arm off. Just say I was wearing expensive jewellery.'

Hazel admits she has always worn lots of jewellery.

'I've got loads of it. If I see a nice stone I'll always have it set into something special. That's why they call me the diamond queen,' she chuckles, in reference, I presume, to the nickname the press gave Hazel during her lengthy 1993 trial for illicit diamond buying.

She was sentenced to a R50 000 fine or two years in jail with an 18-month jail sentence suspended for five years. Although Hazel says she successfully appealed the case in 1994, both sentence and conviction were upheld. The Appeal Court did, however, overturn the compensatory order that required Hazel to pay R101 335 for the eight unpolished diamonds (40,46 carats' worth) that went missing in a bungled police trap.

'I say I'm innocent,' Hazel said later. 'The police were liars and they know it. I paid the fine because I couldn't handle it any more. The press had a field day. But that's one of the joys of being Winnie's friend.'

Charges against Shai in the same case were withdrawn, but he has since been the focus of various fraud allegations.

While I bask in Mrs Crane's jewel-refracted sunbeams, she issues last-minute instructions to Desire for the faxing to the Seriti Mavundla law firm of a press statement that would appear in the papers the following day. (Hazel runs many such errands for Winnie.)

Strangely, it's not an explanation for why Winnie failed to appear in court the day after her divorce to claim a portion of the president's assets, but a denial of earlier criticism that Winnie was incurring unauthorised expenditure on private bodyguards and had failed to return two luxury cars and two cellular telephones when she resigned as deputy minister last year.

'As usual, it's all blatant lies,' says Hazel. 'The government knew the cars and cell phones were at Shell House. Why didn't they just collect them instead of going to the press? And this thing about her bodyguards – she has two like any other MP, even though she should have more. The country would be in complete chaos if something should happen to Mrs Mandela.'

With the press statement out of the way, Hazel dismisses her assistant with an abrupt 'I don't want to be disturbed,' quickly adding the proviso, 'If Winnie phones, call me. There's something I want to discuss.'

Hazel gets as far as explaining that a commodity broker is a high-class middleman who collects commission for putting sellers of coffee, cotton, construction materials, textiles, fancy goods and food in touch with buyers, when her cellphone rings.

'Hi Winnie,' she says, shooting me a well-what-did-you-expect smile. 'How are you?' she continues, leaving the room and closing the door firmly behind her. In an instant my ear is pressed to the door, but I can hear nothing. I consider using an empty glass to eavesdrop Hardy Boys-style, but the prospect of discovery restrains me. The sliding door to the sunroom is wide open and workers are renovating Hazel's glamorous swimming pool, complete with neo-Grecian columns and fountains, ten metres away. Scarlet is also eyeing me from her cage and I'm not quite sure how articulate she is.

Hazel returns about ten minutes later with apologies and a teasing air of mystery that sheds little light on her conversation. Later, the sceptic in me wonders whether the call was a set-up, but Hazel assures me that she and Winnie spend a lot of time on the telephone.

'Mrs Mandela is always checking on my whereabouts. She likes to know if I'm all right.'

The feeling is apparently mutual but, unlike Hazel, Winnie is often uncontactable ... 'even though I know a thousand places where I can reach her'.

Realising that I'm not about to prise any more about Winnie's call from Hazel, I turn the spotlight on her. She responds. Hazel loves talking about Hazel almost as much as she loves talking about Winnie.

Quickly rewinding she reveals that just over two decades ago she was a 23-year-old mother of a four-year-old daughter Hayley and seven months' pregnant with her second child, Anthony, when her husband, a Rhodesian lance corporal, was tragically killed in a land-mine explosion while on a routine military exercise.

'It was like someone pricked my balloon,' recalls Hazel who, by her own admission, was a well-heeled Bulawayo housewife who never wanted for anything.

'But lying in a hospital a few weeks after the funeral with a premature baby in my arms I realised that there were a lot of other people worse off than me. It dawned on me that I was quite capable of making a successful life of my own.

'I could have taken the easy way out and got married again. But I wanted to find my own independence and give my children the best that life could offer.'

Hazel had already been a nurse, a banker and a home-based book-keeper. But she knew that none of these would make her rich. So she says she invested her war-widow's pension in a nightclub and restaurant (and later a hotel), and started acting as a middleman to various unspecified commodity deals.

But Hazel grew too big for Bulawayo, so she relocated to her birthplace, Belfast. Her stay was short-lived because she couldn't stand the chauvinism.

'I couldn't do business with men who treated women as second-class citizens.'

In 1981, Hazel Crane arrived in Johannesburg with four suitcases, two children, R9 000 'and the intention to either make or break'.

Her first job was with a personnel agency. From there she switched to selling short-term insurance for a top company and moved swiftly up the ranks. She realised then that selling was her niche.

'I'm a natural,' she says. 'I sold a policy to an Afrikaans guy using hand signals because I couldn't speak Afrikaans.'

In the mid-'80s Hazel switched to selling life assurance, but by 1989 the pond had again grown too small, so she started her own insurance and commodity broking business. By now she was well off, but this was when Hazel's irrefutable chutzpah, determination and talent for self-promotion started making big money. Today at 45, this pint-sized dynamo claims she is a millionaire, possibly a multimillionaire.

'It's hard to say exactly how much I'm worth because I don't keep check. Once you make your first million you want to make more. I've got my eyes set on becoming a billionairess in about five years from now.

Half an hour later Hazel can no

longer stand the tension.

'You've asked me about me, but you haven't asked me about Winnie,' she says.

'What would you like to know … Is it strange that a white woman can be friends with Mrs Mandela? You see, being a gutsy person I'm not afraid of anything. So when I speak to Mrs Mandela we speak on the same level. When people see this they are amazed and say, "But *that's* Mrs Mandela." But I say it doesn't matter because Mrs Mandela is my closest friend. We get on like a house on fire.'

Hazel then launches into another diatribe against the press for unjustly pillorying Winnie and steadfastly failing to acknowledge that she is 'a caring mother and grandmother and a compassionate champion of South Africa's children'.

The general thrust of Hazel's spiel, repeated at intervals throughout the interview, is that Winnie Mandela is a victim, not of her own calamities, but of a malicious Third and Fourth Estate conspiracy.

Using the infamous 'necklace and matches' speech of 1986 as an example, I remark that Winnie is often the architect of her own bad press.

'I would have made a statement like hers if I had been black and living in the apartheid system,' snaps Hazel irritably.

'All she wanted then was what she wants now: freedom for her people and their upliftment. If you had been in the same situation, you, too, would have stood up and said we'll burn them with matches, we'll necklace them with our tyres or whatever it was. It was the heat of the moment.'

Hazel Crane met Winnie Mandela nine years ago while she was trying to flog insurance policies to the black workers at a Johannesburg paint factory. Apparently it was love at first sight because, after a long chat, they became bosom buddies. As a sign of commitment, Hazel even started to attend ANC Women's League meetings and eventually joined the organisation.

Around this time, Winnie's thuggish bodyguards, under the guise of the Mandela United Football Club, were conducting a reign of terror in the name of liberation. Between 1987 and 1989 they were implicated in more than a dozen rapes, kidnappings and murders, including Stompie Seipei, a 14-year-old activist whom Winnie accused of being a state spy. In 1991 Winnie was convicted of kidnapping Stompie and three other youths and of being an accessory to the assaults on them. On appeal, the accessory to assault conviction was overturned in 1993, and her jail sentence was reduced to a fine and suspended sentence.

It was a testing time for many of Winnie's friends and comrades. But not for Hazel.

'Like the president, I believe Mrs Mandela is innocent. And if I believe in something, *nothing* will change my mind.'

With Winnie's past glibly dispensed with, Hazel turns to the present. But with exasperation I soon discover that behind all her shameless strutting and faux discretion, Hazel Crane is as baffled by her

Although Hazel has admitted to paying for Winnie's clothes (most memorably, the black-and-gold lace Spero Villoti outfit Winnie wore to the president's inauguration), she isn't telling exactly how much money she has dished out. On the other hand, she can't resist making it clear that cash does change hands.

best friend's recent behaviour as the rest of the country. This in spite of the fact that she claims to be the shoulder that Winnie leans on during her troubled times.

Instead of the promised low-down on the divorce of the century, Hazel Crane wants me to believe that she was not privy to her best friend's divorce strategy! That she had no idea why Winnie nominated Kaiser Matanzima (a collaborator she wouldn't have been seen dead with in the '80s) as a divorce mediator, a move that deeply shocked and insulted the president.

This, even though Hazel claims she was grafted to Winnie's side when she left the Rand Supreme Court in March this year a divorced and defeated woman.

Most incredible of all is that Hazel the hardened businesswoman, who by her own admission is a financial wizard, hasn't the foggiest why Winnie failed to appear in court the following day to fight over her ex-husband's assets, estimated to be around R40 million.

Considering that Winnie had indicated that she would claim half her husband's estate, and that Hazel, her benefactor, stood to gain from any settlement that big, it's hard to explain why she didn't marshal every financial and legal resource at her disposal to support Winnie's claim.

Unless, of course, she wished to perpetuate Winnie's financial dependence.

'We didn't discuss the divorce because it's none of my business,' says Hazel. 'I've tried not to take sides or influence her in any way. I'm her best friend, but she's not going to tell me how she's going to end up financially after her divorce. I'll read about it in the press like everyone else.'

Finally, the penny that's been threatening to drop for the last hour descends with a deafening clang. Winnie may be Hazel's best friend, but Hazel is not Winnie's. Dispense with all the smoke and mirrors and it's really nothing more than a paparazzi friendship.

Sure Hazel and Winnie talk. They visit each other frequently, and Hazel wines and dines Winnie in her home and various posh Gauteng restaurants. Occasionally Winnie returns the favour. But their talk, according to Hazel, is frivolous. They swap fashion and beauty tips and chat about their children. But they never talk politics.

It's a friendship of sorts all right, but there are telltale signs that it has about as much substance as Shai's audacious photo opportunity with President Mandela.

There's Winnie Mandela's business card, which Hazel presents to me as proof of friendship. And the framed Christmas card in the sunroom signed 'All my love, Winnie Mandela'.

How many of us frame cards sent to us by our best friends? And how many best friends sign their greeting card with their surname to avoid confusion over their identity? Then again, maybe that's unfair. Hazel might know more than one Winnie.

The bottom line is that this show of friendship makes good business and social sense to a woman who is so self-conscious of her nouveau-riche rank that a journalist sharing her chauffeured silver 260 E Mercedes rides up front with her driver. It's a relationship that turns heads in restaurants and ups Hazel's profit margin.

'My friendship with Winnie doesn't taint my business reputation,' she says, appalled at the suggestion. 'If anything it enhances it. International visitors love to meet Mrs Mandela. Every time they come into the country the first thing they say to me is, "Is it possible to meet Mrs Mandela?" My close friends and associates who have had the honour of meeting Mrs Mandela have always been dazzled.'

Winnie might be Hazel's most trumpeted friendship, but they are poles apart in some respects. What would

Winnie Mandela do if FW de Klerk happened to step into a lift with her? Greet him? Ignore him? Insult him? Who knows? One thing is certain, she wouldn't follow Hazel's example. Bowled over recently by a chance meeting with the deputy president she declared, 'It's a privilege to be sharing a lift with you.'

The other odd feature of the friendship is that Hazel can't stop babbling about it, whereas Winnie seldom acknowledges it in public. After the Bishopscourt house affair, the then deputy minister let a spokesperson speak for her.

During a surprise 50th birthday party organised by Hazel last year, Winnie did, however, toast the friendship with revealing off-the-cuff flippancy.

'Hazel and I both learnt how to run away from the system,' she said as she cut her cake with a fur-wrapped Hazel at her side. 'She with her diamonds and I by fighting the system.'

The comment, reported in the media, served another purpose as well. By casting Hazel as a modern-day Robin Hood, Winnie was justifying their association to her constituency, who must surely wonder what their firebrand is doing courting the kind of rich white woman that this government, in the eyes of Mrs Mandela, is being too soft on.

The quid quo pro for Winnie Mandela is, quite simply, money. Hazel is her financial lifeline, especially when debtors are banging on her door. How else could she balance her private expenditure which, according to documents submitted to the divorce court, exceeds her R90 000 every month?

Although Hazel has admitted to paying for Winnie's clothes (most memorably, the black-and-gold lace Spero Villoti outfit Winnie wore to the president's inauguration), she isn't telling exactly how much money she has dished out. On the other hand, she can't resist making it clear that cash does change hands.

'Let the press gossip about when I've bailed Mrs Mandela out. Only Winnie and I know what we've done together. I am not prepared to say anything more. It wouldn't be right. If I had financial problems and had no money, Winnie would be the first person to help me out. A good way of putting it would be great friends think alike.'

In spite of a marathon four-hour interview that included lunch at a Melrose Japanese restaurant (where Hazel, the charming host, coaxed me to eat sukiyaki dipped in raw egg while regaling me with an anecdote about a live monkey being decapitated for its brains in a Hong Kong restaurant), I'm no closer to Winnie and the drama behind the divorce.

Hazel calls me a day later, though, to tell me that Winnie was very curious about our interview.

'She told me that she nearly came round to the house. But if she had, you would have asked questions, and I told her that she's not ready for that yet. Instead, I've arranged to introduce you to Mrs Mandela the next time we are both in Cape Town, hopefully in two weeks' time.'

The part of me that warmed to Hazel's irreverent wit and polite friendliness wanted to believe her. But more than a month has passed and there's still no word from Winnie Mandela's office. And I guess that once this story is printed, I'll be persona non grata. It's disappointing because the meeting might have produced a great story. But things could have been worse – I could have held my breath after Hazel's tantalising call.

In 2000 Hazel Crane's diamond-dealing husband, Shai Avissar, went missing for three months. His body was later found buried in a shallow grave. He had been beaten to death with a baseball bat. In 2003 Hazel Crane was shot dead in her Mercedes Benz by an unknown assassin while en route to the Johannesburg High Court to sit in on the trial of Lior Saadt, the man accused of murdering her husband.

And so ended one of the more sordid sagas of Johannesburg's high society.

Charges against Mr Saadt were later withdrawn when the investigating officer died of a heart attack and two other witnesses were murdered.

Who's Afraid of Christine Qunta?

Corporate law is highly aggressive and still dominated by white males, so it's not the obvious arena for a black female attorney. Unless, of course, you're as spirited as Christine Qunta and relish stamping out persistent stereotypes.

Marianne van Kuik

Fairlady 12 May 1999

Steely eyes appraise me from between saucy braids when I first step into Christine Qunta's cool, high-rise office in the centre of Cape Town. She's smartly dressed in an ivory-coloured suit and the atmosphere is formal for a few moments – until she breaks the ice with a witty remark and a jazzy laugh that's packed with more energy than a shebeen in full swing. As anyone who has listened to her fortnightly SAfm radio slot already knows, there are few subjects on which she does not hold an impassioned opinion. During our interview we whizz through African history, the forthcoming elections, Nkosazana Zuma, women's magazines, Felicia Mabuza-Suttle and Oprah Winfrey. But it's when we move on to the racism that still bedevils the working lives of black professionals that she is most forceful.

Christine obtained her law degree with flying colours from the intellectually elitist University of New South Wales in Sydney, Australia and is today an experienced attorney and partner in a well-established practice with Dumisa Ntsebeza.

She's also the author of *Who's Afraid of Affirmative Action*, a survival guide for black professionals (Kwela Books). So when a new client, a white man, recently turned to her during a briefing session and enquired, 'Can you do a power of attorney?' Christine felt the blood rush to her head.

Doing a power of attorney is a basic task; her assistants can do it with their eyes closed. Christine's automatic response to any racial or gender insult is to lash out, but she's learning to check herself.

'Stay calm, stay calm, I told myself, he may have meant it as a joke.' But she could tell from his expression that he was dead serious.

'And he had no clue how offensive the question was. He sees a black woman who is supposed to be a lawyer, but in his mind I'm not. If I'd been a white male, he would *never* have asked me that question.'

The insult might have been unintended, but Christine is adamant that his remark – and its implicit questioning of her competence – is 'a sign of how

> Officially, apartheid may have died, but in the hearts and minds of South Africans, she says, echoing Nelson Mandela at the opening of parliament in February, bigotry is still alive and kicking.

damaged we still are as a nation'.

Officially, apartheid may have died, but in the hearts and minds of South Africans, she says, echoing Nelson Mandela at the opening of parliament in February, bigotry is still alive and kicking. And it's not restricted to rural backwaters: Racism continues to rear its primitive head in corporate corridors all over South Africa.

'Whites still hold the power in most of the large corporations, and the problem is that when they deal with black women, a white person's main frame of reference is still domestic workers. They find it difficult to relate to us on any other level. Consequently we black professionals are still faced with hundreds of small, daily humiliations. These may be subtle and often there's no meanness behind them, but they're emotionally painful all the same because they stem from a deeply ingrained belief in the inferiority of blacks.

'The result is that as a black person your self-esteem is constantly being undermined. Just last month, when I was at the airport checking in at the business-class desk to fly to Joburg, the woman behind the counter looked at me and asked, "business or economy?" If I'd been a white male, she wouldn't have dreamt of double checking.'

Charitably, Christine believes most whites would actually be shocked if they knew how much their attitudes hurt.

As an activist in the Black Consciousness Movement during the early '70s and during her subsequent 17 years in exile, Christine learnt to assert herself and be proud of her race. It's the reason why, to this day, whenever she senses that she's being underestimated, she automatically goes into battle mode.

'And I *never* lose,' she declares gleefully. 'In fact, the few who've tangled with me have found it a rather traumatic, life-altering experience!'

A skirmish with Christine is evidently not something anyone, not even her daughters, should undertake lightly.

Two years ago, when her elder daughter, Yolisa (then 17), briefly rebelled by going nightclubbing against her mother's wishes and then flitted off with some of her cousins, Christine acted without hesitation. She stormed to the nearest police station and reported that her daughter had been abducted. For good measure, she called cabinet ministers Dullah Omar and Steve Tshwete too, before setting off to roam the streets in search of Yolisa.

'Constitution or no constitution,' she laughs wryly, 'it's lucky for her that the police found her first!'

Christine's average working day is long – about 13 hours – as well as challenging, so she cannot, she says firmly, afford any emotional distractions.

Isolated incidents apart, she has a very good relationship with both Yolisa (19) and Nzinga (15).

'Yes, they do complain that they don't see enough of me,' she admits. 'They do get short-changed because I cannot short-change my career – too many people depend on me. But I try to make it up to them on Sundays and I make a point of never missing the important school functions.'

What Christine also does is use every opportunity to strengthen their self-esteem. 'I tell them they don't have to straighten their hair or lighten their complexion. They're beautiful as they are.'

The girls are regularly reminded that Ma doesn't like people who are not determined and that she won't tolerate cowards. You don't get anywhere by whimpering, no matter how difficult life gets – that's the message.

It certainly took more than intelligence to propel Christine along her own brilliant career path. If she hadn't had an extra-large dose of relentless determina-

Christine Qunta – 'Most whites would
actually be shocked if they knew how
much their attitudes hurt.'

tion, it's doubtful whether she would have made it all the way from her humble beginnings to the prominent positions she now holds.

(Apart from running her practice, she sits on the Competition Board and on several company boards. She is also active in the Black Lawyers' Association.)

As the middle of seven children of a domestic worker and an absent father, Christine grew up very poor, moving between Kimberley, George and Bonteheuwel on the Cape Flats.

'I went to primary school barefoot because I didn't own any shoes.'

When Christine was in Standard 8 at Arcadia High School in Bonteheuwel, her maths teacher opened her eyes to the possibility of leading a more fulfilling life.

'Many of the girls in my township were pregnant and had no other ambitions, but he tried hard to get through to us. He'd say, "Do you all want to be domestic workers for the rest of your lives?"

'Those words made me realise for the first time that the answer was, "No, I want to do more with my life."'

Her first wish was to become a microbiologist, but she could do so only at the University of Stellenbosch, which in those days admitted very few black students.

So Christine went off to the University of the Western Cape instead to study law, 'because I had the delusion that the law was about justice'.

She became actively involved in the Black Consciousness Movement and in 1975, after being detained by the security police, went into exile in Botswana.

'It's just as well I left because I was distributing pamphlets and defying the authorities so openly that I wouldn't have survived the 1976 uprising,' she says.

A scholarship took her to Sydney, where she graduated with a BA LLB degree and seven distinctions.

'They'd been concerned that I might not cope academically, but I surprised them,' she says demurely.

In between her studies and positions in Sydney, Gaborone and Harare, she married and had her children. After separating from her husband, she returned to Cape Town with her daughters to check out the newly emerging South Africa.

In 1995, after two years in Sanlam's corporate legal department, and the year in which she established her own

When Christine was in Standard 8 at Arcadia High School in Bonteheuwel, her maths teacher opened her eyes to the possibility of leading a more fulfilling life. 'Many of the girls in my township were pregnant and had no other ambitions, but he tried hard to get through to us. He'd say, "Do you all want to be domestic workers for the rest of your lives?"'

law firm, she wrote *Who's Afraid of Affirmative Action*.

The prime motive of the book was to help lessen the isolation experienced by blacks in the corporate workplace and to offer practical advice. But whenever Christine expresses her views, controversy is guaranteed to follow. Many whites, outraged at some of her remarks on radio and in the book, have accused her of racism. Many managers and career advisers too, have criticised as short-sighted her advice to black professionals to refuse to do menial tasks such as typing, race-related tasks (such as translating) or anything that is not stipulated in their job descriptions – not even to help out on a rare occasion.

I'm not surprised to hear that she's unfazed by criticism. Airing views frankly is vital to a healthy society, Christine believes. And when you're speaking out openly and honestly, you can't expect everybody to agree with you.

Between waging legal battles, debunking myths and broadcasting her opinions, there is not all that much spare time for Christine's life. But she does make a point of going to gym three times a week 'because I never want to feel unfit'.

And to balance her life, she practises yoga and goes for massages and 'spending time with good friends does that for me too, and so does listening to music: Sibongile Khumalo, Vusi Mahlasela, Miriam Makeba and West African music.'

She also loves good movies and good books, both fiction (Toni Morrison and Chinua Achebe are favourites) and non-fiction (Egyptian history and astrophysics are her two main areas of interest). One thing she never does is watch television.

'We don't even own a television set. I don't like having people I don't know from a bar of soap in my sitting room.'

Christine even turned down a recent offer from e.tv to present one of its programmes.

'My daughters thought I was crazy,' she laughs. 'They would love the glamour and glitz that goes with being a TV celebrity.'

But for Christine Qunta, a life of controversy and challenge continues to hold far, far greater appeal.

A few 'Qunta-isms':

On ageing
'I don't care about wrinkles. This obsession with looking young is a peculiarly European neurosis. In Africa, youth is regarded as foolish and age is revered. I like being 46, wise and mature! I'd hate to be 20 again. You're so gross when you're young.'

On Africa
'In the history of advanced civilisations – some, like Egypt, are at least 4 000 years old – the 500 years of calamity that we have been through as a continent is but a blink.'

On social functions
'I generally avoid them. The food is usually atrocious, and more often than not one is condemned to sit at a table with guests who are boring.'

On lawyers
'Lawyers are not the most pleasant people around. If I wasn't a lawyer myself, I probably wouldn't mix with them!'

On her body
'When store assistants show me clothes that will hide my hips, I tell them I don't want to hide my hips, I want to show them off! Big hips are beautiful and voluptuous.'

On Oprah
'She's the bland queen of American pedestrian culture, but she may be more intelligent than she appears to be.'

Christine Qunta is currently a partner in the law firm Qunta Incorporated and continues to provoke debate with her regular column in Business Day.

Smooth Operator

Rian Malan

Fairlady 1 September 1999

Chris Barnard is fond of saying the heart is just a pump. There are those who would agree that his certainly is.

I t was by most accounts, a fairytale romance: She was a sweet young model with baby-blue eyes and blonde hair; he a medical legend, tall, dark and handsome, on first-name terms with presidents and film stars, and yes, something of a Don Juan.

Their marriage in Cape Town in January 1998 was a society affair teeming with celebrities. The reception was held at La Vita restaurant, owned by the groom, and Dean Street Mall in Newlands was closed for the occasion.

Of course there were raised eyebrows about their 40-year age difference. At 23, Karen Setzkorn was seven years younger than Deidre, Dr Chris Barnard's daughter from his first marriage to Louwtjie. And while some hoped that after two failed marriages the dashing doctor would find true happiness with lovely Karen, many feared the marriage might end in heartbreak for the ageing heart-transplant pioneer.

They were assuming, of course, that Barnard would lose his hair and his sex drive and spend his dotage playing with his grandchildren, like an ordinary mortal. And, for a while, this appeared to be his destiny. The newlyweds lived quietly and soon started a family.

Barnard appeared to be mellowing with age, taking delight in his babies, Armin and Lara. There were no outward signs of trouble, but in the back of your mind was always the thought that if any scandal was brewing it would be the glamorous ex-model who ran off with a younger man, leaving Chris with crippled hands, a flagging libido and haunting memories of all the film stars and lovelies he'd bedded during his life.

How different is turned out to be. Indeed, Karen was the one to file for divorce, with her husband initially expressing regret while lamenting that there was 'bugger all' he could do about it. But pity for the lonesome ex-surgeon began to vanish when serious speculation began doing the rounds about an alleged Viagra-driven affair with an even younger woman. It seemed the man with an ego bigger than Table Mountain and a legendary

Chris Barnard – 'up there with the
Apollo astronauts and the Beatles'.

(*Photo: Sarie*/Jacques Stander)

There were no outward signs of trouble, but in the back of your mind was always the thought that if any scandal was brewing it would be the glamorous ex-model who ran off with a younger man, leaving Chris with crippled hands, a flagging libido and haunting memories of all the film stars and lovelies he'd bedded during his life.

lust for pretty young girls was at it again.

Don't get me wrong – Dr Chris Barnard was one of my childhood heroes, up there with the Apollo astronauts and the Beatles. Come to think of it, I tended to confuse him with James Bond, to whom he bore a striking resemblance – same dark hair, dazzling smile and air of effortless mastery over speedboats, casinos and women. It's just that as time passed I began to wonder if fame hadn't come to mean more to him than the advancement of science.

Some time ago, I arranged an interview, and we met in his house, on an oak-lined street under Table Mountain. He answered the door himself, dressed in a blue cotton shirt, white slacks and Reebok sneakers. Only weeks earlier some Frenchman had dismissed him as a 'surgical opportunist' who should never have gone down in history as the first man to perform a heart transplant. The real pioneer of heart transplants was said to have been Dr Norman Shumway of California, who'd allegedly spent ten years doing the experimental legwork on which Barnard's triumph was based. Barnard noted, slightly irritably, that the allegations had since been withdrawn and apologised for under threat of legal action.

But it did get him talking about the '50s, when he and Shumway were younger graduate students at the University of Minnesota, studying under the great Dr C Walton Lillehei, a pioneer of open-heart surgery.

To medical students, the heart is 'just a pump', as Barnard is fond of saying. But to laymen, it's the putative seat of consciousness, the centre of one's being, an organ that skips a beat when you kiss, breaks when you're sad and so on. In comparison, the liver and kidneys are just lumps of meat. Cardiac surgeons are the rock stars of operating theatres, and Barnard and Shumway were stars among stars, the brightest of Lillehei's bright young men.

The ambitious young Barnard earned two advanced degrees in less than half the time it took the average student to earn. Shumway, for his part, wrote a pioneering thesis about operating on hearts that had been chilled to 15°C. After that, the two went their separate ways. Shumway took up a post at Stanford University, where he began to lay the groundwork for human heart transplants, perfecting his surgical technique on dogs. Barnard returned to Cape Town, where he performed dazzling operations on the hearts of babies and wrote many letter to his old professor in Minnesota, complaining mournfully of isolation from the frontiers of science.

In 1964, surgeons at the University of Mississippi caused a sensation by transplanting the heart of a chimpanzee into a dying human. The operation failed and the patient expired on the operating table.

Generally, people were put off by the procedure, which seemed a bit freakish, like something out of Frankenstein. Barnard, on the other hand, was inspired, and decided that he, too, would become a transplant surgeon.

There was a lot of catching up to do. He embarked on a feverish programme of animal experimentation, mastering the techniques Shumway had initiated. Then he returned to America to study kidney transplants and immunosuppression. By 1967, he had joined Shumway on the cutting edge.

In one respect, Barnard was lucky to be working in Africa, thousands of kilometres removed from the disapproving scrutiny of jealous peers and over-fastidious medical ethicists. In Cape Town, he was a law unto himself in many ways, inclined to make up rules as he went along. In November 1967, he identified grocer Louis Washkansky (55) as a potential heart transplant recipient. A donor was found on 2 December, when

Denise Darvall (25) was fatally injured in a car accident barely a kilometre from Groote Schuur Hospital. She was young, she was healthy, and now she was brain-dead on a life-support machine. Her father gave permission, and Barnard just went ahead – summoned his surgical team, said a brief prayer, and switched off Darvall's lifeline. Her heartbeat died away to nothing.

Barnard waited for about 30 seconds, then he made the first incision.

And this, in retrospect, was his great achievement, in the estimation of his former colleague Dr David Cooper: He had the courage to venture into the unknown before anyone else and to face consequences which could have been devastating, given that he had neglected to inform his superintendent. Denise Darvall's heart was placed in Washkansky's chest cavity and sewn in place.

For several unnerving minutes, it lay inert, but Barnard applied an electrical stimulus and, at last, the contractions began. Washkansky's chest was closed, and Barnard stepped into a blue summer dawn to tell the world what he had done.

Within days, Barnard was sucked into the social jet stream, the most famous doctor on the planet. As for Shumway, he performed his own first heart transplant three weeks later, and then returned into a sullen silence that stretches unbroken to this day. Cardiac surgeons declined to gossip on the subject, and Barnard has always bristled at the suggestion that he and Shumway were engaged in a race for medical glory.

'We did it because we were ready,' he said. 'None of us ever imagined the publicity that would follow.'

If it is true, as Barnard argues, that the events of 3 December 1967 were exaggerated out of all proportion by over-excited reporters, how will history judge his feat?

Medical writers generally agree that he was lucky to be first. At the time, several surgeons had skills equalling his. Any of them could have beaten him to the draw, but none, in the final analysis, could match Barnard's record. His first three transplant patients survived an average of 443 days each. Those of his arch rival Shumway died on average after 22. Ninety-one percent of Barnard's heart recipients survived for at least 12 months. Dorothy Fischer lived almost 13 years and Dirk van Zyl lived 24, eventually succumbing to diabetes while his transplanted heart still ticked away gently.

These are achievements for which Barnard would have been venerated even if the Washkansky transplant had been delayed for a week or two and someone else had walked off with all the fame. Barnard would have remained a great surgeon, widely honoured. But he would never have had sex with Gina Lollobrigida.

Barnard was 45 on the day of the first transplant, married with two children, and to all appearances a good Afrikaner, son of a Karoo *dominee* and of a woman who believed that dancing was the first step to hell. Then he was engulfed by a fireball of publicity and adulation, and transmuted into a playboy. He traded in his wife of 21 years, a nurse called Louwtjie, for 19-year-old heiress Barbara Zoellner, explaining that 'I can't be enamoured of an ageing body.'

> Barnard would have remained a great surgeon, widely honoured. But he would never have had sex with Gina Lollobrigida.

He seduced actresses and models galore, offering as justification, 'I just wanted to satisfy myself that I could have any woman I wanted.'

Between conquests, he wrote self-help books (*Heart Attack – You Don't Have to Die*) and racy airport novels (*The Unwanted*) whose chief distinction was his name on the cover. His research career went into a decline, and he seemed to be losing interest in medicine entirely by the time arthritis forced his early retirement at the age of 60.

This was in 1983, five years before he married for a third time, and stranger was to come. Dumped by Barbara, Barnard began dating girls barely out of their teens. Searching forlornly for youth's elixir, he attached himself to a Swiss clinic that specialised in rejuvenating injections for the rich and vain, and later he became a consultant to an outfit that used his name to market an anti-ageing cream. When that collapsed, he came forth

'You know,' he said towards the end of our interview, 'the tremendous reaction to Washkansky really did catch us unaware. I was trained to look after patients, but not to handle all that publicity. All of a sudden everybody wants to meet you, you're being invited all over the world, meeting the best and the most beautiful people. At that stage I should have got an agent to guide me and keep me out of trouble. Instead, I decided, well, these things have come to me, let's make use of them while we can. So yes, I made some mistakes.'

with a second autobiography – *A Second Life* – in which he recorded his sexual exploits in scandalous detail. In one memorable passage, for instance, he described sleeping with three women in six hours, one of whom, the French singer Françoise Hardy, had breasts too small for his taste. Even his friends were aghast, and began to mutter about senility.

Years on, I scanned the famous face for signs of same, but none were evident, although the famous brow was marred by several liver spots, and one eye was slightly drooping. The Don Juan of Beaufort West was getting on a bit, no doubt about it, but the swash-buckling aura was still largely intact. Young Karen bustled in and out, looking lovely as ever, hair and fingernails just so. A baby was gurgling in the nursery, and Barnard spoke lovingly of the joy he derived from his new family. Outwardly, he and Karen seemed happy.

The rumours started last summer. Chris was bored; Chris was straying; Chris had been seen with another woman, even younger than the superbabe to whom he was married. Cape Town society was staggered. 'It can't be true,' said one noted hostess. 'The man's 77, for God's sake.' But it was.

Towards the end of July, Karen issued a summons for divorce. As this article went to press, Cape Town was aflame with gossip regarding the impending scandal, with Karen coming in for a great deal of sympathy while heads shook in amazement over Chris's refusal to act his age.

'You know,' he said towards the end of our interview, 'the tremendous reaction to Washkansky really did catch us unaware. I was trained to look after patients, but not to handle all that publicity. All of a sudden everybody wants to meet you, you're being invited all over the world, meeting the best and the most beautiful people. At that stage I should have got an agent to guide me and keep me out of trouble. Instead, I decided, well, these things have come to me, let's make use of them while we can. So yes, I made some mistakes.'

It was an odd note of humility from a man known for his overweening ego. Barnard seemed to be saying, I learned my lesson. But it was clearly too early to be certain.

In 2001, Professor Chris Barnard, aged 78 died of an asthma attack while on holiday in the Cyprus resort town of Paphos.

True Romance

Rory Steyn and Debora Patta

Fairlady 10 May 2000

The wedding of Nelson Mandela and Graça Machel on the former president's 80th birthday on 18 July 1998 was the official seal on one of the 20th century's greatest love affairs. In a new book Rory Steyn, head of Madiba's personal protection team, and journalist Debora Patta trace a romance that continues to delight the world.

Madiba is sitting in his favourite armchair, legs stretched out. His new bride has kicked off her shoes and is sitting on the floor by his side. Graça Machel and Nelson Mandela have been married for only two weeks, but their relationship is characterised by the kind of intimacy shared by couples who've known each other a long time.

'I have only two priorities in my life right now,' the president says. 'Number one, Graça; and number two, eating prawns in Mozambique.'

He may be joking, but his words contain a measure of truth. For a man whose life has been defined by politics, whose every decision has been based on a concern for the greater good and in whose life the personal has always been sacrificed for the political, it's only now, in his 80s, that he's seizing what's left of his life and making it his own. And this delight in the joys of Mozambican cuisine is really a metaphor for the change that's come about in him.

It became clear Madiba was hankering after something more after his divorce from Winnie Madikizela-Mandela, when he said she'd never once come to visit him in their bedroom after his release from jail. The divorce finally took place in 1996, after much ducking and diving by Madikizela-Mandela. After years of doing the right thing for the struggle and South Africa, Madiba followed his heart. The result is a romance that's been billed as one of the last great love affairs of the 20th century.

Initially their relationship was conducted in great secrecy. But it wasn't long before Graça had won the approval of everybody on the president's team.

Bodyguard Quentin Henwick says, 'There was no doubt that it was love. You just had to look at the president's eyes to see the sparkle there.'

The time the new couple spent together was extremely limited. Not only did they have to keep their relationship secret but they both had extremely busy schedules. In spite of these constraints and the physical distance between them, their romance blossomed. From the beginning of their rela-

Madiba and Graça on their wedding day.

(*Photo:* Pool/Walter Dhladhla/Reuters Archive/ The Bigger Picture)

From the beginning of their relationship, they began a practice of never ending a day without talking to each other. The president wouldn't go to bed if he hadn't phoned or faxed Graça, no matter where they were in the world.

tionship, they began a practice of never ending a day without talking to each other. The president wouldn't go to bed if he hadn't phoned or faxed Graça, no matter where they were in the world.

On one occasion, Mandela insisted on personally buying chocolates for his lady love. The bodyguards had to sweep through a plush shopping centre with sniffer dogs, clear the area of any potential danger and then keep back the crowds who mobbed Mandela as soon as they realised who was doing the shopping.

Such pandemonium, but it was nice to see this common, romantic touch. And it wasn't a one-off. Mandela got into the habit of visiting the shopping centre to buy chocolates, flowers and other romantic gifts for Graça. Never once did he delegate this task to any of his staff. He was determined to do it himself, even if it meant turning everything upside down. Eventually, the couple felt it was time to go public. The story was deliberately leaked to the media, and Mandela's office then confirmed it officially a day later. Machel was to be given the title of 'Official Companion' and would accompany Mandela on state visits and other functions when his schedule permitted it. To their delight, news of the love affair was met with widespread support from all but the most sour of South Africans. Whenever they had to say goodbye to each other, it was like a physical wrench. On the extremely rare occasions when Graça managed to persuade Madiba not to travel with her to the airport, he'd come out of the house with her and they'd kiss like teenagers, unashamedly, in front of the entire waiting security contingent.

'She would get into her car and he would continue to wave and blow kisses until the vehicle was out of sight,' says Henwick.

But in spite of intense media speculation, there was still no talk of marriage. And not because Mandela didn't want this. He pestered Machel for months, but she was firm; she simply didn't want to marry, chiefly out of concern for her children and preserving the name of her late husband. So instead, in a thoroughly modern relationship, Machel and Mandela lived together.

What the public didn't know was that by 1998 Mandela had convinced Graça to marry him. But they decided their relationship was an intensely private affair and they would celebrate it by having a wedding that was theirs and theirs alone. Everything had to be organised with the utmost secrecy. They were finally married on Madiba's 80th birthday, on 18 July 1998.

Machel says the secrecy was absolutely necessary. If they'd had a public wedding they would've had to invite thousands of people, and that wouldn't have been possible, she explains.

'We couldn't invite all our friends and because of that we would've hurt some people. We decided to treat everybody equally and not tell anyone until after the wedding.'

Says journalist Jon Qwelane, 'Mandela, a man whose playground is the entire world, could easily have married his Graça in a blaze of publicity, with the world's media networks in attendance and the globe's high and mighty worshipping at the couple's feet.'

Instead, a few close friends and five clerics from the major religious denominations in South Africa were the only witnesses. Walter Sisulu and his wife Albertina were there, as were Thabo and Zanele Mbeki, Ahmed Kathrada, Dullah Omar and his wife Farida, and Jacob Zuma. Graça's two brothers were flown in from Mozambique, accompanied by a government official from the neighbouring state. And Mandela's sister left her home in Qunu specially for the occasion. They were the only family members given the green light to attend.

The only 'outsiders' were Prince Bandar El Saoud of

Saudi Arabia and Yusuf Surtee, friend and tailor to the president. The joyful Archbishop Desmond Tutu made sure Prince Bandar was welcomed into the small community and cheekily informed everyone they'd better treat the royal visitor kindly because 'he should give us oil'.

For a man revered as one of the century's truly great leaders and statesmen, there was no lavish feast or wasteful expenditure. For Madiba it was a double celebration: a wedding and a birthday. And the best present he could ever have wished for was, of course, the hand of his beloved Graça.

Everyone was overjoyed that Mandela had at last found happiness. His personal assistant, Zelda la Grange, says before Mandela met Machel, 'It would break my heart to see him sitting alone at night. There he'd be, in his favourite armchair, with a blanket over his legs, all alone.'

Afterwards, says La Grange, he was a different man. 'There's more balance to his life with Graça around.'

Graça could've chosen to give up her job and live the life of easy luxury as South Africa's First Lady. But instead she remained a working woman, a mother and very much her own person. Within the marriage itself, too, Machel would not be 'told what to do' by her husband.

It's significant that she didn't agree to 'obey' her husband when they exchanged wedding vows. A thoroughly '90s woman, she chose instead to 'love, honour and cherish Nelson Mandela' – a commitment taken from a modern version of the Church of England's marriage ceremony. The woman who put the sparkle back in the president's eyes and a spring in his step is fiercely independent and continues to uphold this independence.

While he was still president, you wouldn't always see Machel at Mandela's side at official functions, for South Africa's new First Lady was determined to continue her

> Machel says the secrecy was absolutely necessary. If they'd had a public wedding they would've had to invite thousands of people, and that wouldn't have been possible, she explains.

work in Maputo. She also continued to travel around the world in her role as ambassador for Unicef (the United Nations Children's Fund), and the couple maintained residences in South Africa and Mozambique.

Before the marriage, Graça would visit Madiba on average about two weeks out of every month, while he would often sneak up to Maputo for a weekend of prawns and sun. Even now, these arrangements continue as if nothing has changed. But perhaps the most remarkable thing of all is how comfortable Mandela is with the arrangements – particularly given the fact that he comes from a generation where men were quite firmly the head of the household, and he's part of a culture not particu-

What she'll tell you is that although she doesn't like comparisons between Samora Machel and Nelson Mandela, she does believe she's been married to the two tallest trees in Africa.

larly hot on equality of the sexes.

Machel's modern approach to life, love and career began long before she met Mandela. She was born Graça Simbine, and went on to become a university graduate who speaks four languages, and a freedom fighter as a member of Frelimo's armed struggle for independence. She married Samora Machel a few months after Mozambican independence in 1975 and was the liberated country's first Education Minister, a post she still held at the time of her husband's death in a plane crash in 1986.

Graça is an intensely private person, seldom giving interviews and carefully guarding her personal life. Even after her marriage to Madiba, she shed little light on their relationship. She'd tell you that while she'd had no intention of ever remarrying, 'only a very special person, as Madiba is, could make me get married again'.

When pressed further as to exactly when and how they'd fallen in love, all she'd say in her charming Portuguese accent was, 'How did we meet in terms of eye to eye, that we have something clinging between the two of us, this is our secret.'

What she'll tell you is that although she doesn't like comparisons between Samora Machel and Nelson Mandela, she does believe she's been married to the two tallest trees in Africa. And she concedes that perhaps what drew them together was a certain loneliness with the hectic pace of their lives.

'Of course we talked and we realised both of us had been lonely. It's true, but more important than being lonely is that we both suffered in life. And if you are lucky, as we are, to get a very happy moment, you will enjoy it much, much more than before. You had the experience of what it is to suffer, what's pain; that's why this relationship is really so, so sweet. We can appreciate much better what it means to be together and to have someone who really, really loves you. So it's different and it's much sweeter than probably, you know, when you are very young. When you are 20 years old, you have all these dreams, it's just dreams, but one thing is reality which you can touch.'

Another reality is the families that surround both of them. The Machel family is extremely close, and was one of the reasons Graça was reluctant to marry Mandela sooner. Since the death of their father, the children (five from Samora's previous marriage and two of her own) have surrounded her with a kind of protective love. But unlike many of the offspring of great leaders, they have none of the usual airs and graces. They are down to earth and enjoy an easy but intellectually stimulating relationship with their mother. Jozina, the youngest, who bears the greatest likeness to Samora, jokes with her mother, spending the time making witty retorts about many of the world's leaders. Graça is a little disillusioned with politics, believing the Mozambican parliament has not accorded her husband his proper place in history. But she confides that she doesn't like to pass on her frustrations to Madiba, who is an optimist and tends to look for the good in people. When she does speak of Madiba, it's always in the most glowing terms.

Their relationship is, in many ways, like that of any other couple. They have to cope with the routine schedules of running a busy household. Mandela supports four of his grandchildren, who live with him. (He has 25 grandchildren and four great-grandchildren.)

They have their lovers' tiffs. But above all, it's a relationship of deep love and respect. They adore each other, with Mandela calling her 'darling' and seizing every chance to express his affection physically. It's Graça who helps keep Madiba young. Straight after their marriage the couple went on a state visit to Brazil. During the official welcome, Brazilian women dressed only in G-strings performed the samba for the newlyweds, much

to Madiba's embarrassment. He kept turning to Graça and saying, 'Darling, do you see what they're wearing?' Graça was unperturbed and calmly told Madiba that it was perfectly natural in Brazil.

On another occasion Mandela was rushing off to meet Prince Charles and the Spice Girls in South Africa. He asked, 'By the way, who are these Spice Girls?' Graça threw her head back and roared with laughter. 'Oh, Madiba,' she said, 'you'd better speak to your grandchildren about them.'

Once they were married, it was obvious that Mandela enjoyed having a wife, someone who's a friend, but also someone to share their domestic duties. And now that she was firmly in his life, Graça made sure he didn't overstretch himself. She'd conspire with his personal assistant to ensure that his schedule wasn't too heavy. Mandela, however, soon got wise to this and would routinely give her the slip, using his bodyguards to do the 'dirty work'. For example, at times he was supposed to be resting he would sneak out of the house to attend to some or other business. Then he'd tell his bodyguard. 'If Mam' Graça calls, just tell her I'm around or sleeping.' Then off he would go. And if Mandela wanted to organise something without Machel catching on, he would speak to his guards in Afrikaans in front of her – a language that she has no knowledge of at all.

It seems that Graça manages to charm others wherever the couple go. Over the last of his term of office, Madiba's bodyguards would comment constantly on what a fitting end to his presidency the couple's relationship was. A woman of grace, elegance, style and deep compassion, Graça is easy to love and admire. And most people would agree that she was a fitting First Lady for South Africa and an ideal companion for the world's favourite president. A reminder to all of us that anything is possible at any age.

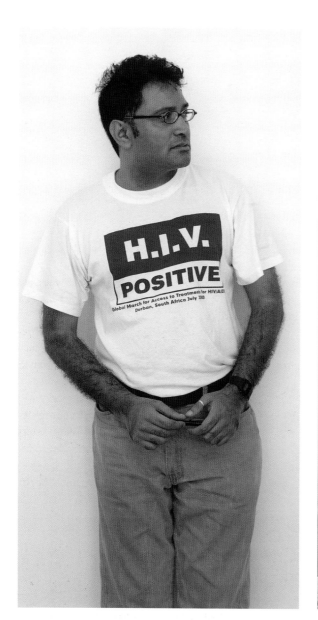

Zackie Achmat and Mirryena Deeb.

(*Photos:* Dale Yudelman)

David & Goliath

As some 40 international drug companies take the South African government to court to protect their patent rights, a handful of activists are fighting for the lives of the world's poorest people. Chené Blignaut meets both sides.

Chené Blignaut

Fairlady 11 April 2001

Zackie Achmat's home, situated in Cape Town's less glamorous seaside suburb Muizenberg, is a hive of activity. I arrive at the same time as a beggar and a journalist from the *Washington Post*.

Zackie heads up the Treatment Action Campaign (TAC), the body representing AIDS activists which has been given permission to join the court proceedings in support of the South African government in its defence against the action brought by the international pharmaceutical industry.

He's not in, we're told, but his sister, Midi, invites us into the friendly, old stone house. We wait in a chaotic office, which proudly houses the trophies and tools of previous campaigns – newspaper clippings and leftover posters from assorted protest marches. Incessant phone calls, a blaring radio and a lively fax machine spewing out mounds of paper lend a frenetic, purposeful atmosphere to the makeshift office, which serves as the informal headquarters of the TAC.

Finally, an apologetic Zackie arrives, half an hour late. Hovered over by a cameraman from an overseas television station, who's making a film of the activist's life, Zackie is dressed in a white T-shirt advertising his HIV-positive status in bold purple letters, and a pair of slacks. He flashes us a sheepish grin from beneath his fashionable specs. With a warm handshake he invites us upstairs to the living quarters of the house-cum-office he shares with ex-boyfriend Jack Lewis. With a hectic schedule of interviews, protest marches and an illegal stint importing cheap generic AIDS drugs from Thailand last year, this outspoken activist has become synonymous with the fight for cheaper drugs for South Africans dying of AIDS.

Zackie himself appears to be far from dying, but he refuses to take the life-saving drugs until they're within the means of the people he's fighting for. With his boyish charm, handsome good looks and passion for life, he seems to be positively bursting with energy and health.

The contrast between Zackie and his opponents could not be greater. As

With his boyish charm, handsome good looks and passion for life, he seems to be positively bursting with energy and health.

I arrive at the upmarket Midrand offices of the Pharmaceutical Manufacturers' Association in South Africa, it strikes me forcibly. This is where I'm scheduled to meet Mirryena Deeb, CEO of the organisation representing local and international drug companies.

After a quick telephone call to Mirryena's office, the security guard lets me through the gates leading to the modern, salmon-coloured office block. The reserved parking bays in front of the building sport a fleet of expensive German-engineered cars.

The quiet, stylishly decorated reception area is separated from the rest of the office by a glass door marked 'Staff only'. Another set of doors leads onto a balcony that overlooks a manicured garden. This is where the photographer has set up her equipment.

Mirryena arrives, attended by a broad-shouldered, smirking young man who never lets her out of his sight and says his role is to 'be friendly'.

Posing for pictures in her black power suit and kitten-heel pumps, Mirryena appears to be distinctly uncomfortable – 'I always look so terrible in pictures' – and as if it were grim torture she jokes: 'Is this how you soften up all you interviewees?'

Later, seated opposite each other across a huge boardroom table, Mirryena begins by telling me what her industry has done for developing countries and how it doesn't deserve its demonic public image. She blames 'biased' reporting and professional activism for the international backlash the industry is currently facing from human rights activists and developing countries, who accuse them of being greedy and putting profits before lives.

Mirryena and Zackie are key personalities in what is sure to be one of the most important and far-reaching ideological fights of our time with market capitalism pitted against the right to health and life for poor people. In recent months they've squared up to each other numerous times, defending their viewpoints on radio, television, paper and in court.

Up to now their interaction has been reasonably good-natured, as illustrated by a recent incident during a live television debate. During an advertising break, Zackie said: 'You can't expect to win a debate with a hairstyle like that. You need a gay hairdresser.'

Mirryena responded with a well-timed: 'Your fly's open,' just as the ads ended.

However, the relationship is likely to cool down considerably with the start of a precedent-setting case in the High Court of SA last month, which is scheduled to continue on 18 April.

The Pharmaceutical Association representing about 40 drug companies, is fighting the SA government over a piece of legislation that would ignore their patent rights – rights awarded for the invention of new drugs. The government says the law is needed to improve access to cheaper drugs for all, because the same drugs could be made or imported at lower prices. Zackie's TAC supports the government's stance because it means cheaper AIDS drugs for millions of dying HIV-positive South Africans.

Although equally passionate, Zackie and Mirryena, both 38, have very different ways of promoting their respective causes.

Zackie is something of a born activist, a fate he could hardly escape after having to survive being openly gay in the predominantly Muslim community of Salt River, Cape Town, where he lived with his grandparents.

He kicked off his political 'career' by being expelled from school in Standard Seven after his school went up in flames during the 1976 uprising, followed by at least five stints in prison before the age of 18. Having perfected his skills in rhetoric by now, he relies heavily on emotional, heart-wrenching arguments about life and death, interspersed with a sharp sense of humour, often at his own expense. 'I had 50 extra T-cells after the march (by the TAC against President Thabo Mbeki's stance on AIDS) last year. I'm hoping to have 100 new T-cells after the court case.'

T-cells are the ones killed off by the HI virus.

While adamantly defending his viewpoints, he still manages to stay calm and shows willingness and the patience of Job in explaining the complexities of the case, as well as sharing intimate details about his personal life.

'I don't see myself as a hero,' he says. 'I have HIV and it's difficult to live with. So this is as much about my own survival as to be able to sleep peacefully at night.'

On the other hand, Mirryena, a trained lawyer and former financial journalist, has a no-nonsense, businesslike approach. Blaming 'shoddy, lazy' reporting for the industry's bad public image, the third-generation Lebanese woman believes the media is 'vandalising' her industry because it's 'in vogue' and because they 'don't do their homework'.

Presenting herself as a 'factual person' she says she only deals 'with the facts and if people don't like them, too bad'.

Her tactics require a stack of technical pro-market arguments and documents. And although it's obviously easier to evoke sympathy for dying people than for multi-billion-dollar industries seeking to protect their profits, some people believe a warmer approach wouldn't do any harm at a time when the industry needs all the friends it can get.

Mirryena, who won an award for excellence in journalism that advances the health status in 1996, sees no irony in defending the drug companies now, even to HIV-positive friends, because she believes it's 'factually defendable'.

And although she once joked in an interview about feeling like Cruella de Ville when she picks up her two boys, aged ten and seven, from school, Mirryena is adamant she's never come under personal attack as a result of her job.

But is this a clear-cut case of good guys versus the bad guys?

After two hours each with Mirryena and Zackie respectively, it becomes apparent that the issue exists in a grey area.

For once, the convenient image of good versus evil ignores the failure of the SA government to prioritise

During an advertising break, Zackie said: 'You can't expect to win a debate with a hairstyle like that. You need a gay hairdresser.' Mirryena responded with a well-timed: 'Your fly's open,' just as the ads ended.

AIDS as a crisis by choosing to allocate only R300 million to the curbing of the pandemic in this year's health budget.

In comparison a cool R43 billion was spent on a single arms deal in the same year during a time of peace. With more than four million South Africans sick or dying of AIDS, this is not the face of the benevolent caretaker. Prioritising arms over lives obviously makes a mockery of the government's pleas of poverty in refusing to pay for the treatment of HIV-positive patients who can't afford life-saving drugs.

As it is, the lack of political will in tackling AIDS is one of the few things Zackie and Mirryena actually agree upon.

'When the government does something wrong, we challenge them. We're not scared. We stood firm against the government when the link between HIV and AIDS was questioned, but when they do something right, they require our support,' says Zackie.

And passing the Medicine and Related Substances Control Amendment Act was right, he says. Without it the drug companies would be putting the government in a position of 'presiding over a holocaust' by charging 'exorbitant' prices for essential drugs.

This is disputed by Mirryena who blames the government for not even trying to negotiate better prices for big volumes of AIDS drugs through

Mirryena and Zackie are key personalities in what is sure to be one of the most important and far-reaching ideological fights of our time with market capitalism pitted against the right to health and life for poor people.

the State tender system.

The government has also 'spurned numerous' offers to obtain the drugs at 'rock-bottom' prices. Many of the ten or so companies selling patented AIDS drugs in the country have also offered their drugs free to patients in the public health sector for a couple of years, says Mirryena, but government has been slow in accepting offers.

Recently they'd just spurned another offer of R50 million's worth of free AIDS tests by an American company, she says.

Although Zackie agrees that government should accept offers of free drugs, he says the companies' 'generosity' results from world pressure and attempts to protect their patents. The bottom line is that companies overcharge for essential drugs, he says.

'The only way to overcome the unjustifiably high prices of AIDS drugs is not through the charity of the drug companies but a legal framework that will allow the government to fulfil its constitutional duty to all South Africans,' says Zackie.

But Mirryena maintains prices are reasonable and the companies deserve the protection of patent rights, allowing them some time to recover some of the US $1 billion they spend to put a new drug on the market. Not to mention the effort – the laborious process involving clinical drug trials and product development can take up to 14 years.

'For every 5 000 drugs we research, only three make it to the market and for every three that make it, only one is a commercial success,' says Mirryena. 'So when we have a success it has to pay for the failures.' But not in the developing world, she adds. Instead, the companies charge more in America and Europe to subsidise lower prices in Africa and Asia.'

Why don't generic companies innovate new AIDS drugs?

'Because it's not so easy to invent and make quality drugs on a sustainable basis.'

Therefore, she doesn't believe patent rights stand in the way of access to cheaper drugs. Without patents, drug companies would stop research all together, she says, with the result that no new drugs would come onto the market, causing more people to suffer and die in the long term.

Zackie is not convinced. Very little of these research costs are spent on drugs for diseases in the developing world, he argues.

'What the drug companies don't seem to understand is that God gave the right to life before he gave the right to patent.'

The government (and the TAC) won this round but it brought little comfort for the thousands who urgently needed medication when government appeared to keep stalling the anti-retroviral rollout in the public sector. Two years later, in November 2003, the Department of Health announced the 'Operational Plan for Comprehensive HIV and AIDS Care, Management and Treatment for South Africa'. Later that same year, Zackie Achmat finally opted to begin taking life-prolonging anti-retrovirals.

In his State of the Nation address to parliament on 21 May 2004, President Thabo Mbeki said government hoped to reach the initial 53 000 target a year later, that is in March 2005. However, seven months after the November 2003 announcement, less than 10 000 people had commenced ARV treatment in the country.

In the meantime, the Minister of Health, Dr Manto Tshabalala-Msimang, continued to make confusing and contradictory public statements about the 'toxicity' of anti-retrovirals and preferred the promotion of nutrition and vitamins over anti-retroviral medication.

In 2004, the Treatment Action Campaign, with Zackie as chairman, was nominated for the Nobel Peace Prize.

He lives in Cape Town and continues to challenge government on issues of health, citizenship and democracy.

SA's Fiscal Spice

Jamie Carr

Fairlady 11 April 2001

Maria Ramos is 'utterly babe-tastic', says Jamie Carr. With no money for university, South Africa's Director-General of Finance started out as a bank clerk but now does us proud at those international gatherings of global money men.

I've met a few economists in my time. At university, they ranked somewhere between the chemists and the engineers in the league of ill-judged facial hair and dubious personal hygiene.

At work, they're immediately recognisable by their dialect, designed to leave ordinary mortals unable to judge whether they're talking utter garbage because only about one word in six is remotely comprehensible.

So I was more than a little nervous to be allocated an hour with Maria Ramos.

She's not only collected universal plaudits for her performance as Director-General of the Finance Department, she's also the author of a thesis on 'Clower's Dual Decision Hypothesis and Keynes's General Theory'.

This put me at a slight disadvantage. I have at least heard of Keynes, and am as capable as anyone else of nodding respectfully when his name is mentioned, but I wouldn't know Clower if he (or is it she?) whacked me over the head with a demand curve in broad daylight.

But I needn't have worried. In the whole hour there was only one reference that went completely over my head, when she mentioned the iniquity of Joan Robinson having been denied the Nobel Prize. I went into a frenzy of sympathetic tutting, but my mind could get no closer than another Mrs Robinson, who surely deserved more than she got for taking Dustin Hoffman's virginity, though a Nobel Prize might have been a tad over the top.

The first thing you notice on meeting Maria is that she is never likely to represent any country other than Lilliput on the basketball court. What she lacks in height, however, she makes up in spades with a languid charm that, if I were a Spaniel, would have had me rolling around on the floor waiting for a tickle.

Our Director-General of Finance is utterly babe-tastic.

It gives me a warm fuzzy feeling inside to think that the country with the coolest ex-president in the world is represented in the economic stratosphere

Maria Ramos – 'If I were a Spaniel, she would have had me rolling around on the floor waiting for a tickle.'

(*Photo:* Angie Lazaro)

In the whole hour there was only one reference that went completely over my head, when she mentioned the iniquity of Joan Robinson having been denied the Nobel Prize.

by a fox like Ramos. The rest of the world infests Davos with a bunch of fat, balding suits, while we send along our very own Fiscal Spice. This is clearly a good thing.

But it is all a long way from the arrival of the Ramos family in SA when Maria was a nipper, following her grandparents in search of better economic opportunities than Portugal could provide. The debate as to just how African one has to be to classify as an African doesn't seem to cause her too many sleepless nights, though.

'I am South African first and foremost, I have a commitment to Africa, I feel African, and certainly don't want to live anywhere else or aspire to any other culture,' she says firmly.

Maria was the eldest of four children in a working-class family, so when she finished school there was no money to send her to university. She went to work as a clerk at what was then Barclays Bank, processing cheques in the aptly named waste department. She says she was attracted to Barclays because of its scholarship scheme to send promising employees to university, but was a touch peeved when she first applied in 1979 to discover the scheme was not open to women.

In a bold and progressive moment, Barclays then suggested that women should be allowed to try their pretty little hands at Unisa, while scholarships to Wits were still restricted to men. When Chris Ball finally opened the scheme up fully to women, Maria was the first through the door.

She first thought of becoming a lawyer rather than an economist, but her mind was made up in an interview with one of her managers whose son was struggling with the BCom they were both taking.

With the immortal line, 'This BCom thing is very hard; it must be even harder for a woman,' he made it impossible for her to change to law. She completed her degree in 1986, with Honours in 1987.

By 1991 Maria was in the enviable position of being able to choose between a Fulbright Scholarship for a doctorate in economics, and the Helen Suzman Award, which she chose.

By this stage she was deeply involved in setting up the ANC's economics department, and it made more sense for her to spend a year in London doing her Master's than to disappear into the bowels of American academia for the interminable period of a doctorate.

She was involved with the ANC's department of economic planning from 1990 to 1994, with responsibility for monetary and fiscal policy.

'We were taking on board the fact that we were going to be in government in a time when there was rapid change in the global economy,' she says. 'SA lost out on a lot of the global change of the '80s, and we had to play catch-up.'

When she was appointed deputy DG in 1995, she was the only woman in a management position in the department. This caused a few short circuits in the brain cells of the old guard, such as the genius who popped his head round her door and said: 'Such a big office for such a little girl.'

Maria wasn't deterred.

She says of SA now: 'We have a huge amount of credibility world-wide. We are one of the few emerging countries with stable economies, and we have more than just a seat at the table; in many cases we set the agenda. We've been through some tough times and come out pretty well.

'Now we can look at social transformation projects from a position of strength. We've made commitments and delivered on them; now we can speak openly and decisively because we remain in charge of our own destiny, and people respect that.'

She describes her six years at Finance as 'incredibly

She first thought of becoming a lawyer rather than an economist, but her mind was made up in an interview with one of her managers whose son was struggling with the BCom they were both taking. With the immortal line, "This BCom thing is very hard; it must be even harder for a woman," he made it impossible for her to change to law.

exciting' and the department as 'the strongest black economic resource in the country'.

She says she regards putting together such a strong team as her greatest personal achievement: 'I get the credit, they do all the hard work and the thinking.'

This is clearly not true, since Maria has a reputation for putting in hours that would make an American lawyer pale.

In July this year, Maria's contract with the Finance Department runs out. So what's next?

It would take her about three minutes to pack up the contents of her office if she were to leave. It contains a laptop, an ANC team photo, a suspiciously pristine-looking copy of President Mbeki's latest page-turner, a couple of economics tomes and a large glossy book on Magritte, which suggests an interest in the surreal that must be a great help in South African politics.

For all the rumours about her intentions, however, she says her job has been so all-encompassing that she hasn't had a chance to think about what she might do outside it. She can, however, categorically deny that she is going to the IMF or the World Bank, and says she wants to stay in this country.

One thing I can guarantee is that if she so much as winks towards the private sector, there will be so many head-hunters around it'll look like market day in Papua, New Guinea.

But let's hope government doesn't lose Portugal's finest export since Eusebio. We need to differentiate ourselves in a competitive global economy.

And nobody else has got anyone like our Maria.

This profile originally appeared in the Financial Mail. *In 2004 Maria Ramos was appointed as the CEO of Transnet.*

Chasing Amy

The remarkable story of the death of Amy Biehl and the life of her parents and siblings, featured in the award-winning documentary *Long Night's Journey Into Day*, has become a symbol of hope and forgiveness in the new South Africa. In the midst of all the media attention and the community work done by the Amy Biehl Foundation, Nechama Brodie discovered a family fighting for more than just a good cause …

Nechama Brodie

Fairlady 11 April 2001

High noon in the Mother City and Linda, Peter and Kim Biehl are standing at the fruit-and-vegetable market outside Cape Town's train station, posing for a picture.

'We need more people in the background,' says the photographer, Jacques.

'Who wants to be in the photo?' I shout. One sulky fruit seller raises his hand reluctantly. Another scuttles to the front, ripe melon in his hand. A passer-by notices the commotion and decides to join the fray. He stands right next to Linda, placing his hand on her shoulder with a familiar air.

'Do you know these people?' I ask him. 'Yes,' he replies. 'This is Linda and this is Peter,' he says, touching their shoulders.

'Have you met them before?' I enquire. 'No. But I know them. I have seen their pictures in the newspapers, and on TV.'

He is smiling from cheek to cheek.

It's the same wherever we go. I introduce the Biehls to a taxi full of men finishing their lunch.

'Sorry for what happened to your daughter,' says the driver.

'Ja, sorry hey,' echo the men in the back.

The Biehls don't flinch at the mention of their daughter. It's been nearly eight years since she was murdered, and the family's pain seems to have been replaced by the healing forces of responsibility. Peter and Linda travel from the United States to South Africa between 11 and 12 times a year, doing work for the foundation they set up in their daughter's name.

The Amy Biehl Foundation is involved in a number of projects – everything from youth development and education to community building and empowerment.

In death, Amy Biehl has transcended the boundaries of mortal flesh; she's become Amy, the myth; Amy, the legend. Amy, the movie …?

Linda Biehl – 'Linda and Peter seem to
have dealt with the phenomenon of
their daughter Amy.'

(*Photo:* Dirk Pieters)

The Biehls don't flinch at the mention of their daughter. It's been nearly eight years since she was murdered, and the family's pain seems to have been replaced by the healing forces of responsibility.

Could be. Rumours have been flying since 1997, hinting that South Africa's own Spielberg, Anant Singh, is 'in production' with a movie about the life, and death, of Amy Biehl, complete with a star-spangled American celebrity cast. Singh and the Biehls have both been branded as Hollywood sell-outs as a result but, unsurprisingly, the truth is far less objectionable. Yes, Anant Singh has discussed the possibility of making a movie with the Biehl family. No, it's nowhere near being 'in production'. There's no fancy cast in place; there isn't even a working script.

'We visited a lot of schools, and the kids have always wanted a movie about Amy,' Peter says.

'But today's movies need a lot of action. The problem with dramatising this story is getting a script that is appropriate for us, and artistically viable.'

The Biehl family is adamant that they will not let the need for a 'good story' get in the way of the facts. Amy's family and friends are frequently confronted with media reports on Amy that take liberties with real life.

'They notice everything that comes up,' Peter comments, of his children, and they say, 'That's not Amy. We have worked hard, and Amy worked hard, and there's no way to control the outcome of a film once it's in production. I think what we don't like are the ethics of the film industry in general.'

The family admits to being far more comfortable with a documentary film format, like that of the Oscar-nominated *Long Night's Journey Into Day*. The film looks at post-apartheid South Africa, focusing on four TRC hearings, including the one where Amy's killers were given amnesty (a move that Amy's parents famously supported).

'I thought they did a pretty good job,' says Linda, of filmmakers Francis Reid and Deborah Hoffman.

'Everyone we know of has learned from it,' she adds before saying, 'Our friends have said to us that *now* they are beginning to understand.'

Kim Biehl, Amy's sister, attended the film's premier in Los Angeles. 'I think it's a very powerful film overall. I cry every time, at certain parts. It's hard for me to deal with some of it, but the rest of the film is very moving,' she says.

Kim and Linda tell me that Zach, the youngest of the Biehls, initially chose *not* to see the film.

'It's not that he's against what we're doing,' says Linda, 'but he's been misquoted so often by the press that he's become gun shy.'

Zach was 15 when Amy was killed.

'Because he's a boy, I think there's more anger sometimes,' Linda says.

Linda and Peter seem to have dealt with the phenomenon of their daughter Amy. It's not necessarily so easy for the other children, or for those who were close to Amy.

'My life is very much "before this happened" and "after this happened",' says Kim.

'My sister [Molly] and my brother and myself have fought really hard to maintain our own lives. I have to wear a name tag to work, and not a day goes by when someone doesn't recognise my surname, or make a comment like, "you're the sister of that girl" or, "your parents do really good work". Sometimes I want to say, "Guess what? My sister and I do good work too ... The hardest thing for me is that they just didn't know Amy. Nobody even knows her as a person any more. Now she's just become this *thing*. I hate that. I try to tell people about her, when I get the chance. And my parents have done a great job of communicating that through their work ... but Amy was a character.'

What does she tell people about Amy?

'I tell them that she was a very difficult person. She

'I never hated these guys,' Linda says. 'I actually love them. They are real children of South Africa. I sense that, indeed, they can carry Amy's spirit. There's a heart in there ...' Linda says that they have often told her, if they'd known who Amy was, they wouldn't have killed her, as she could have helped them in their cause.

really always knew what she wanted ... even when we were very little. I was older than she was, but when I started to walk, she was walking with me. I think she rode my two-wheel bicycle before I did. She was a very dominating personality.'

'She still is!' says Linda, smiling as she walks back in. Linda is also happy to contradict the image of a saintly daughter and a righteous family.

'We argue all the time,' she says.

When I comment that it's a healthy thing, Kim responds: 'We're a *normal* family,' as if anything else would be idiotic.

'It *has* consumed much of our lives,' Linda gradually admits. 'In a strange, horrible sense, our life has taken on a new meaning. But I look at people who play golf all day, or watch the stock market ... and it's so *boring*!'

With her bright yellow shirt and luminous persona, Linda is comfortable with being singularly identified as 'Amy Biehl's mom'.

Recalling the days after Amy's death, when reporters were busy digging up the details about exactly what had happened in South Africa, she says, 'The detail is not what's important to us; we were never into the *details* of what happened; it was a *situation*. If you start letting that take over, you'll give in to victimisation. People always say: "You're a victim of violence." I am not a victim of anything! I didn't let things keep happening to me ...'

While we talk, a young man walks into the room and

Linda introduces him to me, as she has done with every other volunteer in the office. She pronounces his name badly, but it rings a bell. When he leaves, I ask Linda to spell his name for me. She looks at me and pronounces it again, slowly, before adding that he was one of Amy's killers. Ntobeko Ambrose Peni, whom the Biehls call 'Peni'. Ntobeko works for the Foundation together with Easy Nofomela, another one of the four men convicted of the murder. Despite the fact that I'd known about this arrangement for some time, it was still a shock to come face to face with the reality.

'I never hated these guys,' Linda says. 'I actually love them. They are real children of South Africa. I sense that, indeed, they can carry Amy's spirit. There's a heart in there ...' Linda says that they have often told her, if they'd known who Amy was, they wouldn't have killed her, as she could have helped them in their cause.

'In reality,' Linda says, with a touch of irony, 'she was more helpful dead than alive.'

'Peter and I have a great sense of pride that we're her parents. And we miss her. There are certain times when we ask: why did this happen? Then you start thinking: things happen for a reason. So I'm going to celebrate her life.'

Peter Biehl died of colon cancer in 2002. The Amy Biehl Foundation continues to be involved in various projects in South Africa.

Patricia de Lille – 'the country's
favourite political underdog'.

(*Photo:* Angie Lazaro)

Meet the Mettle

In one week, PAC chief whip Patricia de Lille took quite a beating. Subpoenaed to back up her claims of government corruption, blamed for the Rand's demise, voted 'Mampara of the Week' and forced to make a public apology, she tells Chené Blignaut how she plans to bounce back.

Chené Blignaut

Fairlady 23 May 2001

When I phone Patricia de Lille to set up an interview, she sounds weary.

'I've taken today off. I need to clear my head,' she says. 'Things have been quite hectic, you know.'

I speak to her assistant June the next day and I'm told Patricia's at home, confirming my suspicions that the country's favourite political underdog is licking her wounds after what must count as a particularly disastrous week in any politician's diary.

It started with a nasty fall-out in the media about the PAC chief whip's long-standing allegations about government corruption in the R43 billion arms deal.

The first blow came when well-respected national treasury director Maria Ramos accused the outspoken politician of causing the frail Rand to drop because of her 'unsubstantiated rumours'.

This followed allegations made at a PAC press conference that the heads of five senior ANC members embroiled in the arms deal controversy would roll before the end of that week.

It also led to Patricia and her colleague, PAC secretary-general Thami ka Plaatjie, being slapped with subpoenas to appear before the team investigating the deal to back up their claims with hard facts.

Within days national headlines boldly declared what appeared to be a humiliating and uncharacteristic about-face for Patricia: 'De Lille sorry for allegations over arms deal'.

Adding insult to injury, a Sunday newspaper afforded her the dubious honour of being voted 'Mampara' of the week for what they called 'shameless publicity mongering'.

They criticised the 'will-she-won't-she, push-me-pull-me, carrot-dangling exercise' she'd played with the media by 'threatening' to reveal the names and then backing off with her tail between her legs.

> 'I've been blamed for many things in my life,' she laughs, 'but it's the first time I've been blamed for the Rand. I was saying to my son last night, one of these days they're going to blame me for the increase in the petrol price,' she says, followed by another infectious burst of laughter.

For someone who's fought her way bare-fisted into the hearts of ordinary people across racial and other chasms by taking on even the most daunting political opponent, a public apology must have been quite a bitter pill to swallow. Or at least, so I thought.

But after only my second probing question to find out how much strain the woman behind the politician is taking after the week from hell, Patricia de Lille explodes with laughter at my carefully considered mention of her 'Mampara' status. Slapping the desk in her parliamentary office in Cape Town, she roars with delight. The spontaneous outburst of laughter lights up the sharp eyes behind her glasses and scrunches up her face into a series of cute dimples, making her look much younger than her 50 years.

'I've been blamed for many things in my life,' she laughs, 'but it's the first time I've been blamed for the Rand.

'I was saying to my son last night, one of these days they're going to blame me for the increase in the petrol price,' she says, followed by another infectious burst of laughter.

A little taken aback by her obvious enjoyment of her predicament, I nonetheless continue to look for signs of stress underneath the politician's mask, but they're well disguised by oiled rhetoric and breast-beating bravado.

Shaking her head vigorously at my question as to whether any of this is getting to her personally, Patricia – having swapped her trademark African prints for an elegant khaki suit and black boots and today with her braids tied back – looks me straight in the eye.

'I give the punches all the time,' she says, 'so, when they come my way, I must be brave enough to take them.'

Comparing her stand-offs with the ANC government to a boxing match, she says for every one round they win, she wins five.

'I don't complain at all.'

But surely a public apology must sit a little uncomfortably with her?

Not really, she insists. In fact, she assures me, it's part of her tactical approach to turn around what could easily be interpreted as a serious setback for her crusade against corruption.

Undeterred, she's been spending her time plotting the next move to put the investigation 'back on track'.

Her first salvo was drafting letters to the editors of papers she believes created 'false impressions' by suggesting she'd capitulated to attempts to discredit her.

Although she'd used the word 'sorry', says Patricia, the context in which it was used was wrongly reported. She said she was sorry for the *confusion* resulting from remarks made by a PAC colleague, who claimed the party would identify senior members of the ANC about to 'fall'.

Personally, insists Patricia, she never intended making the names known.

'I give information to the media, they investigate and run with the story. When they announce the names, I confirm it and I'm vindicated.'

As for allegations that her claims had been 'unsubstantiated', Patricia begs to differ. 'Many of the allegations in the briefing document which was handed over to me by concerned ANC members two years ago have subsequently been substantiated.'

Her decision to apologise, even if she was not personally to blame, says Patricia, was 'the right thing to do'.

'You show me one politician in our history who ever apologised for anything. They're all too big and above the people. I just think you have nothing to lose by admitting you've made a mistake,' she says.

Asked if she thinks her credibility has been affected, Patricia looks down at the table for the first time before responding, 'How do you measure that, you know?'

'But,' she says, spreading her hands over the pile of pink message slips on her table, 'I'm still getting messages from people. I've got files full. I haven't had a chance to respond to any of these yet.' She's also reassured by phone calls to local radio talk shows from people congratulating her.

Patricia – who fancies herself as the conscience of the nation – has no regrets about the role she's played in the arms deal investigation so far and says she's just doing what every elected Member of Parliament should be doing. She refuses to be intimidated by bad press, personal attacks and even death threats – these have since stopped.

But scratch a little deeper and her thick-skinned approach becomes more ambivalent.

'It's not my brief in life, you know. Honestly, I don't want to go around exposing corruption.'

She'd be much happier involved in socio-economic issues, such as children and AIDS, she assures me.

'But I can't disappoint the people who put their trust in me. Whistleblowers must be protected. I can provide that shield, even though it was difficult the past 18 months because I had to take the punches on behalf of others. And with hindsight, seeing how viciously government responded to me, can you imagine what they would've done to the actual whistleblowers, some who are in their own ranks?' she says.

From the beginning, Patricia adds, government has been far more interested in finding out which the whistleblowers are than investigating the allegations of corruption.

'But they can forget it. I'll never give them the names.'

Her main regret is that she can't shield her close family from the punches she's determined to take for what she believes in.

'The only real casualty in this whole thing is my family. They're the sacrificial lambs in this,' she says seriously.

Apart from the fear of endangering their lives through her work, Patricia also regrets the fact that her commitment takes her away from her husband Edward, son Alistair (29) and her three German Shepherds.

And even when she's at home in Pinelands, she's often so wired by what's been happening at work, she struggles to unwind.

'I sometimes have to remind them that I'm home because they get so used to being without me,' she jokes.

She also has little time for her latest hobby – golf – affording her little chance to improve on her 42 handicap.

In December last year, she never really managed to switch off, especially after Judge Willem Heath came under attack on the day after Christmas, making Patricia see red and causing her to jump to his defence.

She's come under fire from some circles for her unstinting support of the 'white' judge and his special investigation unit, even going as far as challenging Presi-

'If there's one thing that doesn't work with me, Patricia de Lille, it's the race card. I don't care who the hell you are,' she declares.

dent Thabo Mbeki's decision to exclude the SIU from the arms deal investigation in the constitutional court.

At the mention of this criticism, Patricia's smile is replaced with a frown and her eyes flash with anger. Her until now soft-spoken voice rises in pitch, getting dangerously close to the shrill shrieks normally reserved for lashing out at her enemies in parliament.

'If there's one thing that doesn't work with me, Patricia de Lille, it's the race card. I don't care who the hell you are,' she declares.

For her, competence is what counts.

'If they want to accuse me of hobnobbing with a white judge, I'd rather hobnob with a white judge than with criminals, thieves and crooks. And that's what they want me to do, to leave the crooks alone,' she says.

'My experience is that people protect one another. They say: "He was with me in exile, or in the trenches. He's my comrade, therefore I can't split on him." That's wrong.'

Corruption and exploitation of the poor are the threads that run through most of her fiery public crusades, and the next one will be no exception.

Casinos, she says. 'It's the worst decision we ever took.'

And what really irks her is that the community component of the shareholding of the luxury gaming palaces are bound to include some of the same names linked to the investigation into the arms deal.

'It's the same black elite. The same names always pop up. They'll stop at nothing to make money. I want to go to them and ask them how they can sleep at night – taking money from the poorest of the poor,' she says.

Is there anything that scares her, I ask?

She answers without hesitation. 'No. Fear makes you weak. It makes you compromise. If you believe in yourself and come to terms with yourself, you can stand in front of anyone – and not be scared. We're all human beings after all,' she says.

Believe it or not, but the voice of the voiceless, who's been compared with erstwhile political firebrand Helen Suzman, was once so shy she couldn't open her mouth in class.

'There's no book to teach confidence. You can only become confident through experience and exposure.'

Yes, but first you need the courage to be honest with yourself and the world around you – and there aren't too many politicians who can claim honesty as their hallmark.

Patricia de Lille was vindicated in June 2005 when, after a lengthy public trial, Schabir Shaik, Deputy President Jacob Zuma's personal financial advisor, was convicted by Judge Hilary Squires of charges of fraud and corruption relating to the 'Arms Deal'. Judge Squires also found that the relationship between Zuma and Shaik was one that was 'generally corrupt'.

Meanwhile, in 2003, Patricia left the PAC to start her own party, the Independent Democrats. She managed to secure seven seats in the National Assembly in the 2004 general election. The party is also represented in the Western Cape, Gauteng and Northern Cape legislatures.

Betwixt and Between

What does it mean to be coloured in South Africa? Iman Rappetti speaks to three artists about issues of identity.

Iman Rappetti

Fairlady 22 May 2002

Born in Africa but
Mixed equals inferior, rearrange that exterior
Scorned for the secret exposed by my skin
Enslaving beliefs this child was bathed in.
MALIKA NDLOVU

Malika Ndlovu exudes calmness and balance. A poet, playwright and director, among other things, she's clear about what being coloured means to her.

'Coloured, not only in South Africa but also across the globe, means people of colour or people born of mixed descent. There are many other names in other languages for that. In our context that's inextricably linked to the luggage of apartheid race classification, and that's where the ambivalence or "mixed feelings" (excuse the pun) come into play. If we have to use terminology: I am a woman of colour, a black woman, an African from the south!'

Malika says her work gives her the freedom to explore issues that push the envelope on what people expect of her.

'Being an artist is for me the most liberating and fulfilling way to express myself and my thoughts, and to make my contribution to my society, to the world. As a writer and director, the relative anonymity you have is a bonus. My work is not judged by my age, my appearance or what others conclude from what they see.

'My play, *A Coloured Place,* and several poems I've written around identity issues, expose the impact of growing up in a coloured area and staying within its mindset. These works encourage people to define themselves rather than live under the oppression of other people's definition of who they are. Why miss out on a deliciously unpredictable journey of self-discovery or even recovery?'

Malika believes coloured people can and should discard the negative identity foisted upon them.

'The first sad irony is to believe the lie that to be born coloured is to be born a half-breed; a lost, in-between soul; one of God's leftovers; or other such hideous translations. We mourn and moan about the very thing that is our asset!

'We're privileged to be alive at a time when prisoner-to-president and

'Our identities are constantly evolving and in flux, even if we do choose to cling to one label in defining ourselves – we grow, we change, we are affected by change whether we recognise that or not. It's our choice to remain stuck to a fixed frame of who we are.'

ghetto-girl-to-business-executive-type success stories are constantly unfolding. We need to open our eyes, our ears and our minds. We need to replace our blame-and-complain syndrome with critical questions, such as: Why can he or she do it and I not? Finding answers for yourself is the path to freedom on so many levels; and the process never ends, not as long as you want to keep growing.'

Boxed attitudes and negative comfort zones contribute to the malaise of failure and inferiority, but these can be changed if coloured people look around and observe the universe of possibility around them.

'Our identities are constantly evolving and in flux, even if we do choose to cling to one label in defining ourselves – we grow, we change, we are affected by change whether we recognise that or not. It's our choice to remain stuck to a fixed frame of who we are.'

In a country like South Africa, where apartheid history marginalised black achievers, Malika says she still manages to find people who inspire her and through a synergy of talents show her the great possibilities that exist.

'I find myself drawn to people or their work. Our parents may not always be ideal role models, but often you can learn from who they are, even if it means recognising behaviour and qualities that you'd rather avoid than emulate.'

Most of all, Malika encourages people to just be themselves.

'In my work dealing with this issue, there is never a total rejection of the term "coloured" and what that means in South Africa specifically, but it provokes people to go beyond that limited horizon. If you dig the label, wear it with pride and know what it means for you.'

Vanessa Jansen is a filmmaker and chairs an organisation called The Women of the Sun, which advances women of colour in the film and television industry. Vanessa grew up in Swaziland, free from the policies of apartheid South Africa. Her upbringing, albeit by a Zulu mother and white Afrikaner father, did not prepare her for the racial mind camps she encountered when she attended school in the KwaZulu-Natal midlands.

'I did not grow up in a coloured community and my social surrounds were never classical. My parents left South Africa in 1971 so they could get married. My father passed away when I was very young, so I grew up with my mother. I attended schools classified as coloured here in South Africa, and that's where the whole thing became clear. In that setting, what always struck a chord was that you would have these really light-skinned coloureds with green eyes and blonde hair and then on the other hand you'd have these dark ones, and they were all coloured. I could never quite figure out what this whole coloured thing was about.'

Currently working on a documentary tentatively entitled *Mixed Relations*, told from her perspective of being on the borderline of black and white, she tries to unravel a definition of the word coloured.

'I've never really considered myself coloured – it's always just been a name on a paper somewhere. You come to SA and people call you coloured. The term "mixed-race" for me is much easier to handle because there are none of those connotations from the past and it also frees me up to say I am a unique individual because I am mixed. Vanessa loves the surprise she encounters when subverting stereotypes.

'I learnt Swazi at school and grew up speaking Zulu. When I came back to South Africa in 1993, I noticed people speaking to me in Afrikaans, a language I speak poorly, or I'd speak to Zulu people in Zulu and their eyes would pop. That's where the notion of doing this documentary came in. When you're an anomaly in this situation, it's so nice to break down stereotypes and go

Malika Ndlovu,
Vanessa Jansen and
Gail Smith.

(*Photos:* Leila Amanpour)

beyond the presumptions and make people see that I am a unique individual.'

Her work has been driven by the desire to give exposure to coloured talent and diversity, and to affirm their success through the media.

'Our job as filmmakers and people in media is really to source our intellectuals and put them on the covers of magazines and on television. The Americans, for instance, have done a history series on all their prominent black American leaders so that everyone knows who they are. I think that's a task we have to take upon ourselves in this generation – to uncover those people.

'My vision ultimately is to have a society where people can interact with each other without the baggage that we have. I have a son who is mixed. He's at a school where they speak Sotho and Zulu and other languages, giving him alternatives so that at least he has a communication tool, if nothing else, to help him to deal with different communities.'

Gail Smith is lithe, sensuous and cool. She's a woman with insight. Currently a lobbyist for social security rights for children as well as a feminist writer and researcher, she's passionate about the issue of coloured identity.

'I have been for a long time, because I was politically conscious from the time I was about 12 or 13. I completely rejected the label "coloured", but as changes have happened in the country, I've had to reconcile myself with that aspect of myself and begin to see the good things about it and to feel less defensive.

'In the '80s we were black, a political term that included Africans, coloureds and Indians speaking against apartheid. I would never describe myself as coloured; I would say I am black, and that is my self-identity. For identity is something you choose.'

Gail explains: 'The thing I dislike most is that most people don't understand what colouredness is about, and so it becomes the catch-all phrase for a lot of negativity about mixed-race people. I've never seen myself as mixed race ever. For me coloured people are not even a mixed race, between black and white, but people who meet at the intersection of many races. So we are multi-ethnic in our identity. Most foreigners assume I have a white parent and a black parent. I do have white blood, but

three generations ago. I get very offended when people ask, "You're coloured, aren't you?" Because I know what I mean but not what they mean by that term.'

Gail works hard to keep dialogue alive and constantly re-evaluates the stereotypes she encounters during her research.

'I did my Masters' dissertation on Winnie Mandela, and that really kick-started a whole lot of questions for me around identity. She made some seriously negative and anti-coloured comments during the '80s and it took me by surprise. I didn't expect that to come out of my research. I started thinking, "but hang on", I need to answer to this, and to think about the millions of young people who don't have anyone to look up to.'

Role models are crucial for providing direction to people still immersed in the ghetto, without hope of escape from the drugs, alcohol and violence that are the cesspool of communal life.

Gail's mantra is excellence, excellence, excellence.

'Excellence is the antidote to racism of any sort. More young people need to have positive role models. At the moment we have Breyton Paulse, Patricia de Lille and Trevor Manuel. Historically, coloured people have been part of the fabric of this society in a very overt way and I think that it's just a matter of remembering the diverse members of our community who've made valuable contributions to this country over the years.'

Gail says her influences are many, and that her work has taught her to be analytical.

'One of the reasons why I get angry about misconceptions around coloured identity is because this is something that has been written about for decades. There's a body of work around it. People conveniently forget about it and continue to perpetuate a whole lot of rubbish. They continue to go back to the "God's stepchildren" ideology. Coloureds are constantly being seen as tragic mulattos.

'I don't think there's a problem with being someone of multi-ethnic origin. In fact I revel in it. I love the fact that a lot of coloured people subvert expectations. They look a particular way but are actually something else. Or they sound one way and then flip into an African language fluently. It shows that identity is a very fluid thing.'

Primed Minister

Dr Nkosazana Dlamini-Zuma is the most powerful woman in South Africa and whisperings in parliamentary corridors are of her becoming the next deputy president – that is if she doesn't pip her ex-husband, Deputy President Jacob Zuma, to the presidential post. Chris Barron tries to get a sense of our Foreign Affairs Minister's mettle.

Chris Barron

Fairlady January 2004

Minister Dr Nkosazana Dlamini-Zuma sounds relieved when I tell her that I'm not going to be critical about the décor in her office at the Union Buildings in Pretoria. 'I promise.'

She breaks into a smile that is unrestrained, warm and just a little shy.

'Okay then,' she says. 'We can go to my office.'

She leads the way, sailing along the corridor like a stately galleon, heavily laden and low in the water.

It has taken us ten minutes to get this far and I'm feeling edgy. Her entourage – a couple of secretaries, a protocol officer and a personal assistant – can't tell me how much time the minister will give me, but knowing her truly astonishing schedule – Japan one week, New York the next, India, Canada and France in the weeks thereafter – I suspect it won't be more than a couple of hours.

The reason she doesn't want me in her office is that it's being renovated. The reason I particularly want to see her office is that it is being renovated. One of the first calls on her budget when she became Foreign Affairs Minister was R70 000 for a customised lavatory. The mind boggles. What is she prepared to spend on an entire office?

In the event, I don't notice any renovations in progress, so I don't see what she was so coy about. It's a spacious enough office with wood panelling and French doors leading onto a small balcony or two. But it's much more modest in its dimensions and furnishings than the lavish suites occupied by many South African chief executives.

She was in former Foreign Affairs Minister Pik Botha's office but didn't like it. She's just moved to this one, which explains why it seems a bit impersonal. The only personal touch is an obviously loving birthday card signed by her children. Dlamini-Zuma is in her mid-50s.

I haven't the heart to ask where the famous loo is, whether she's going to have it transported to within striking distance of her new quarters, build a

The reason she doesn't want me in her office is that it's being renovated. The reason I particularly want to see her office is that it is being renovated. One of the first calls on her budget when she became Foreign Affairs Minister was R70 000 for a customised lavatory.

new one or just learn to walk a bit faster.

Instead, I ask if she enjoys being Foreign Affairs Minister.

'Initially I was worried,' says Dlamini-Zuma. 'I didn't think I had the experience.'

Indeed, she didn't. And if *she* was worried, then many in the country were downright alarmed. Foreign Affairs is about tact and diplomacy, and if her tempestuous term as Minister of Health demonstrated anything it was that she had about as much of either as a rampaging bull elephant.

The first victims were closest to home; in her own department, in fact. Director-General Jackie Selebi hit the road within months of her arrival, and desk officers began whinging about her autocratic style.

Next to occupy the DG's hot seat was the talented but sensitive Sipho Pityana. He left before the end of his contract, admitting that he found Dlamini-Zuma 'a very difficult woman to work with'.

Whether because of her reputation or because she couldn't find the time to interview candidates, it was 18 months before anyone else stepped into the breach.

'I love and respect Nkosazana too much to take the job,' remarked one front-runner. 'Our friendship would not survive two months.'

Further from home, however, the results have been more mixed. She is credited with doing a wonderful job to bring peace of sorts to the hellishly riven and complicated Great Lakes region. She relates well to the warring parties. She's no grimacing, shuffling, fork-tongued, Whitehall-type dissimulator.

'Are you positive about democratic prospects in Africa?' a foreign hack asked her within minutes of her appointment.

'I am not euphoric,' she answered dryly.

It's this kind of direct honesty that has won her the huge trust she has in Africa. And it's this ever-so-slight glint of dry, dry humour that very occasionally shows through an otherwise stolid façade that gives her an unexpected appeal.

If she's learned one thing in office, though, it is that no matter what she does or how she does it, she's going to be criticised. And sure enough, her relentless search for a way out of the central African morass has led to the accusation – within her department – that she is too 'obsessive' about the DRC.

How the Foreign Affairs Minister can be too obsessive about trying to bring an end to a conflict that has killed three million people in the last five years boggles the mind. It also suggests that there are a goodly number of functionaries in her department whose worldview is still, quite frankly, inappropriately Eurocentric.

Talk in inner ANC circles is of her close relationship with the Mbekis which, coupled with her ability and gender, bodes well for her to become the deputy president, if not the president after the 2009 national election.

When President Mbeki asked her to take Foreign Affairs, Dlamini-Zuma also 'worried about it being a generally very male-dominated area'.

Days before our interview she'd sparked a minor furore by refusing to be body-searched while on a visit to the United Nations in New York. Would there have been the same fuss if she'd been a man?

'The security services of most countries make you feel you're a woman in this job. They have geared themselves that foreign ministers are men.'

She's got used to having her way barred.

'They say, "Spouses go this way; foreign ministers and presidents go that way." I have to explain that I'm actually not a spouse. When they have your name on a list, they say, "Are you standing in for Dr Zuma?" I say,

Nkosazana Dlamini-Zuma – 'It's this
kind of direct honesty that has won her
the huge trust.'

(*Photo:* Picturenet)

"What do you mean am I standing in for Dr Zuma?"'

It must infuriate her, I say.

'If it's done in a way that does not cross the line between security and humiliation, I don't mind.'

The latest incident crossed that line, she felt.

Zuma was born in humble circumstances in the Natal midlands. She was the oldest of eight children and her dad was a Roman Catholic rural primary school teacher. She studied medicine at the non-European medical school of the University of Natal, arriving there in 1972 just as Black Consciousness leader Steve Biko was leaving.

She became vice-president of the South African Students' Organisation, but left prematurely to join the ANC in exile.

She became a medical doctor in Britain, and ANC leader Oliver Tambo and a young Thabo Mbeki were among her patients.

While in exile, she met Jacob Zuma and they married. Like many 'struggle' marriages, this one came under severe strain and eventually cracked. Clearly, it remains a highly sensitive area – not the least sensitive aspect being that she was not his only wife by some margin – and Dlamini-Zuma's body language projects an unmistakeable message when one tries, ever so circumspectly, to broach it: 'Keep out.'

Right, then. So, what was it like going from freedom fighter to government minister?

They knew what kind of society they wanted to create, she says, and from that point of view were well prepared. The tortuous process of translating what they wanted into reality was something they were not ready for and was made worse because most of the civil servants they had to rely on might as well have been from another planet.

'An administration that yesterday was calling you a terrorist, that yesterday was sanctions-busting, that yesterday was shunned by the world; an administration that was there to oppress you – and you suddenly have to use this administration for the total opposite of what they've been doing all their lives.'

There were leaks to the press that were calculated to make trouble and embarrass. When Dlamini-Zuma made it clear that the all-white, all-male composition of her staff couldn't remain intact, a provocative report appeared in *The Citizen* the next day saying she was going to get rid of all white males.

Or there'd be a question in parliament on an issue she'd just discussed in agreed confidence with her staff.

Or her phones would be disconnected the moment she left for Cape Town, and she'd come back to find they weren't working. She'd get it sorted, then have to go back to Cape Town for a few days. On her return, she'd find the lines had been disconnected again. This happened 'for weeks', she says.

Eventually she asked to see the person responsible.

'I just want to understand why,' she said to him. He produced an old rule book that said that when the minister goes to Cape Town, his Pretoria line must be transferred to the Cape Town office.

But these rules were written when the minister's entire staff used to relocate to Cape Town for six months, she pointed out. Hadn't he noticed that since the new government came into office, parliament had been in session the whole year and ministers travelled up and down all the time?

She asked her DG why someone who worked for the government 'and was therefore presumably not a fool' stuck to a rule that was obviously no longer applicable.

'He explained that in the past if you did something creative and things went wrong, you'd be sacked. But if something went wrong and you'd done it according to the rules, you would not be sacked.'

Some of this was 'not deliberate hostility', but some of it was.

Her predecessor at the health ministry and fellow medical doctor Rina Venter 'didn't make herself available' to Dlamini-Zuma. She left no message, no report, no briefing, no offer of assistance and no contact number.

'She left nothing.'

One can't help wondering what a difference it might have made to the new minister's outlook had Venter made a more gracious exit.

'Maybe she was a bit bitter,' suggests Dlamini-Zuma without rancour.

At this point things are going swimmingly and it seems impossible to believe that this fundamentally decent, clearly compassionate, intelligent, soft-spoken,

But two words change all that.

'*Sarafina*' and 'Virodene'.

Mention them and the effect is immediate. The shutters come down. Her expression, which is habitually undemonstrative, becomes unnervingly so. A bewildering unreason takes over.

rational lady was once the most vilified person in South Africa.

But two words change all that. '*Sarafina*' and 'Virodene'.

Mention them and the effect is immediate. The shutters come down. Her expression, which is habitually undemonstrative, becomes unnervingly so. A bewildering unreason takes over.

Just over a year into her term as Health Minister, it emerged that her department had given R14 million to playwright Mbongeni Ngema to produce an anti-AIDS play called *Sarafina 2*. None of the necessary processes had been followed and no tenders had been invited. The bulk of the money was from the European Union and its use should have been cleared with them first but was not.

Whichever way you looked at it, it was a clear breach of trust on the part of Dlamini-Zuma as the minister in charge. Instead of apologising, she demonstrated an arrogance that had media and politicians baying for her head.

She remains entirely unapologetic and even suggests, outrageously, given her immensely damaging refusal to provide antiretrovirals at the time, that those who forced her to withdraw her funding of *Sarafina* are to blame for the extent of the AIDS crisis.

'I knew we had a serious epidemic coming, and I knew it would cost our people a lot of lives. And I knew that if we had *Sarafina* going it could have been able to influence a lot of young people before they were infected.'

AIDS campaigner and High Court judge Edwin Cameron described this thinking as 'dangerous tosh'.

The criticism, says Dlamini-Zuma sanctimoniously, came from people (the media and opposition politicians) 'who didn't care about some people's lives'.

Then there was Virodene. She bypassed all regulations in order to get multimillion-rand government funding for a bunch of Pretoria University scientists who claimed to have discovered a cure for AIDS.

Basic tests revealed that Virodene contained a toxic industrial solvent that caused fatal liver damage and cancer.

Dlamini-Zuma became a figure of derision. Her angry response suggested a complete failure to understand either the role of the press in a democracy or the principle of accountability.

She lashed out at her critics and dissolved the Medicines Control Council when it refused to sanction Virodene tests on humans.

'I still don't know what the fuss was about,' she responds blithely.

The MCC, headed by the world-respected Professor Peter Folb, deserved what it got, she says. 'It was unhelpful in many things, not just Virodene.'

Dlamini-Zuma's minder, who has been shooting me looks as poisonous as any dose of Virodene, stands up and Dlamini-Zuma tells me that time is up. And anyway, she adds, sounding aggrieved, 'this is not what you said you were going to talk about'.

I've had barely an hour and I remonstrate feebly. I feel I've hardly touched the surface of this complex, intriguing bundle of contradictions.

'You would have had time if you hadn't talked about Virodene and *Sarafina*,' scolds her assistant.

On the way out, I step on Dlamini-Zuma's heel and apologise profusely.

She touches my arm and smiles. For a second the clouds part and another Dlamini-Zuma altogether, I have no doubt the real Dlamini-Zuma, emerges.

Maybe she was happy to see the back of me.

The Prince of Darkness

Rian Malan

Fairlady February 2004

JM Coetzee, winner of the 2003 Nobel Prize for Literature, is inclined to speak, if he speaks at all, in riddles and codes.

Once upon a time, quite a long time ago, the literary editor of a London Sunday newspaper prevailed upon JM Coetzee's agent to persuade the reclusive author to grant an interview, an exercise to which Coetzee was known to be totally allergic.

But an understanding was reached and a date was set, and I was deputised to ask the questions. This was a great honour, given that Coetzee was to my mind the greatest living author in the English language. I'd read all his books in a single sitting engaged on a psychic level so deep I can only liken it to hypnotism. They were awesome, those early Coetzee works, lit from within by a cold and terrible light, haunted by unanswerable questions. I could make a case for Conrad's *Heart of Darkness,* but otherwise, these were the greatest novels ever written about what my friend Jessica used to call 'our expedition of consciousness', by which she meant the struggle of whites to figure out their destiny in Africa.

We met in his office, the great novelist a pale and austere presence in his gray slacks and tweedy sports jacket, and I under strict instructions from his agent to avoid questions about his personal life. We were to talk only of literature, but my opening question was answered by dead silence.

Coetzee was writing the question on his notepad. He pondered it for a minute or two, then proceeded to analyse the assumptions on which it was based, a process that offered penetrating insights into my intellectual shortcomings but revealed nothing about Coetzee himself. All of my questions were similarly treated, and I wound up sounding like a reporter for a fanzine.

'What kind of music do you like?' I asked, desperately. The pen scratched, the great writer cogitated.

'Music I have never heard before,' he said.

Ja, well, what can I say? I wasn't the first to come short on the hard rock of Coetzee's aloofness. He never did public signings or book tours, kept

Anyone who wanted to understand John Maxwell Coetzee was forced to turn to the books, an area in which the master was kind enough to offer some guidance: 'True interpretation,' he has written, 'is inseparable from true understanding of the culture and historical matrix' from which any writing emerges.

his political opinions to himself, kept his private life secret. Maybe there wasn't much to reveal. He worked, he cycled, delivered the odd lecture at the University of Cape Town, lived quietly in Rondebosch with fellow academic Dorothy Driver. Beyond that, his privacy was impenetrable, his distaste for the limelight so extreme that he failed to turn up to receive either of his two Booker prizes.

Anyone who wanted to understand John Maxwell Coetzee was forced to turn to the books, an area in which the master was kind enough to offer some guidance: 'True interpretation,' he has written, 'is inseparable from true understanding of the culture and historical matrix' from which any writing emerges. At the time of that interview, I thought I understood Coetzee's matrix pretty well. I was white and half-Afrikaans; so was he. We both lived in Cape Town. Yonder was a freeway bridge that bore a striking resemblance to the one under which Mrs Curren lay dying in *Age of Iron,* drifting in and out of consciousness while street children probed her mouth for gold teeth. A few miles in the opposite direction was Sea Point, surely the white suburb ransacked in the opening chapters of *The Life and Times of Michael K.* Over the mountain was UCT, where Coetzee had recently taken a brave stand against leftists who wanted to bar Salman Rushdie from speaking on campus on the grounds that the cultural boycott should not be violated.

It was this act, as much as anything he had written, that caused me to think of Coetzee as something of a kindred spirit; a Suzmanite white liberal, disgusted by apartheid but not particularly enthusiastic about the revolution, either. People get upset when I say things like that, but it's true. Coetzee was never anything so mundane as a sloganeer, a trendy shouter of 'Viva, Mandela'. His dark, veiled parables usually gave you the sense that our problems might be beyond solution, and

that we were heading into a nightmare of burning cities, roadblocks, barbed wire and concentration camps.

This wasn't the future envisioned by Nadine Gordimer and André P Brink, but then they were at pains to present South Africa in a way that made sense to outsiders, often peopling their novels with black characters who spoke perfect English and subscribed to fashionable ideas about democracy. Coetzee always offered something more disturbing.

Consider the story of Susan, an Englishwoman cast away on a desert island in *Foe*, Coetzee's 1986 retelling of the Robinson Crusoe fable. On the beach, she encounters an African slave. She is eager to talk to him, but Friday's tongue has been cut out, so he can't answer. Susan becomes obsessed with Friday's silence. Who is he? What is he thinking? In the closing passages, she prizes his jaws open and presses her ear to the mutilated mouth, but still no sound emerges. Foreign critics thought *Foe* was a clever commentary on the evolution of the novel, but I discerned something else in its depths: an unbearably painful parable about the country where most whites and Africans had no language in common and hence no way of reaching understanding.

'Is this not what you are saying?' I demanded in our interview. A pen scratched on paper and again the great writer cogitated.

'I would not wish to deny you your reading,' he said.

Coetzee was equally opaque about Mrs Curren, the central character in *Age of Iron,* then his most recent fiction. Mrs Curren is a decent woman, a white liberal of the sort everyone seems to disparage these days. Whenever an apartheid cabinet minister appears on her television screen, Mrs Curren stands up to listen; otherwise it is like being urinated on while kneeling. She loathes the 'savage, unreconstructed old boars' who run the country, but she's never really done anything about them (other

JM Coetzee –
'a pale and austere presence'.

(*Photo:* Newspix)

An artist told of a three-day trek into the mountains during which Coetzee said not one word to anyone.

than be 'nice' to everyone) and now there is a price to pay: 'I have cancer from the accumulation of shame I have endured in my life,' she says. 'That is how cancer comes about: from self-loathing.'

Do you and Mrs Curren have anything in common? I asked Coetzee.

'My position is as confused as hers,' he replied.

That is the most revealing quote I was able to wring out of him, but I counted myself quite lucky – in a previous interview he'd refused even to disclose his middle name. I went home and wrote a piece in which Coetzee came across as coldly intellectual and possibly a bit weird. His friends were not impressed.

'You got him wrong,' they said. 'He's great company if he's among people he likes. Cooks great vegetarian dishes, cracks jokes. You should have met him in the old days, before he gave up drinking; he could be incredibly funny.'

Others thought my sketch was quite accurate. Another writer described dinner parties ruined by Coetzee's ominous silence.

'He just sits there,' she said, 'listening, judging.'

An artist told of a three-day trek into the mountains during which Coetzee said not one word to anyone. A fellow academic wrote to say he sympathised with my attempts to extract a coherent set of positions from a man he called 'the Great Elider'.

'There are legions of stories to back you up,' he continued. 'A friend of mind was an MA student of Coetzee's. She had to deliver a paper to his home. As she approached the door, she noticed the blinds moving, but her ring remained unanswered for a long, long while. When she finally gave up and was walking away, she turned around to find the crocodile-eyed genius contemplating her implacably from a window. She became a lesbian, but I am not sure if there is any connection.'

Do we detect a streak of cruelty here? Well, yes. Coetzee has published two slim volumes about his early life. *Boyhood* was about growing up in Worcester. 'An undistinguished rural family,' he writes. 'Bad schooling.' Boring parents who dance to 'clodhopping' music at the Metro Hotel with 'goofy' looks on their faces.

At the age of 15, John decides he will become an artist, and beyond that point, anyone who offers comfort or causes distraction is shoved ruthlessly aside – cloying girlfriends, backward Afrikaans relatives and even his mother, who refuses to understand that young John is 'remorselessly' determined to extinguish the very memory of his family. In *Youth,* the second volume of autobiography, an entire country is dispensed with. 'South Africa was a bad start, a handicap,' he writes. 'If a tidal wave were to sweep in from the Atlantic and wash away the southern tip of Africa, he (John) will not shed a tear.'

John wants to be an artist, you see, and to his mind, artists have certain characteristics. They understand that 'civilisation since the 18th century has been an Anglo-French affair,' and live in London, New York or Paris. Ideally, they should be able to read the classics in the original Greek or Latin, but above all, they must suffer agonies of loneliness and alienation. In *Youth*, Coetzee describes himself sitting in a bitterly cold London flat, eating bread and apples, writing dreadful adolescent poetry and dreaming of making love to film stars. Not Hollywood stars, of course. Exotic creatures in European art films with subtitles.

'Is true art born only out of misery?' he asks himself. The answer is yes, but misery somehow fails to ignite his creative fire.

Some reviewers found *Youth* depressing, but I thought it was full of witty self-deprecation, as if Coetzee were amused to remember what a pretentious little twit he had been, and how awkward his first sexual gropings were. But, as always in Coetzee, things turn dark towards the end. John turns 24. John is a failure as a lover and writer. His soul is 'cold, frozen'. He's so miserable he might as well die. Alas, poor John, always drawn to darkness in much the way that helpless spacecraft are sucked into black holes in science fiction. At some point in the 1970s, he was sucked back into the darkness of South Africa, and the rest is history – a string of eight terrible and beautiful novels, each darker than its predecessor.

When the apartheid drama began to lighten, after 1990, he turned towards darkness in his own life for inspiration. His ex-wife, Jubber, died of cancer, and he created Mrs Curren, who visualises the tumour as a crab inside her body, eating her alive. His son died in a mysterious fall from a building, and he produced *Master of Petersburg*, a novel about a father similarly stricken.

This relentless bleakness eventually began to worry me. I did my own share of agonising, but after the long dark night of the soul there was usually a bright sunny morning followed by a nice braai and a dop with cheerful, backward rugby fans in short pants. It pained me that Coetzee was too civilised to enjoy such things. As critic Shaun de Waal observes, 'He cracked a joke in the opening line of his first novel ("My name is Eugene Dawn. I can't help that.") and never laughed again.'

In fact, looking back over Coetzee's writings, I can pinpoint only two moments when he appears to be happy. One came in the summer of 1964 or thereabouts. Coetzee is lying on the greensward of Hampstead Heath. The air is warm, birds are singing. He drifts into a state of consciousness he has never experienced before. 'At last,' he thinks. 'At last it has come, the moment of ecstatic unity with the All.' Thirty years later, in the delirious aftermath of Mandela's election, Coetzee goes on a bicycle tour of France and experiences a second epiphany. I can't find the article where he describes it, but the way I remember it, he says something like, 'I am so deeply grateful to be alive.' I got tears in my eyes. I thought, heck, the oke is finally coming right.

Alas, it didn't last. A year later, Coetzee came forth with a caustic dissection of the folkloric spectacles staged around the 1995 World Rugby Cup. These were supposed to celebrate the birth of the Rainbow Nation, but Coetzee found them farcical, a parade of ethnic clichés designed to promote the interests of 'an international cartel embracing a "philosophy" of growth no more complex than that of a colony of bacteria.' In retrospect, this was the first sign that Coetzee was not entirely at ease in the New South Africa. It was a common feeling among those of us buried in the matrix of white maleness. Our ancestors bestrode Africa like giants, slaughtering game, digging holes for gold, subjugating everyone. When the tide turned, we steeled ourselves for Armageddon, but nothing happened. The enemy came to power, but no vengeance was taken. They were even willing to forgive us, provided that we fell to our knees and said sorry. I experienced this as totally humiliating. White males had become ridiculous, and we were heading towards irrelevance.

Since I still considered Coetzee a potential kindred spirit, I wondered how the changes were affecting him. One gathered that the winds of change had begun to buffet UCT. A black woman became vice-chancellor, new ideologies swept the campus. The classics were out, 'outcomes' were in. For a writer who once feared the Europeans might regard him as a 'barbarian' if he couldn't read Aristotle in the original Greek, things were not necessarily moving in a favourable direction. Coetzee took to spending much of his time abroad and started referring to the University of Chicago as 'my intellectual home', an insult to UCT, as far as I could see. Something was brewing inside him, something unforeseen.

It burst forth in 1999 in the form of *Disgrace*, the story of a Cape Town academic who falls out with university administrators who want him to apologise for a sexual indiscretion with a young student. This would save his job, but Lurie is arrogant and secretly contemptuous of the new order, so primly gender-sensitive, so smugly PC. So he walks away, intending to devote himself to writing an opera about Byron, only to be hammered into a cringing abjection by murderous blacks. His daughter is gang-raped, Lurie himself doused with methylated spirits and set afire. Left harrowingly vulnerable on an isolated small-holding, the daughter has no choice other than to offer herself and half her land to her former boss boy in the hope that he will 'take her under his wing' and protect her against further attacks. Lurie winds up a nobody, feeding the corpses of stray dogs into a furnace.

On the surface, *Disgrace* is a withering dismissal of the fragile hopes on which the Rainbow Nation is based. Had the real Coetzee finally revealed himself? The African National Congress thought so, denouncing him for portraying blacks as 'savage, violent' and 'propelled by dark, satanic impulses'. Whites responded by turning *Disgrace* into a best seller. Academe was convulsed by debate, and there was nearly a fist-fight around my braai one night. My china Ernest shouted, 'Lurie is an effing coward. He should have taken up arms and gone to fight for a Boerestaat.' My china Dan said, 'No ways! Something religious has happened! Once Lurie loses his suburban baggage, he's, like, free, like, on his way to enlightenment.' I stood between them, marvelling at the uproar a good book could cause.

As for Coetzee, he naturally said nothing, and nobody was particularly surprised when he quietly left a year or two later.

Now he lives in Australia, and I sit in his abandoned matrix reading *Elizabeth Costello,* his first post-South African novel. It is a very odd book, a novel about a famous novelist who goes around the world delivering lectures, informed by a cold distaste for everything: journalists; fans; people who eat meat, write about the violence, indulge in pretences of second-rate African novelists, carry on ceaselessly about literary theory and, worst of all, keep inviting the writer to award ceremonies that have become pointless and unbearable. In this novel about a writer, the writer is 'old and tired', 'an old, tired circus seal', a 'dying whale', surrounded by parasites, disenchanted by the entire literary/academic enterprise.

'We are just performances speaking our parts,' says the writer. 'The core discipline of universities is money making. The lecture hall itself may be a zoo.' Is this the voice of Coetzee, emerging from the mouth of one of his characters? When he stepped up to receive his Nobel Prize in December, was he secretly thinking, like Elizabeth Costello, I wish you'd just sent the cheque in the mail?

Because Coetzee is Coetzee, we will never know. He is a grand master of the literary game of truth and illusion, inclined to speak, if he speaks at all, in riddles and codes that I'm far too dense to decipher. Besides, it's a game that spares everyone the ordeal of confronting reality. I suspect the truth is quite simple: Coetzee has written many great novels, but *Disgrace* is the one they will talk about for decades because it cuts so dangerously close to the bone. I think he was saying it will take centuries for whites to live down the consequences of centuries of oppression. Might not be the sort of thing anyone particularly wants to hear, but it's true, isn't it?

All that seems odd is that Coetzee has chosen to remove himself from the drama while it's still under way. I'm sure Australia is very nice, but it is said to be bland and boring. Any reading of *Elizabeth Costello* confirms this impression: a place where an intellectual has nothing better to do than pick silly fights about vegetarianism. Perhaps Coetzee should have listened to his own Mrs Curren. Midway through *Age of Iron*, she takes up a snapshot of her grandchildren, two little boys who have been taken away from the terrors and ecstasies of Africa to live in America, where they are playing in snow. She studies this little tableau of life in a place where almost everyone is safe and secure, and curiously, she shudders. 'They will die when they are 75 or 85,' she says, 'as stupid as they are today.'

Of Rockey Roads and Democracy

Rian Malan

Fairlady April 2004

'Tis the season to take soundings on the state of South African democracy. Some maintain there's only one place to do it …

Once upon a time in Africa, there was a Camelot that was officially termed 'grey', even though it was really a vivid and colourful urban village where people said what they felt and did as they pleased in defiance of their hard-hearted rulers.

It was a place where forbidden love flourished, where every conceivable rule was broken, and for a brief shining hour, ten years ago, it was the capital of South Africa.

Welcome to Yeoville, founded in 1890 on a ridge just north of the world's richest gold reef.

'Magnificent views,' said the developer. 'Healthy air.' He was a Scotsman named Thomas Yeo Sherwell, and he was hoping to attract the rich. Never quite managed that, but he did get the infant lower-middle classes and, after the turn of the century, the Jews, who came mostly from the Baltic states and gave Yeoville an intellectual and cultural ambience slightly out of the colonial ordinary. Some Jews went on to become capitalists, but others were Bolsheviks who immediately set about organising revolution, first and rather embarrassingly under the slogan 'Workers Unite for a White South Africa' but after 1927, on behalf of 'the natives'.

The presence of this small band of rebels attracted kindred spirits in the form of Bohemians (most famously, Herman Charles Bosman), jazz musicians and dope fiends, all of whom lived furtively until 1978 or so, when a gay nightclub called Casablanca opened in Yeoville's main road. In the larger scheme this was a nothing event, but it was one of the first signs that the ruling Calvinists were losing their grip. Casablanca was joined by Rumours, a jazz bar that daringly featured black musicians. When Rumours got away with it, similar joints sprang up nearby, and by 1986, Rockey Street was the hippest place in South Africa – racially integrated in proportions comfortable to whites, infested with fashionable nightspots and overrun by trendies.

Everyone lived in Yeoville. Okay, everyone who was anyone in the al-

> On any given night, Yeoville was awash with famous actors, human rights lawyers, Marxist academics, gay activists and radical feminists whose unshaven legs were known locally as 'Yeoville stockings'.

ternative society that styled itself as the vanguard of political and social change. A small boy learnt Zulu guitar on Yeoville's rooftops and grew up to be Johnny Clegg. Barney Simon lay in his bed on Muller Street, dreaming up stories that became famous plays. All the seminal anti-apartheid movies were cobbled together in Yeoville, and it even had its own Beat poet, Sinclair Beiles, a witty old madman who'd knocked around the Burroughs in Paris. On any given night, Yeoville was awash with famous actors, human rights lawyers, Marxist academics, gay activists and radical feminists whose unshaven legs were known locally as 'Yeoville stockings'.

Reshada Crouse did not wear Yeoville stockings, but then she was always contrary. Beautiful and talented, she was smitten at an early age by the paintings of grand masters and decided, after art school in Cape Town and London, to become a portraitist 'in the tradition of Goya, Caravaggio and Michelangelo'.

In South Africa in the '80s, such an ambition was almost insanely inappropriate. Taking their cues from the great overseas, the local art police had declared Eurocentrism a dirty word and figurative painting largely passé. Artists were expected to become 'cultural workers' de-

picting the struggle of the masses against capitalism. To stand up in such a revolutionary climate and call yourself a painter in the grand tradition of Dead White Men was a provocation that invited savage retaliation.

'Highly skilled; highly horrible,' said one leftist critic of Reshada's early work.

'Absolutely masterly,' said another, 'but I am reminded of political works done under Hitler.'

One night, at a party, I was bitten by a dog. Reshada offered to take me for a tetanus shot, and I was delighted to hear that she was at war with the art police because I was at odds with them, too. I moved into her spare room a while later, and we became a team of sorts, roaming from bar to bar in Yeoville's combat zone, picking arguments with leftists.

By the end of the 1980s, Yeoville was a liberated zone of sorts. Bars stayed open till dawn, defying the liquor laws. Rastas sold dope on the street corners. It was like Amsterdam in Africa, and it got even better after February 1990, when Mandela was released and the exiles came home.

Yeoville was cheap and ideologically congenial, and almost the entire executive corps of the ANC settled there. Wally Serote, the movement's cultural commissar; Pallo Jordan,

its leading intellectual; Geraldine Fraser, Jabu Moloketi, Derek Hanekom, Albie Sachs, Zola Skweyiya, Joe Slovo … Living amidst such a dense concentration of political talent was amazing. In the nerve-wracking run-up to our 1994 election, insiders started saying, ignore what you read in the papers; a deal has been struck in high places and Mandela will soon be state president. I said, oh, really? At the time, right-wing Boers and Bantustan dictators were plotting to take over the military and annihilate the ANC, which was in turn embroiled in a bloody fratricidal war against Inkatha.

One morning, we were woken by war cries and raced out to find a Zulu impi marching down Cavendish Street, brandishing spears and clubs and looking to bash Mandela loyalists' heads in. I was sure we were doomed.

'Civil war is inevitable,' I wrote.

'We are walking the plank.'

What can I say?

I was wrong. Seven weeks later, Reshada and I strolled through the cathedral calm of a bright autumn morning and cast our ballots in South Africa's first elections. Given my erroneous predictions, it was not my proudest moment, but I had to concede that what was embarrassing for me promised good for others. Here's the thing, see: At that moment, Yeoville was the epicentre of everything. Six residents of the suburb and its immediate surrounds were about to be drafted into Mandela's cabinet. Another 40 or so became national or regional MPs, and hundreds, perhaps even thousands, were headed for big jobs in the civil service. It's hard to convey how odd this was. The Yeoville power zone was so small you could walk across it in 20 minutes, its 35 000 people a drop in the ocean of the nation's 40 million. It was as if a single extended family had taken control of the country, and great things seemed to lie in store for Yeoville residents. In my mind's eye, I saw the suburb becoming a bright, shining, showpiece of the Rainbow Nation, with fine schools and clinics, an efficient police station and plaques on buildings saying, 'Childhood home of Joe Slovo', or 'Here lived Barbara Hogan, first white woman jailed for advocating the overthrow of apartheid.' Three years later, Yeoville was a hellhole. Read on ...

'Let's cartwheel, everybody!' shouted the posh guy with the posh British accent, draining his wine glass and calling for more. It was May 1994, and Reshada and I were in the throes of a party that started on election day and contin-ued without letup for weeks on end. This one took place in a Moorish courtyard under a big tree, and the polished, dark-skinned personage turned out to be Trevor Tutu, wayward son of the famous Archbishop. Like most men, Trevor was smitten by Reshada and became a regular at our semi-daily 'tea parties', which started around sunset and continued indefinitely. Another courtier was Samuel Johnson, an amiable giant who'd come out from Britain to fight apartheid only to find himself fighting off white girls who saw him as something of a dream date – big, black and very threatening with his Mohawk and biker leathers but a gentle poet once you got to know him.

Sam liked to shoot pool. I dimly remember doing a lot of that in the post-election period, also hanging out at the Blue Parrot, a Yeoville bar patronised by the local black nobility and touring celebrities. I think I met Peter Gabriel there one night, but my brain was so addled by booze and euphoria that I wouldn't swear to it. There was a lot of irrational crying in that period, especially on the day of Mandela's inauguration, itself cause for further bouts of indiscriminate celebration.

But all good things end eventually, and there came a day when I woke up sober and noticed that something odd was going on in Yeoville. It suddenly seemed more crowded. Traders were setting up fruit-and-vegetable stands anywhere they pleased, or knocking holes in garden walls so they could sell cheap phone calls to passers-by. One day pirates tapped into Reshada's telephone connection, and she couldn't make any calls for two days on account of voices speaking in tongues on her line. Shortly thereafter, Telkom presented her with a bill for R8 000 to cover hundreds of calls to Ethiopia, Zimbabwe and Nigeria. The amaKwereKwere had arrived, joining a stream of local blacks in search of cheap accommodation.

Unfortunately, cheap accommodation often consisted of a single room divided by curtains so that eight or ten people could share it. Looking back, Yeoville patriot Maurice Smithers identifies this as a root cause of the suburb's woes. As apartheid crumbled, laws enforcing residential segregation were ignored, and Yeoville became in official parlance a 'grey area', where racial mixing was legal. This caused an upsurge in demand for accommodation, which in turn enabled landlords to double or triple their rents. The newcomers, being poor, could only pay by stuffing sub-

The Fairlady Collection

Of Rockey Roads and Democracy, 2004

tenants into every nook and cranny. Overcrowding was illegal but the municipality lost interest in enforcing the by-laws.

Post-election, not much changed, and the area's housing stock deteriorated further, spurred on by epidemics of apathy in the liquor licensing department, among health inspectors and especially among the police, who seemed incapable of controlling crime. Until 1993, it was safe to walk around Yeoville at night. By 1995, walking was almost suicidal. One by one the trendy bars and restaurants on Rockey Street called it a day.

One day they were there, and the next – poof! – they'd vanished. I refer here to the Bohemian leftists and art police with whom Reshada and I once sparred so pleasantly. It's probably unfair to blame the politicians for leaving, because parliament is located in Cape Town, but the broad mass of anti-apartheid activists, academics and journalists had no such excuse. They'd spent years jeering at anyone who resisted integration, but now that it had come to Yeoville, they packed their belongings and fled en masse. 'Couldn't stand the noise', they said. Or, 'My daughter's school friends wouldn't come to play any more.'

And so on.

I took malicious delight in all this and never lost an opportunity to remark on the hypocrisy attendant. On the other hand, I was growing uneasy myself. Visitors to Reshada's house had their cars stolen. Reshada's car was stolen, too, and mine had its windows smashed. I would lie in bed at night listening to distant gun battles and wondering how big my own balls were. One day, I found my laptop gone, nicked through an open window. I bought a replacement, but within a week it was stolen too, and I said, that's it, I'm out of here. I invited Reshada to come with me, painting a picture of a rambling commune in some safe, leafy suburb where we would continue to host tea parties behind high walls and an electric fence. But she was made of sterner stuff. I went; she stayed.

On the other side was Aletta Khubeka, who was born in a mud hut and spent most of her life as some white madam's maid. Now she and her janitor husband were the burstingly proud owners of a three-bedroom home with tiled bathroom and a kitchen so clean that every surface could be eaten off.

And so it came to pass that by 1999, my circle of Yeoville friends had dwindled from hundreds to half a dozen, and all of them were struggling. David Heitner sank his life savings into an advanced edit suite with plush private cinema attached, only to find that customers were too scared to come to him. Adriaan Turgel was robbed so often that he turned into a vigilante, prowling the streets of nights with his Zulu sidekicks, doing work the police were too lazy to do. Tony Richards, a legal aid lawyer, was woken one morning by shouting and pounding on his garden gate. He went out to find an angry mob standing guard over a naked, terrified wretch who'd been caught breaking into cars. 'You're a lawyer,' they said, 'you pass sentence.' Sensing that the crowd was in a murderous mood, Tony presented the captive with a choice: private punishment or the police station. He sobbed, 'Police station! Police station!' and his life was saved. Tony decided it was time to go. But he'd left it too late. The area had been unofficially red-lined by banks, and there were no buyers at any price. Tony gave his house to a friend and walked away.

Which left Reshada the last white person on her street, bar one or two, and harrowingly vulnerable – or so it seemed to me. No gun, no perimeter wall, not even a gate to keep her and her children safe from the forces of darkness. Every time I opened a newspaper I half-expected to read that she'd been murdered. Why did she stay? It would have been easier to understand if she were poor, but she wasn't, not really. She was just difficult. 'I'll do what I want to do when I want to do it,'

she said. She wouldn't ever admit to being afraid.

And so, as Yeoville disintegrated and white capital fled, Reshada started investigating its restoration. Her house was a grand old Victorian with generous rooms and high ceilings, but the roof leaked, the wiring was wonky and hot water came from an old coal stove. Reshada rolled up her sleeves and set to work.

She fixed the wiring, nearly electrocuting herself in the process. The donkey stove gave way to a rooftop solar geyser, and then came a semi-formal English garden in the back yard, strewn with sculptures and overhung with wisteria

'It's not a house,' she explained, 'it's a love affair.'

I said, yes, Reshada, but it's in Yeoville. She shrugged and said, 'I'm not willing to leave just for the sake of having white neighbours.'

Ah, yes. The neighbours. Owen Phiri was a boilermaker who had emigrated from Malawi. He was a sweet, soft-spoken man, very concerned about crime. One night, he woke up to find sinister shadows clustered around Reshada's car.

'Go away,' he said. They whispered, 'What's wrong with you? She's white.' Owen shouted, 'Go away or I'll shoot,' and they went.

On the other side was Aletta

Khubeka, who was born in a mud hut and spent most of her life as some white madam's maid. Now she and her janitor husband were the burstingly proud owners of a three-bedroom home with tiled bathroom and a kitchen so clean that every surface could be eaten off. They were also burstingly proud of their son Sibusiso, who attended King Edward VII, the school that produced the artist William Kentridge plus any number of billionaires and South African cricket captains.

'Dis aangenaam hier,' Aletta told me.

'What's it like to have white neighbours?' I asked.

She giggled shyly and said, 'It's nice.'

A while back, a Buddhist dropped in for tea while I was visiting. 'Yeoville is sick,' he informed us, sitting in the lotus position in Reshada's studio, swathed in robes. 'It's not evolving in a way most people perceive as positive or in keeping with the changes taking place in South Africa.'

Reshada bit his head off.

'Excuse me,' she said, reeling off a string of small acts of kindness she'd recently experienced. Her car broke down some distance away. Instead of robbing her, a group of young black men pushed her home.

Next morning, a backyard mechanic made a house call, crawled under the car with a gun on his hip, reconnected some wires and waved away Reshada's offers of payment.

'Something good happens almost every day,' she said. 'It's like living in an African village. People look after each other. Children play in the street. I bet you don't even know your neighbours' names!'

The Buddhist and I rolled our eyes. In truth, he and I thought Reshada had long since gone off her rocker, throwing good money after bad. His name was Patrick Booth – a coloured boy from a small country town, largely self-educated, ravishingly charming. In 1999, he moved to the big city, becoming Reshada's protégé and houseguest. She introduced him to people who were involved in spiritual pursuits, and next thing, Patrick was out in the formerly white suburbs, laying his mystic healing hands on the stressed bodies of politicians and executives in an exclusive health retreat. He lived in Illovo, as I recollect, which was not far from Rosebank, where on Friday nights the achingly beautiful and sophisticated young black nobility gathers at Katzy's for drinks, followed perhaps by dancing at Kilimanjaro, a club so exclusive they

didn't let grubby old whites like me in. But I've lurked on the fringes of that set and listened to their conversation. From time to time, they mention Yeoville, pull faces, and go, 'Yech, I'd never live there.' You often hear such opinions recycled by whites who fled the area.

They say, 'Hey, it's not a race thing. My black friends also regard Yeoville as a no-go area.'

Well, yes, for people like us. The lucky few. People with money, given half a chance, will try to convince you that ours is the real South Africa, but I'm not sure we should be listened to. South Africa has always been a country where most people are poor and desperate, and Yeoville a weather vane that points where the whole is going. It was one of the first places where you saw racially mixed couples, one of the first white areas to turn grey, and then one of the first grey areas to topple into what struck me as a typically African state of anarchy. On the eve of democracy's tenth birthday, I returned to Yeoville to divine what next.

Much was as I remembered it – streets clogged with fuming taxis, live chickens for sale on the pavements, formerly illustrious nightspots boarded up or reduced to smoke-blackened holes out of

which emerged blasts of kwaito. But here and there, piglets were taking wing. After years of agitation, Joburg's municipality was pulling its socks up. Banks had reversed their no-loans policy, which led, just the other day, to a truly confounding development: Yeoville property prices pulled out their decade-long nosedive.

All this coincided with the triumphant conclusion of Reshada's renovations, which included, by the time she was done, a rose garden on the front lawn, an imposing palisade fence, and lights to play on the house's ice-white facade. It looked astonishing after dark, a gleaming shrine to art and beauty, looming over a street thronged with prophets, cut-throats, Senegalese traders in flowing robes and street people in rags and tatters.

Word of this oddity reached certain arbiters of style, and Reshada's house became the subject of a spread in the opulent pages of *Home & Garden*. The headline read, 'Artist in residence', and the rich and famous were green with envy. Reshada looked upon what she had done and pronounced herself satisfied.

'I just hope it doesn't get boring now,' she said. 'I'd hate to have to move away.'

One Scoop too Many

Chris Barron

Fairlady April 2004

Principled journalist or handmaiden of the pro-Zuma faction of the ANC? Will the real Ranjeni Munusamy please stand up.

Eight months ago Ranjeni Munusamy had it all: youth, looks, intelligence and, seemingly, a brilliant career.

She was senior political writer of South Africa's biggest, most influential newspaper, the *Sunday Times*, and head of the presidential press corps. Her ability to produce front-page leads, with an apparent ease and regularity that, perhaps, should have been more closely examined, assured her a stellar profile. She wasn't at the pinnacle of her career yet but she was clearly getting there fast.

And then one day in September 2003 she self-destructed.

She took a story she'd been working on for the *Sunday Times* and handed it lock, stock and barrel to a rival Sunday newspaper, *City Press*.

The story implied that Bulelani Ngcuka, Director of Public Prosecutions and head of the elite police investigations unit, the Scorpions, had been an apartheid spy. It said an ANC intelligence unit had compiled a damning dossier, which pointed to Ngcuka as Agent RS452. The man in charge of the unit's investigation had been Jacob Zuma. Deputy President Zuma, as everyone knew, was being investigated by Ngcuka for allegedly soliciting a filthy great bribe from a French company involved in the South African government's multibillion-rand arms deal.

The story would have been hugely damaging at the best of times. Given the context in which it appeared, it was political dynamite. By so severely compromising Ngcuka's credibility it seemed to invalidate the prima-facie evidence he claimed to have against Zuma and his financial advisor, Schabir Shaik.

Their strongest, or at least their loudest, line of defence against the bribery allegations had been to question Ngcuka's motives for launching his investigation.

The *City Press* story seemed to confirm their worst suspicions. Munusamy could hardly have done a better job for them if they'd paid her. But she

When Munusamy (31) fetches me at the gate of her flat in Illovo in the northern suburbs of Johannesburg there is no sign of sackcloth and ashes. 'The car that Schabir bought me,' she cracks cockily, as we pass her silver BMW coupé. The least he could have done, some might retort.

hadn't done herself any favours.

Firstly, by taking her 'scoop' to a rival publication, she'd committed what for a journalist is a cardinal, unforgivable sin. In one stroke she'd smashed just about every glittering prospect she'd had in the profession. She was effectively fired and her former colleagues competed to see who could plunge the knife into her departing back deepest and twist most savagely.

Secondly, she unleashed the Hefer Commission, which was called by President Thabo Mbeki within days of her story appearing. By the time it had played itself out in Bloemfontein, Munusamy was a celebrity, but her status as a journalist was the butt of many jokes.

So, now that the commission is history and the TV circus has moved on, one wonders how the star of the show is coping?

When Munusamy (31) fetches me at the gate of her flat in Illovo in the northern suburbs of Johannesburg there is no sign of sackcloth and ashes.

'The car that Schabir bought me,' she cracks cockily, as we pass her silver BMW coupé. The least he could have done, some might retort.

The only picture in her sparsely furnished apartment is a shot of her flanked by former President Nelson Mandela and Foreign Minister Nkosazana Dlamini-Zuma, all looking very chummy together. Mandela is, supposedly, a big fan of hers, worrying about her love life and, not necessarily related, whether she's getting enough rest.

His lawyer, Ismail Ayob, represented her in her disciplinary hearings at the *Sunday Times*. These had hardly started when *Sunday Times* publisher Mike Robertson called her to his office and offered her a financial settlement. Former editor, Mathatha Tsedu, had supposedly messed up by announcing her resignation before she'd agreed to resign. She took swift advantage of this technical loophole and, with what many felt was breathtaking arrogance under the circumstances, threatened to bring the paper before the Council for Conciliation, Mediation and Arbitration. Advised that the *Sunday Times* didn't have a leg to stand on, Robertson paid Munusamy the amount she herself proposed. Staffers – and not only those who thought her arrogant and manipulative – were outraged and Robertson had to descend from mahogany row to pacify them.

'She did something which is criminal for a journalist,' complains one. 'That the paper paid her to go boggles the mind.'

There was more to come. When the Hefer Commission started and Munusamy mounted a desperate battle to avoid taking the stand, the *Sunday Times*, with

Ranjeni Munusamy – 'In one stroke she'd smashed just about every
glittering prospect she'd had in the profession.'

(Photo: Charle Lombard/*Volksblad*)

The effect of her betrayal was to neutralise a well-placed source of information about arms and corruption.

astonishing chivalry considering what she had done, paid her legal costs – 'in support of the principle that journalists must not be obliged to reveal their sources', says Robertson.

Her 'journalistic principles' were all she had left by this time, reflects Munusamy with a scarcely believable lack of irony. And never to reveal a source was a principle she regarded as particularly 'sacrosanct'. If the *Sunday Times* had not paid her to uphold this sacred tenet of journalism, she hopes she would have had the courage to go to jail if necessary.

'I didn't want to destroy my career in journalism completely by being the person who destroyed this principle and set a legal precedent.'

Munusamy has honed the expression of noble sentiment into a fine art. Sadly, however, she'd ditched its practice long before Hefer beckoned, when she betrayed former ANC intelligence operative Bheki Jacobs. Jacobs had agreed to speak to her about arms deal corruption after she gave him a solemn undertaking that she would never expose him as her source.

She was a journalist, she told him: 'Trust me.' He did. And she ratted on him to the presidency, then she exposed him to five million readers of the *Sunday Times*. She didn't merely expose him, she denigrated and ridiculed him, presenting him as a pathetic, half-mad 'Walter Mitty'.

Munusamy says she blew his cover after realising that Jacobs was an 'information peddler' and that the 'lies' he was peddling were 'causing serious divisions within the presidency'.

'As far as I was concerned it was a story that he was doing this.'

The effect of her betrayal was to neutralise a well-placed source of information about arms and corruption.'

Far from being 'lies', Jacobs' information had 'checked out nine times out of ten', according to another investigative journalist. Her betrayal served as a warning to other would-be informants and reinforced the suspicions of the *Sunday Times* investigative unit that Munusamy was 'playing a different game'.

By the time the Hefer Commission was called to examine the authenticity of her story about Ngcuka, Munusamy had revived her belief in the sanctity of sources and wild horses couldn't get her to testify. Hefer's assurances that she wouldn't be forced to reveal her sources cut no ice. She'd received death threats, she announced with a wonderful sense of theatre, a sense that never faltered throughout the entire proceedings.

'Who would have threatened her?' asks Tsedu. 'Mo Shaik? Because her sources were Mo.'

Munusamy insists that she had 18 sources. We now know that one of them was the sinister former apartheid security policeman Gideon Nieuwoudt. She didn't know at the time that Mo Shaik had paid Nieuwoudt R40 000 to 'confirm' the spy allegations against Ngcuka. Pressed, she admits that of the 18 only one, Mo Shaik, was a 'primary source'.

And it's hard to imagine her taking seriously a death threat from a man she likens, with whoops of laughter, to a 'tree stump'. One is left with the suspicion that Munusamy's real reason for not wanting to testify has less to do with lofty principles or fear of death than with the prospect of being publicly humiliated. Given what happened to her accomplice, the then *City Press* editor Vusi Mona, who can blame her?

'I firmly believe that (evidence leader) Kessie Naidoo and those guys were baying for my blood,' she says.

'They wanted a gangbang. They couldn't wait to get their hands on me. It would have been torture.'

Indeed. But there's also the possibility that she knew she risked being exposed as more than handmaiden of a pro-Zuma faction in the ANC than a journalist seeking to uncover the truth without fear or favour.

Munusamy seems to have had many of the attributes of a good journalist. She was sharp, wrote well, worked hard and was brave. She covered the bloody violence in KwaZulu-Natal in the mid-1990s and was the first journalist on the scene after warlord Sifiso Nkabinde was assassinated in Richmond. She visited his bodyguard in hospital and got a story that help lead police to the killers. She also had extraordinary contacts, built up during her three years as spokesperson for KwaZulu-Natal transport minister and later ANC leader in the province S'bu Ndebele. She was part of a close inner circle that rotated around Jacob Zuma, then provincial leader of the ANC.

It was because she boasted such contacts that she was offered a senior position on the *Sunday Times* in Joburg with not much more than four years' journalistic experience behind her and only a year after joining the paper's KwaZulu-Natal office.

But contacts can be a double-edged sword. They try to manipulate journalists to satisfy their own agendas. They call in favours. Get too close to them, and it becomes very difficult to resist. Mathatha Tsedu believes that Munusamy's obsession with the Ngcuka spy allegations should be seen in this light.

'She gets too close to her sources and bought into their arguments. It was no longer a matter of a story; it was more than that.'

Munusamy's account of why and how she became so fixated with the story suggests, at best and not for the first time, some confusion between the role of a journalist and that of a party public relations officer.

'These corruption scandals [around the arms deal] were cancelling out any possible successor to Mbeki. I thought it was frightening that in 2007 the ANC was going to have to elect a new president and they had no

There've been requests for her to model sexy lingerie and even endorse a cardiac machine, 'because I make men's hearts race'.

clue who it was going to be. I thought it was unhealthy for the country and the ANC.'

It was in this context that she thought it in the national interest that the story about the spy allegations against Ngcuka should be brought into the open. The trigger was Ngcuka's failure to invite her to his confidential briefing with 'this brotherhood of editors', as she scathingly puts it.

'I'd been writing a lot of this and suddenly I get left out,' she says with shrill anger in her voice. 'That pissed me off.'

With Zuma's former comrade-in-arms and close friend, Mo Shaik, egging her on and giving her leads, she began to dig. When she finally had her story, or so they both believed, he became 'agitated' when it failed to appear.

'He was blaming me,' she says, adding that he put 'pressure' on her to get it published.

Mathatha Tsedu believed her 'facts' didn't check out. 'There was no story,' he says.

Up to this time, Munusamy and Tsedu had been so conspicuously affectionate that they'd attracted jealous mutterings and all kinds of unsavoury conjecture in the newsroom. (Munusamy insists it was devoid of truth, although her career has been marked by what many believe to be a number of strategically useful affairs.)

When Tsedu refused to publish her story she was furious and accused him of colluding with Ngcuka to block it.

'She threatened to call a press conference,' says Tsedu. 'I said, "Go ahead."'

By now Munusamy had decided she had no future at the *Sunday Times* and didn't want one.

'I had a serious gripe with how the paper was being run. Ethics had gone out the window and I knew I couldn't work in this environment any longer.'

When her 'story' hit the streets in *City Press*, Munusamy, who likes you to know what a devout Catholic she is, was attending Mass.

'I go every week, no matter where I am,' she explains with a suitably angelic smile.

And did she go to confession, I ask?

'I didn't feel the need,' she retorts.

The world of journalism has turned its back on Munusamy and she's aggrieved, or at least pretends to be. Ever since circulating the gossip she picked up in her father's barber shop in the small KwaZulu-Natal mining town of Dannhauser she's been driven by a compulsion to find and report stories. Being a journalist is in her blood. But don't cry for Ranjeni.

'There are so many irons in the fire,' she sighs happily.

There've been requests for her to model sexy lingerie and even endorse a cardiac machine, 'because I make men's hearts race'.

More prosaically, the president's brother, Moeletsi Mbeki, has approached her to start a southern Africa current affairs magazine and maybe also a TV channel. Business people and politicians have flocked to her with book requests, and local film producer Anant Singh wants to make a film about her.

With her as herself? She laughs. 'They want me to write the script for the moment.'

The plot against Bulelani Ngcuka ended spectacularly when agent RS452 was exposed as Vanessa Brereton, a former human rights lawyer who worked at the Port Elizabeth Legal Resources Centre and who now lives in London. After the Hefer Commission, established to test allegations that Ngcuka was an apartheid government spy, Ranjeni was employed as by the short-lived, Nigerian-backed daily, This Day.

During Schabir Shaik's trial on charges of corruption relating to the arms deal, Ranjeni suddenly emerged as his 'media advisor' and sat in on the proceedings 'as an observer'.

In May 2005, Judge Hilary Squires found Schabir Shaik guilty of charges of corruption and fraud and also found that his relationship with President Jacob Zuma had been 'generally corrupt'.

Ranjeni currently runs her own PR agency in Joburg.

Disgraced City Press *editor, Vusi Mona, has disappeared from public view while Mathatha Tsedu, who was fired by the* Sunday Times, *has gone on to fill Mona's seat.*

In the meantime, former President Nelson Mandela has taken his lawyer, Ismail Ayob, to court in an attempt to stop him from selling artwork and other merchandise in his name.

Not by the Book

Chris Barron

Fairlady December 2004

Withdrawing authorisation she'd given to a controversial author to write her biography rekindled interest in Nadine Gordimer, Nobel Laureate, grande dame of the pen and famously private person.

I'm a bit apprehensive about meeting Nadine Gordimer.

South Africa's Nobel laureate is famously private. She hates interviews and, only grudgingly, agrees to them when she has a book to plug.

One thinks of her as being austere, aloof, witheringly impatient of human weakness.

'He just didn't have the guts to become much of a personality,' she once said of her Lithuanian father who arrived in South Africa at 13 and scraped enough from fixing watches on the mines to start a jewellery shop.

Alan Paton, who liked her personally, found her writing very cold – 'I cannot remember experiencing any emotion while reading anything she has written.'

He is not the only one, and undoubtedly this has helped engender the hard image one has of her – the perceived lack of warmth in her work a reflection of her personality.

Being barked at by a big brown German hunter called Tilla behind the high gate of her double-storey house in the genteel, leafy, Johannesburg suburb of Parktown West does little to ease one's mild sense of foreboding.

There is no bell and, apart from the dog, no sign of life. One has an appointment, laboriously negotiated with her publisher, and this is the appointed hour. I try a soft, plaintive hoot, followed by a slightly sharper one. Still nothing.

Then, thank God, a housekeeper appears. I give her my name and she vanishes inside. The dog has put a sock in it by now and there's an ominous pause during which I imagine Gordimer wondering just how badly she needs to punt her new book after all.

The housekeeper reappears and leads me through the kitchen and along a narrow corridor lined at some point in the distance with African clay pots.

We pass a small room with a small desk and a typewriter (no computer) facing shelves of books. I slow down for a better look but the housekeeper

Nadine Gordimer – 'One thinks of her
as being austere, aloof, witheringly
impatient of human weakness.'

Alan Paton, who liked her personally, found her writing very cold – 'I cannot remember experiencing any emotion while reading anything she has written.'

firmly escorts me past what is clearly forbidden territory and into a sitting room.

It is sparsely furnished with a couch and some chairs that have been around for a long time, one guesses, and are there to support serious intellectual discourse rather than to be admired for their trendiness and aesthetic appeal, or lounged on for comfort.

There are some black and white drawings, which the family of her late husband, art dealer Reinhold Cassirer, managed to take with them from Berlin, she tells me, when they left urgently just ahead of the Nazis.

Cassirer, her second husband, died in 2001 after they'd been married for 48 years.

There's absolutely nothing in the room that speaks of Gordimer's fame. No ostentatious collection of books, no pictures of her receiving the Nobel Prize, or with royalty or other famous writers, or Oliver Tambo, Nelson Mandela or any of the numerous luminaries she could claim as close friends.

Suddenly, quietly, here she is. Very small and delicately built, but not at all fragile or bent as one might expect of someone just weeks short of 81. Her face has no makeup and looks relatively young. She's wearing dark glasses because she's just had eye surgery for cataracts.

She shakes my hand firmly, gives me a smile that is unaffected and warm, beckons me to the couch and sits in an upright chair close by, considerately mindful, perhaps, of how soft her voice is.

She comes to the point quickly, which is the book of short stories she has compiled in aid of AIDS, called *Telling Tales*.

'I have been very disturbed about our president's attitude over the AIDS crisis.

'I think the government's response and especially that, unfortunately, of our president, has been inadequate and based on a total misunderstanding.

'I don't understand how somebody of his intelligence and his wide reading can doubt the fact that HIV causes AIDS. The figures are staggering. Six hundred people die a day in our country.'

Where, I say, would we be without Zackie Achmat and the Treatment Action Campaign?

'Indeed,' she says.

And so she asked 20 writers to submit short stories, not necessarily with an AIDS theme, free. She persuaded their publishers to play along, and all proceeds will go to the TAC.

Most of the writers she knows personally, and they're an impressive bunch: Chinua Achebe, Hanif Kureishi, Amos Oz, Salman Rushdie, Paul Theroux, John Updike ...

Why no JM Coetzee? I ask mischievously, knowing that he and Gordimer had a fall-out 16 years ago when she told Rushdie not to visit South Africa because of objections from local Muslims.

'He's not really a short-story writer,' she says.

How are things between you? I wonder.

'Oh, he's an old friend, you know. Not intimate. But writers in South Africa, we've never been a sort of clique. I've been closer to André Brink. But they're of a different temperament, aren't they? He's a more gregarious person.'

She and Salman were friends when the *Weekly Mail* and Congress of SA Writers invited him out to give a talk.

She'd visited him before in his hideaway in London. 'To me it was incredibly sad and terrible that he had to live like this under that fatwa.'

When 'some mullah came along with his henchmen' and made it 'categorically' clear to her and fellow members of Cosaw that Rushdie's visit would not be tolerated, she called the author of *The Satanic Verses* and asked him, 'Can we be responsible for your life? These people seem to be very serious.'

Rushdie refused to take the hint, so she had to phone him again and spell it out:

'Salman, we think that you shouldn't come.'

The reaction was one of outrage, some of it aimed at Gordimer.

'JM Coetzee was one of the people who said it was terrible that writers, and especially naming me, had disinvited someone that we ... and that this was giving in to the oppression of freedom of expression and so on.

'So we should have let him come, and perhaps be killed?'

I ask what she thought of the government's reaction (in effect labelling him a racist) to Coetzee's book *Disgrace*.

'When you publish it's publish and be damned and you write what you want to write, what you believe in. If it offends, you have to take the criticism.'

When Coetzee got his Nobel she wrote to congratulate him – 'and gave him some of my own criticisms of that book'.

She won't say what they are, but the book, which won Coetzee his second Booker Award, is clearly not one she liked. One can imagine the politically correct Gordimer – one of her favourite books is Joseph Conrad's *Something of the Narcissus*, she says – wincing.

> She says she told Coetzee, who moved to Australia after the government's denunciation, that she wished he would return.

She says she told Coetzee, who moved to Australia after the government's denunciation, that she wished he would return.

'He wrote back. He obviously had reasons of his own, and I left it at that.'

Like it or not, *Disgrace* was read by more South Africans than ever read one of Gordimer's books. She's never been well read in this country, and I ask her why she thinks this is.

'If this is true, there are many books that are not widely read in South Africa. South Africans are not big readers. We do not have a "reading culture". I don't think that any of us who are "serious writers" in South Africa are widely read. No books are widely read except what I call the airport books.'

Unless more money is spent on libraries, she doesn't see this changing.

Gordimer herself did not come from a literary background 'at all'. Her mother, who came to South Africa from England at the age of six, was a great reader 'at a popular level'. But Gordimer had to wait for her birthday money to buy the kind of books that interested her (Chekhov and DH Lawrence were early favourites).

For the rest she depended on the Springs municipal library.

'If it hadn't been for the local library, I would never have been a writer. Every Saturday I was down at the library borrowing books. Of course blacks couldn't go into the libraries. Now there are no libraries for them to go into.'

She is clearly disillusioned by the government's arms spending which is so 'hugely disproportionate to the tremendous needs that we have'.

'There's always money for arms. I'm not a military strategist but I really can't see what threat there is to us.'

She's angry that not even a fraction of the money that is poured into sport can be found to support a single literary journal.

She cut her teeth on such journals, she says. Without them our young writers will struggle to make it.

She mentions the number of people she knows – 'no names, no pack drill' – who were 'wonderful' champions of a book culture while members of Cosaw, but now have government positions and have gone quiet.

Gordimer describes herself as 'a loyal member of the ANC'. Loyalty implies the responsibility to criticise when necessary, she says.

Why hasn't she criticised more loudly and more frequently, one wonders, the government's shameful record on AIDS, as well as its abysmal failure over Zimbabwe?

'What's the good of bitching about it?' she says of AIDS. A fund-raising exercise such as her book is a more effective response.

And 'you must please separate' AIDS and Zimbabwe, she insists.

They're both major human rights issues, surely? I ask.

Maybe so, but 'the idea that President Mbeki could really have influenced Robert Mugabe to change his policies is a dream. I think if God came down from heaven and went to Mugabe, He wouldn't get through to him. Mugabe would say, I know better, you're not the real God.'

Gordimer talks in a precise and ordered way. There are no superfluous words or gestures. It comes as no surprise to hear that she does very little rewriting because by the time she sits down at her typewriter she has the sentences worked out in her head.

'I do it when I'm awake in the middle of the night, I do it when I'm driving somewhere. The discards have been made by the time I get to put it down.'

Does she love writing, I wonder, or, like some successful writers, does she hate it?

'I don't think of it that way. It is just so much part of my being and my life.'

Nevertheless, even after 13 novels and nine short story collections, she has to discipline herself to sit down at nine every morning, as she still does, and keep going until lunchtime. There's no lying around waiting for inspiration.

'All there really is to know of the writer is in the work. How the writer lived as an individual and as a human being is entirely his or her private affair. You don't have to find out whether Tolstoy's wife had a hard time with him or not. It's irrelevant to the achievement of the book.'

'The idea that you suddenly have some epiphany or eureka or something – I doubt whether that happens.'

She's never had writer's block, she says, and only once has she started a novel and abandoned it. Even then nothing was wasted. She turned the aborted novel into a short story which she called *Not For Publication*.

Gordimer has two children who live abroad, and five grandchildren for whom, she chuckles, English is a second language.

When the children were young she had to be 'rather ruthless' to ensure the solitude she needed, which meant sending them to boarding school.

But she's careful to maintain a balance between the solitude of writing, which she once confessed she found 'quite frightening', and engagement with the outside world.

So she makes a point of doing 'the ordinary things of life' like shopping or going to the dry cleaners. And she travels overseas a lot.

'I don't want to live life in my invented world. There is a tension between what's inside you and what is impinging on you from outside. You need these two things. Your relation to the world, to other people, to society, to everything that goes on in your country and beyond.'

Around seven years ago Gordimer allowed a young West Indian writer, Ronald Suresh Roberts, into her life to write her biography. As is now well known, she withdrew her authorisation after a disagreement about the content of the book he wrote, which, one gathers, was more personal than she'd intended.

She flatly refuses to say anything about it.

How much are readers entitled to know about the private life of writers? I ask.

'There's no entitlement at all,' she says shortly.

Even if knowledge of a writer's private life might shed light on the work?

'All there really is to know of the writer is in the work. How the writer lived as an individual and as a human being is entirely his or her private affair. You don't have to find out whether Tolstoy's wife had a hard time with him or not. It's irrelevant to the achievement of the book.'

She looks at her watch, a telltale sign that she's had about enough.

Gordimer wrote once in an essay how she was inspired to visit Madagascar after learning that in their language they have the same word for soul and butterfly.

Does she believe the soul leaves the body like a butterfly from the chrysalis? I ask

'You mean do I believe in life after death? Unfortunately I don't. I wish I did. When the body dies, unfortunately, everything dies.'

As we get up we start talking about newly retired Chief Rabbi Cyril Harris, whom Gordimer – a non-religious Jew – thinks is wonderful. She's concerned that his 30-something successor sounds 'rather conservative'.

We both wonder why they picked such a youth to take over from Harris.

'The strangest things happen,' remarks Gordimer.

She chortles. 'Yesterday I got a great colourful invitation – and it was to the inauguration of Carl Niehaus as a pastor in the Rhema Church!'

She sounds both horrified and fascinated at the same time.

Unfortunately you will not be reading a Gordimer short story called *Talking in Tongues* any time soon. She was 'not able to go', she says, when I phone her later.

Country Girl, City Girl

Khanyi Mjindi

Fairlady December 2004

A week before I go home to rural Transkei, I have to shove food down my throat as if getting ready for slaughter. I do this to gain some weight because where I come from, a woman's weight is not a big deal – it's a huge deal. The bigger, the better. I, however, am as thin as a rake. I am definitely not a city girl, but I could say that I have adapted fairly well.

I feel the tension I have caused when my neck fails to carry a 20-litre bucket filled with water. My friends, women my age, are carrying theirs while I pathetically walk with them carrying a half-empty bucket.

The last time I was home, which was before I started studying, we carried 5-litre calabashes. I want to be a woman of my community, and if it means carrying a 20-litre bucket on my head to prove my womanhood, I will.

All I want is the same feeling I used to have when we fetched water from the same river, the same girl who would come to this same river, take off all her clothes and dive in, with or without crowds around – the innocent girl who was free from the pressures of today's busy living, the little girl that used to laugh from the heart. All I want is a grown-up version of that girl.

It's a hot Sunday afternoon and my friends are going to play netball. I am filled with excitement when I find out that we are finally allowed to go to the grounds. I am only going to watch, but I'm extremely excited about it anyway.

I bend to fasten my Nike sneakers when I realise that everyone is barefoot. Hell, no! I ain't walking ten kilometres with my bare feet. This is the only luxury I am not depriving myself of. The white mud from the river that I have to smear on my face will not gel well with my three-step Clinique products. Those are my thoughts as I smear the natural sunscreen on my face anyway.

Every last Sunday of the month we have games. This is a big social gathering. When I left for the city, we were still not allowed to go to this event because we weren't old enough. I'd almost forgotten how I would have killed to see myself there. This is where young men and women meet. After a very long, exhausting walk, we finally get to the grounds, which are filled with young men and women.

Growing up, I envied the older girls who were allowed to come here, but never had I imagined such beauty. I cannot help the excitement I'm

Here or there – writer Khanyi Mjindi
explores the conflict between
urban and rural life.

(*Photos:* Brett Eloff)

I am trying to fit in. I'm trying to fit in with my own people.

I have to make an effort to be accepted by my own people.

I feel like an outsider in a place I call home.

feeling. It's all finally in front of me. I don't wish to be anywhere else in the world at this point in my life. What an event!

Women are gathered on one side of the grounds and men on the other side. Songs are coming from both sides. I suddenly realise that my over-excitement has made everyone move away from me. I am trying to fit in. I'm trying to fit in with my own people. I have to make an effort to be accepted by my own people. I feel like an outsider in a place I call home.

A week before I come back to the city, I have to starve myself so I'm trim. Again conforming to society's standards of living. Which society am I supposed to conform to? Which society do I belong to? Is where I come from more important than where I am going?

I feel a slight relief as I get into my car after saying all my goodbyes. That bothers me the whole way. This is home. I should feel sad to leave. As I am tearing through the Free State's dry veld, I shed a tear. I am filled with shame and fear of losing my sense of belonging. I start to ask myself who am I and where I am going. Am I so busy that I have forgotten who I am? Am I so caught up in my own little world 'trying to keep my head above water' that I have lost myself to it? Am I too busy to take time, look back and just show appreciation of the place that has made me what I am today, to the people who have moulded me into who I am today?

It is almost dark when I suddenly see the lights. My phone starts ringing. I'm driving into Joburg when a group of friends call to invite me to a party they are having. Excited, they ask how home was and what I got up to.

'Home was nice and I got up to a lot of things,' is all I can say.

They tease me about my drastic weight gain, and my friends and I make arrangements to renew our membership at the gym.

This is a social gathering, but the difference between this one and the one I attended last Sunday is humungous. After a couple of minutes I exit silently, as I have to work tomorrow.

A few weeks have passed. I have not been to the gym in ages, but I have found other things to keep me active and happy. I've joined a horse-riding club. The smell of the horse poo makes me feel at home. It brings back to life the free and innocent girl I used to be. The woman that I have long buried suddenly awakens when I'm there. The sight of the grazing horses keeps me calm and the small, muddy dam makes me want to take off all my clothes and dive in. Why would anyone want to go smell some horse poo when you could be having a dude for a personal trainer at the gym? It's a mystery to many.

I've really come a long way towards understanding who I am, but I don't yet have a complete understanding. It is a journey, but it gets better with age. Every day I learn something new about myself and the affection that I have for myself grows daily. I have come to understand that I'm neither a city girl nor a farm girl. I am a woman, a complete woman who is part of society and, most importantly, who belongs to two different communities. I'm proud to be where I am today and I am proud of where I come from.